The Cambridge Introduction to
Postmodern Fiction

Postmodern fiction presents its readers with a challenge: instead of enjoying it passively, they have to work to understand it, to question their own responses, and to examine their views about what fiction is. Yet accepting this challenge is what makes postmodern writing so pleasurable to read and rewarding to study.

Unlike most introductions to postmodernism and fiction, this book places the emphasis on literature rather than theory. It introduces the most prominent British and American novelists associated with postmodernism, from the 'pioneers', Beckett, Borges and Burroughs, to important post-war writers such as Pynchon, Carter, Atwood, Morrison, Gibson, Auster, DeLillo, and Ellis. Designed for students and clearly written, this *Introduction* explains the preoccupations, styles and techniques that unite postmodern authors.

BRAN NICOL is Reader in Modern and Contemporary Literature at the University of Portsmouth and has previously taught at Lancaster and Chichester. He has published on D. M. Thomas, Iris Murdoch, postmodernism and stalking in contemporary culture.

The Cambridge Introduction to
Postmodern Fiction

BRAN NICOL

CAMBRIDGE
UNIVERSITY PRESS

CAMBRIDGE UNIVERSITY PRESS
Cambridge, New York, Melbourne, Madrid, Cape Town, Singapore,
São Paulo, Delhi, Dubai, Tokyo

Cambridge University Press
The Edinburgh Building, Cambridge CB2 8RU, UK

Published in the United States of America by Cambridge University Press, New York

www.cambridge.org
Information on this title: www.cambridge.org/9780521679572

First published 2009

Printed in the United Kingdom at the University Press, Cambridge

A catalogue record for this publication is available from the British Library

ISBN 978-0-521-86157-1 Hardback
ISBN 978-0-521-67957-2 Paperback

For Karen, Joe and Jamie

Contents

Chapter 8 Fiction of the 'postmodern condition': Ballard, DeLillo, Ellis

Acknowledgements

I would like to thank Ray Ryan of Cambridge University Press for his enthusiasm and patience, colleagues in the English department and in the Centre for European and International Studies Research at the University of Portsmouth for their support, and my wife and our boys for their laughter and love.

Preface: reading postmodern fiction

> The commonest complaint about the narratives of Beckett or Burroughs is that they are hard to read, they are 'boring'. But the charge of boredom is really hypocritical. There is, in a sense, no such thing as boredom. Boredom is only another name for a certain species of frustration. And the new languages which the interesting art of our time speaks are frustrating to the sensibilities of most educated people.
>
> Susan Sontag, 'One Culture and the New Sensibility' (1965)

> Sometimes I suspect that good readers are even blacker and rarer swans than good writers. . . . Reading, obviously, is an activity which comes after that of writing; it is more modest, more unobtrusive, more intellectual.
>
> Jorge Luis Borges, Preface to *A Universal History of Infamy* (1935) (trans. Norman Thomas di Giovanni, 1972)

In an essay about postmodern fiction a student once declared that Beckett's writing 'doesn't go down easily'. As I was the marker, I had to point out that this phrase was not exactly appropriate academic discourse. But I could also see her point. If reading Jane Austen is like having a nice Sunday lunch, and *The Da Vinci Code* is the equivalent of a McDonald's, then reading Beckett is, for some, like being asked to complete the 'Bushtucker Trial' in the TV show *I'm A Celebrity . . . Get Me Out Of Here.*

Besides the parallel between literature and food, her statement implied a definition of fiction. A novel should be something accessible, easy to read. Literature should be *digestible*. But why is this? Why shouldn't literature be a *challenge* to the reader? Who said reading a novel has to be easy? After all, we accept more readily the fact that modern art, the kind we are confronted with in the Tate Modern or the Turner Prize, does not communicate straightforwardly, that we have to work to interpret it. Even poetry, part of the staple diet on university literature courses, is something we accept from the outset is not going to give its meaning over to us without a struggle.

If asked why they read, most people (including myself) would say that they read fiction for pleasure. It is hard, though, to determine exactly what the pleasure of reading a novel or a short story is. It may be the pleasure of escapism, of experiencing what it would be like to be another person, indulging one's fantasy-life, or exercizing the intellect. If asked why they choose to study literature at university, most students reply that it is because they enjoy reading fiction. (For the kind of reasons just mentioned.) But very quickly they realize that 'reading' literature at university is not simply about enjoying reading. In fact, for some students, it turns out to be the exact opposite. Many students feel that the process of studying literature empties reading of the enjoyment that caused them to study literature in the first place. Why do we have to ask so many questions about a book? Can't we just accept that an author wrote something because he or she felt like it, or wanted to make money?

Postmodern fiction presents a challenge to the reader. This is true even though most of it is actually not as hard to comprehend as Beckett, and many of the authors labelled as postmodern (and examined in this book) are among the most popular, acclaimed, and, I think, enjoyable, writers in contemporary fiction: Thomas Pynchon, Angela Carter, Margaret Atwood, Toni Morrison, William Gibson, Paul Auster, Don DeLillo, Bret Easton Ellis.

But postmodern writing challenges us because it requires its reader to be an active co-creator of meaning rather than a passive consumer. More than this, it challenges its readers to interrogate the commonsense and commonplace assumptions about literature which prevail in our culture. Though it is a product of the latter half of the twentieth century, studying postmodern fiction can deepen our knowledge about literature on a wider scale. To read postmodern fiction is to be invited to ask: what *is* fiction? What does reading it involve? Why do we read? Why, for that matter, do novelists write? Why do they create innovative, experimental forms rather than just stick to traditional ones?

Postmodernisms

This book is an introduction to postmodern fiction, offering accounts of its various 'waves' in a period stretching mainly from the 1950s to the 1990s and providing in-depth readings of texts which have been consistently associated with postmodernism by literary critics and theorists.

Though the term 'postmodern' is still an important one in a number of academic disciplines and remains essential in the literary-studies lexicon, the topic of postmodernism is no longer hotly debated in academic journals and research monographs. Linda Hutcheon, one of the major theorists of postmodern fiction, has suggested that postmodernism is now, in the twenty-first century, 'a thing of the past' because it has become 'fully institutionalized, it has its canonized texts, its anthologies, primers and readers, its dictionaries and its histories' (Hutcheon, 2002, 165).

This is not quite true, since the conditions of 'postmodernity' (as detailed in the Introduction) still seem to shape the contemporary world, and much aesthetic and cultural production (novels, film, TV, etc.) still clearly deploys strategies and generates effects which have been defined as postmodern. And while it is no longer the subject of cutting-edge academic debate, postmodernism is now more than ever a fixture on literature courses in universities around the world, and studying it remains one of the most valuable ways of making sense of contemporary writing.

But there is an advantage to thinking of postmodern fiction as something effectively in the past, like modernism, something we can treat as a more or less 'complete' historical movement with its own set of core texts (though this 'teleological' idea is entirely against the spirit of postmodernism). Now, in other words, a welcome sense of retrospectivity is possible in relation to the postmodernism debate.

This book does not seek to produce an exhaustive, exact chronological survey, taking in every significant writer who has been labelled 'postmodern', but tries to isolate and examine the main varieties of postmodern fiction. My strategy has been to divide postmodern fiction into groups of authors who deal with similar questions and favour similar formal techniques. Depending upon the particular theme, some chapters consider specific authors and offer readings of one or two or their key works, while others focus on specific representative texts. The order in which the book considers these varieties of fiction preserves a loose sense of chronology, though the book is not intended as a literary history.

The book concentrates mainly on Anglo-American fiction. This means that some of the non-English-speaking writers who have been convincingly co-opted into the postmodern 'canon' over the years, such as Alain Robbe-Grillet, Carlos Fuentes, Italo Calvino and Gabriel Garcia Marquez, are largely absent from the discussion. This is partly due to spatial constraints, but it is also because postmodernism has always chiefly been a phenomenon in theory and criticism produced in England and America and on university literature courses taught in these countries.

The book, then, attempts to determine what postmodern fiction is – or *was* – by looking back at key examples. Its aim is not to provide a final definition of an entity named 'the postmodern novel'. This book treats 'postmodern fiction' as a category which contains a number of different kinds of postmodern fiction, a range of *postmodernisms*, in fact, rather than alternative ways of expressing a single, unified postmodernism.

Postmodern fiction is far too diverse in style to be a genre. Nor is it a historical label, like 'Victorian fiction', as to speak of the late twentieth century as the postmodern 'period' would be to misrepresent a great many contemporary writers whose work cannot usefully be related to postmodernism. I would prefer to think of postmodern fiction as a particular 'aesthetic' – a sensibility, a set of principles, or a value-system which unites specific currents in the writing of the latter half of the twentieth century.

To explain this, it is useful to follow the example of Brian McHale (another major theorist of the postmodern novel) in his approach to defining postmodern fiction, and use the Russian Formalist theorist Roman Jakobson's concept of 'the dominant': 'the focusing component of a work of art' which 'rules, determines, and transforms the remaining components [and] guarantees the "integrity" of the structure' and which shifts over literary history (McHale 1987, 6).

Identifying postmodern texts is a matter of determining which elements within them are especially dominant, in this sense. In my view, the most important features found in postmodern texts are:

(1) a self-reflexive acknowledgement of a text's own status as constructed, aesthetic artefact
(2) an implicit (or sometimes explicit) critique of realist approaches both to narrative and to representing a fictional 'world'
(3) a tendency to draw the reader's attention to his or her own process of interpretation as s/he reads the text

The reason why the concept of the dominant is useful is that none of these features are exclusive to postmodern fiction. Self-reflexivity is common in the eighteenth-century novel, modernist fiction rejects nineteenth-century realist techniques, and a great many novels from all periods invite the reader to interrogate the reading process. The question is really one of degree. It is also important to consider how these dominant features correspond to the specific historical context of postmodernism – in other words, how certain social and cultural factors have *caused* them to be more dominant than they are in, say, modernism.

I should point out that this book contains less about modernism than perhaps one would expect from an introduction to postmodern fiction. This is not to deny that postmodernism – as its name clearly indicates – bears a close relationship to modernism. Many of the most important definitions of postmodernism, such as those by McHale and Hutcheon, Jameson, Jencks, and Eco, are founded upon a comparison with modernist values and aesthetic techniques. In fact, the precepts of modernism will figure in the Introduction and in Chapters 1 and 2. However, my view is that the starting-point for understanding postmodern fiction is to compare it chiefly to realism – or at least the kind of 'ideal', 'straw-target' version of the nineteenth-century realist novel, which may not always resemble more complex actual examples of literary realism but nevertheless has figured as an antagonistic force in the development of postmodern writing.

Distinguishing between modernism and postmodernism is again a question of the postmodern 'dominant'. Patricia Waugh has argued that where modernism is preoccupied by *consciousness*, showing how the workings of the mind reveal individuals to be much less stable and unified than realist psychology would have us believe, postmodernism is much more interested in *fictionality* (Waugh, 1984, 14). Fictionality refers to the condition of being fictional, that is to say, the condition of being constructed, narrated, mediated. Fiction is always all of these things, which means that the represented world is always framed, presented to us from the perspective of another. In particular, fictionality involves a concern with the relationship between the language and represented world of fiction with the real world outside. This is what especially interests postmodern writers (though an interest is visible in some modernist texts too) and the reason why they position their writing against realism rather than modernism is because, in realism, the question of fictionality is generally ignored or suppressed.

To try and isolate what is effectively a 'canon' of postmodern fiction might naturally lead to disagreement about which authors or texts have or have not been included. Yet my method is more conservative than it might seem: I have not tried to incorporate any novelists or texts into the postmodern tradition who have not seriously been identified as postmodern already by theorists and critics over the last few decades. To try to keep the discussion accessible I have offered my own readings of these writers and texts, supported by relevant theory and criticism, but without being overloaded by references to the readings of others.

This brings us back to the question of reading. I hope my analyses will be useful to you in *your* reading of the postmodern fiction discussed in this book. I believe the twenty-four novelists it examines are not only twenty-four of the most important postmodern writers but twenty-four of the most remarkable novelists in twentieth-century writing as a whole. I hope this book will enhance your enjoyment of them, making their writing go down a little bit more easily.

Postmodernism and postmodernity

There is an episode of *The Simpsons* in which the barman, Moe Szyslak, tries to transform his dingy bar into somewhere 'cool' and futuristic, decorating it with randomly chosen objects such as suspended rabbits and eyeballs. His regulars don't get it. Faced with their non-comprehending stares, Moe explains: 'It's po-mo!... Post-modern!... Yeah, all right – weird for the sake of weird' ('Homer the Moe', *Simpsons Archive*).

The Simpsons is widely considered one of the most exemplary postmodern texts because of its self-reflexive irony and intertextuality. But postmodernism is not weird for the sake of being weird. Nor is it simply 'the contemporary' or 'the experimental'. It *may* be 'avant-garde' (though many critics, myself included, think it isn't), or it may be a continuation of the values and techniques of modernism (but then again it may just as plausibly be a break with modernism). It may be an empty practice of recycling previous artistic styles... or a valid form of political critique.

Postmodernism is a notoriously slippery and indefinable term. It was originally coined in the 1940s to identify a reaction against the Modern movement in architecture. However, it first began to be widely used in the 1960s by American cultural critics and commentators such as Susan Sontag and Leslie Fiedler who sought to describe a 'new sensibility' in literature which either rejected modernist attitudes and techniques or adapted or extended them. In the following decades the term began to figure in academic disciplines besides literary criticism and architecture – such as social theory, cultural and media studies, visual arts, philosophy, and history. Such wide-ranging usage meant that the term became overloaded with meaning, chiefly because it was being used to describe characteristics of the social and political landscape as well as a whole range of different examples of cultural production.

This begs the question: why has an obviously problematic term continued to be used? I think the reason is that there has been a genuine feeling amongst theorists, cultural commentators, artists and writers that our age, has, since the 1950s and 1960s onward (opinions vary as to when exactly), been shaped by significant alterations in society as a result of technology, economics and the media; that this has led to significant shifts in cultural and aesthetic production as a result, perhaps even (though these are even more difficult to measure) changes in the way people who exist in these changed conditions live, think, and feel. To try to capture this sense of change, vague and multi-faceted though it may be, is why the term postmodernism has been invented, adopted, defined and redefined.

More precisely, one of the key questions behind the postmodern debate is how the particular conditions of postmodernity differ from or have arisen from those of *modernity*. Theorists have tended to portray modernity (i.e. from early to mid-twentieth century) as increasingly industrialized, mechanized, urban, and bureaucratic, while postmodernity is the era of the 'space age', of consumerism, late capitalism, and, most recently, the dominance of the virtual and the digital. Such generalized portraits of modern and postmodern society have been paralleled by similar comparisons of the specific aesthetic styles which have dominated in these periods. Where modernist art forms privilege formalism, rationality, authenticity, depth, originality, etc., postmodernism, the argument goes, favours bricolage or pastiche to original production, the mixing of styles and genres, and the juxtaposition of 'low' with high culture. Where modernism is sincere or earnest, postmodernism is playful and ironic.

The discussion in this book aims to move beyond such generalizations (and, in any case, after this chapter, will concentrate on prose fiction), but it is important to acknowledge that the question of how postmodernism relates to modernism remains a highly contentious one, not least because the term itself – 'post-modern' – implies, confusingly, that modernism has either been superseded or has entered a new phase.

The problems with the term postmodernism are complicated further because when reading about it we are actually dealing with three derivatives – not just 'postmodernity', but also 'postmodernism' and 'postmodern'. This latter term gives this book its title and is favoured throughout. 'Postmodern' is an adjective that refers both to a particular period in literary and perhaps cultural history (though this book is more interested in the former than the latter) which begins in the 1950s and continues until the 1990s (though inevitably there is disagreement about this too, as some would argue we are still in the postmodern period now), and to a set of aesthetic styles and principles which characterize literary production in this period and which are shaped by the context of postmodernism and postmodernity. Where 'postmodernity' refers to the way the world has changed in this period, due to developments in the political, social, economic, and media spheres, 'postmodernism' (and the related adjective 'postmodernist') refers to a set of ideas developed from philosophy and theory and related to aesthetic production. To provide a context for the discussion in the rest of the book, this chapter will now turn to a more in-depth consideration of prominent theoretical uses of these latter two terms.

Postmodernity and 'late capitalism'

Postmodernity can be described most usefully in terms of the political and socio-economic systems which develop in what the Marxist thinker Ernest Mandel called the 'third stage' of capitalist expansion (Mandel, 1975).

In the period following the Second World War, the first two stages of capitalism, 'market capitalism' and 'monopoly (or imperialist) capitalism', were superseded by 'postindustrial' or 'late' capitalism. In effect late capitalism sees the accumulative logic of capitalism extend into every possible area of society, and into every corner of the globe, eliminating any remaining pockets of 'precapitalism'. It means that areas of society which were previously unaffected by the logic of the market, such as the media, the arts, or education became subject to the laws of capitalism (i.e. requiring growth, profits, and business models) and the advance of what we now call the 'globalization' of consumerism. The result of this is a cultural eclecticism, as summarized in a much-quoted sentence from the philosopher Jean-François Lyotard: 'one listens to reggae, watches a western, eats McDonald's food for lunch and local cuisine for dinner, wears Paris perfume in Tokyo and "retro" clothes in Hong Kong' (Lyotard, 1984, 76).

The key factor behind this expansion, as Larry McCaffrey has argued, is the rise of technology. As competition is so intense amongst multinational organisations, it follows that the most important resource of all – more than actual materials or products – is information which can be used for marketing, research, and production purposes. Ever more sophisticated means of gathering and analysing information, McCaffrey suggests, has meant that postmodern society has become increasingly 'high-tech', saturated by products such as medical supplies, weaponry, and surveillance technology (which protects the interests of multinational corporations) and consumer goods such as mobile phones, computers, plasma screen TVs, high-spec cars, etc.

McCaffrey argues that even more significant than these high-tech products are 'the rapid proliferation of technologically mass-produced "products" that are essentially *reproductions* or *abstractions* – images, advertising, information, memories, styles, simulated experiences' (McCaffrey, 1991b, 4) and which rely upon other technologically engineered products such as computers, televisions, digital music, etc. to package and transmit them to consumers. These are much cheaper to produce and consume than more tangible products, and are the speciality of the advertising, information, and the media/cultural industries.

The consequence of living in a postindustrial, information-driven, media/ culture-saturated world, according to theorists of postmodernity, is that we have become alienated from those aspects of life we might consider authentic or *real*. While our working lives are still 'real' (we go to work and pay the bills) they are not as real as, say, farming or building a ship. Instead we spend most of our time at our desks in front of a computer screen processing 'information' of one kind or another, engaging with symbolic representations rather than real, tangible objects. Much of our leisure time is spent engaging in simulated experiences or consuming more information. Existence has become more 'virtual' than real.

Baudrillard and simulation

We tend to think of 'virtual reality' in a 'sci-fi' sense as an experience to be available in the near future, once computers are sophisticated enough to enable us literally to inhabit a fake version of the world but interact with it as if it were real. It is conventionally imagined (curiously in terms of sado-masochistic fantasy) as a situation in which we don gloves, a helmet, or a suit and then interact with our real body in a fictional world. But as the postmodern philosopher Jean Baudrillard has argued, we don't need to wait for these devices to be possible: virtual reality is already here, and we all live in it almost every moment of our lives (Baudrillard, 1994a). We 'experience' the world through TV news or 'reality TV' shows, engage with other people we have never met (in internet chatrooms, or in our fascination with celebrities), use e-mail to communicate virtually to real people.

Central to Baudrillard's theory is the idea that we have entered a new phase of history, though he develops this thesis in a different and rather idiosyncratic way from Marxist thinkers like Mandel. What characterizes our world is that the last traces of the 'symbolic structure' that reigned in the pre-industrial world are disappearing. Baudrillard here draws on the economic theory of Marcel Mauss. Mauss's famous work *The Gift* (1953) explores the way primitive society was founded upon the logic of the gift-exchange rather than commodity-exchange. Where commodity-exchange is a system that works according to the exchange of goods for money, gift-exchange involves a threeway system of obligation: the gift must be given, received, and reciprocated. Most importantly, reciprocation means effectively giving back more than is received, in order to avoid the receiver being placed in an inferior position to the giver and to ensure that the triangular pattern of exchange may continue (Mauss, 2001).

In early societies this logic underscored every aspect of life, from harvest festivals to military service to weddings, and meant that even people could be gifts. Where Mauss believed that remnants of this economy still operate in our own money economy (e.g. weddings, dinner parties), though they have largely been replaced by a formalized notion of commodity-exchange, for Baudrillard this form of symbolic exchange has died out completely. Now there is only the endless and meaningless exchange of *signs*, which are even less 'real' and more ambiguous than commodities or currency (often they are images or words): everything can be exchanged for everything else, every sign is potentially interchangeable, reversible. There is no surplus element as there was in symbolic exchange.

Baudrillard's term for this overall interchangeability of signs is 'the code'. Its function is to 'codify' reality according to the 'law of value'. In other words it establishes a system of signs which provides (or tries to provide) everything with a meaning and a value relative to other things. It establishes the binary oppositions upon which Western culture is founded (life over death, good over evil, cause over effect) and produces an apparent stability in essences, identity, difference, and meaning. In this way the code actually *produces* reality: we experience the world through the sign-system of values set down in its underlying metaphysic.

The special ability of the code is to duplicate things so that the copy is indistinguishable from and indeed replaces the original. It is visible in science (in biology or DNA) and in computer and information technology which enables perfect reproduction (e.g. of biological tissue or of a photographic image). Previously, copying something that is real resulted in a version of the real thing which was still recognizable as a copy. Yet because the code can produce an exact replica, the difference between the original and the copy is eliminated. This effect is a typical one in contemporary culture which is characterized by a process of reproduction Baudrillard terms simulation. He points to numerous instances in the contemporary world in which the ability to distinguish between the real and representation is compromised: for example, Disneyland, opinion polls, President Nixon, Michael Jackson. Perhaps the most powerful example is the way that the actual events of twentieth-century warfare have become replaced by their representations: we 'consume' the representations as if they are real. The Vietnam War, the Gulf War, even, retrospectively, the Holocaust, are visible only in simulated form: with Vietnam, Baudrillard argues, 'the war became film, the film becomes war, the two are joined by their common haemorrhage into technology' (Baudrillard, 1994b, 59).

Baudrillard's idea of simulation is often assumed to be the state of affairs when we engage somehow with a representation rather than the real thing. So that if one drinks a synthetic version of Irish beer in an Irish theme pub, one may be comically seen as consuming the hyperreal rather than the real. In fact, simulation refers to the process by which the technologies which dominate the contemporary world attempt to make aspects of the real, natural world around us into tangible, distinct entities. Paradoxically simulation tries to make the real properly *real* by attempting to explain everything in the world, eliminating mystery and the unexplained, and dividing the world up into a system of oppositions, differences, and values. Simulation does not just eliminate the real, it creates it.

Poststructuralism, postmodernism, and 'the real'

The idea that postmodernity separates human beings from 'the real' has important resonances with poststructuralism, a theoretical movement which has been hugely influential in literary studies (and other humanities disciplines) in recent decades, and which, like the work of Baudrillard, revolves around the separation of the realm of language from the real world.

It is important not to overplay the link between postmodernism and poststructuralism as some do and regard them as being 'really' the same, or the former having emerged out of the latter. Poststructuralist thinkers such as Derrida and Foucault are sometimes, erroneously, co-opted into the roll-call of postmodern theorists. As Brian McHale has put it, 'poststructuralism and postmodernism are more like cousins than parent and child' (McHale and Neagu, 2006, n.p.)

It is unnecessary here to consider the similarities and differences between postmodernism and poststructuralism beyond stating generally that poststructuralism favours a creative approach to interpreting the literary or artistic text that demonstrates how its meanings are always multiple and deferred rather than fixed, and this is in tune with the 'postmodern' approach to interpreting texts (considered in more depth in the next chapter).

But we can note here that one way in which postmodernism is indeed 'poststructuralist' is because in problematizing the question of 'the real' it signals that it comes after *structuralism*, the implications of which also triggered poststructuralist theory. The theories of Ferdinand de Saussure, the linguist whose ideas are the starting-point for structuralist theory, emphasize that language and the world are always separate, and the gap between them impossible to bridge. Saussure's theory argued that language was a system made up of signs.

He defined the sign as composed of two elements: the 'signifier', a distinctive combination of sounds or images (i.e. a word or a visual image), and the 'signified', the concept or definition that the signifier calls to mind. The signifier and the signified are yoked together arbitrarily (there is no reason why a book should have this name rather than a 'rook' or a 'magazine') but once connected they could not be divorced because for language to function as a form of social communication agreed meanings have to be maintained. Language works principally by convention.

The real implication of Saussure's theory is that language doesn't *need* the world to function; it works independently of it. What this means is that when someone is speaking about a real thing he or she is only understood because of the code of the signifier. So if I point at a book and say 'this book', the reason you understand what I am referring to is actually not because of 'the referent' (the actual book I may be pointing at) but because you comprehend the *signifieds* evoked by the signifiers 'this' and 'book'.

Saussure's ideas would seem to offer a foundation for the postmodern conviction, articulated most powerfully in the theories of Baudrillard (even though he was strongly critical of Saussure) that we inhabit a virtual world always already divorced from the real. In postmodernity, to quote Baudrillard, the map 'precedes the territory': in other words reality is determined by its simulated version. More directly relevant to postmodern fiction (as we shall see in the following chapter) is the structuralist idea that meaning is derived from the relations between elements in the system rather than their capacity to refer to something outside it. A book gains its meaning from how it differs from other terms both phonetically (i.e. it is not a rook or a boot) and conceptually (it is not a magazine or a leaflet) rather than inherent value: this is what Saussure meant when he described language as a 'system of differences with no positive terms' (Saussure, 1966, 120). This provides a theoretical underpinning for the idea which preoccupies postmodern fiction, that specific words in a literary text mean what they mean because of how they relate to other words in the text and to other literary texts rather than how they relate to the real world.

As the work of poststructuralist theorists such as Jacques Lacan and Louis Althusser demonstrates, Saussure's theory also has profound implications for the way we conceive of human subjectivity. Indeed the very notion of the human 'subject', unlike the humanist idea of the autonomous 'self', emphasizes how we exist in the world as a kind of linguistic unit in a sentence, our 'meaning' derived from our position in the overall system rather than any inherent substance. The most powerful development of this idea is Lacan's psychoanalytic theory of how we derive identity from our position in what he calls the 'symbolic order', the system of 'meanings', codes, conventions, and rules that structure society.

We only gain a meaningful identity once we are inscribed in the symbolic order – most obviously because we are given a name, but also because our actions and assertions of identity can only signify in the terms of an agreed-upon network of signification. But entering the symbolic order separates us from 'the real' (our bodily drives) and means that everyday life is essentially virtual as everything real is made recognizable and meaningful by language and the codes of the symbolic order.

The outcome is the creation of desire and the unconscious and the whole symptomatology of neurosis and psychosis which are the special objects of psychoanalysis and are determined by our efforts to deal with what cannot be 'symbolized' (i.e. what does not 'make sense' to everyday reality, such as trauma or death). The most 'postmodern' articulation of this state of affairs is provided by the Lacanian philosopher Slavoj Žižek, whose work emphasizes how everyday reality – the world of our name, our consciousness and our social identity – is nothing but a necessary fiction which is designed to keep our *real* selves (i.e. the inaccessible part of ourselves located in unconscious) at bay (Žižek, 1991).

Sociology and the construction of reality

There is an interesting convergence between the Lacanian presentation of reality as a necessary fiction and sociological (and non-structuralist) theories about the 'social construction of reality' which have been used by some literary theorists (Waugh, 1984, 51–3; McHale 1987, 36–9) to provide a context for the self-reflexivity of postmodern fiction. Most influential of these is Peter L. Berger and Thomas Luckmann's idea that reality is not 'given' but is a fiction that we collectively subscribe to (Berger and Luckmann, 1991). Reality is manufactured as a result of the interaction between given elements of the world and social convention, language, and individual vision. This produces a fairly stable version of reality which we inhabit in everyday life – what Berger and Luckmann call 'paramount reality' – though they contend that contemporary reality is especially subject to being reimagined and reshaped.

The idea that it is more accurate to speak of multiple *realities* in the post-modern world than a single reality is developed by Stanley Cohen and Laurie Taylor in their 1976 book *Escape Attempts*. Their study explores how we con-tinually 'escape' from the world of paramount reality to inhabit other realities, which we project as we engage in different social activities, for example, reading about celebrities in newspapers, planning a holiday, playing games, watching a film, having sex, etc. In a world increasingly dominated by advertising, pop culture and the media it means that 'miniature escape fantasies' are constantly available to us and switching from one to another effectively turns us into 'split personalities' (Cohen and Taylor, 1992, 139).

Jameson and the crisis in historicity

The experience of being 'split off' from reality, living in a 'hyperreal' world (Baudrillard's term for the culture in which the logic of simulation has become all-pervasive) might be expected to have profound consequences for the way we live – the way we *feel*, in other words. Indeed a loss of reality is a symptom of a range of psychic disorders, from mild depression to full-blown psychosis. This seems to explain a peculiar tendency amongst theorists of the postmodern to employ the language of mental disorder to describe its effects. Postmodernity has been described as 'schizophrenic' (Jameson, 1991), 'multiphrenic' (Gergen, 1992), 'telephrenic' (Gottschalk, 2000), depressive and nihilistic (Levin, 1987), paranoid (Burgin, 1990; Frank, 1992; Brennan, 2004), and liable to induce in those who live in it 'low-level fear' (Massumi, 1993), or 'panic' (Kroker and Cook, 1988).

This psychopathological terminology is easily explained, on one level, by the fact that the majority of theorists of postmodernism and postmodernity have tended to regard their effects as harmful. Most prominent of these is the Marxist thinker Fredric Jameson, whose diagnosis of postmodernism trumps all other theorists of the postmodern in its references to pathological conditions, associating the phenomenon with schizophrenia, hysteria, nostalgia, paranoia, and a 'waning of affect'.

Highly rhetorical as Jameson's style is, there is substance to it. His diagnosis is backed up with an extensive analysis of the impact of the conditions of late capitalism on individual perceptive and cognitive faculties. The starting-point for his analysis is that postmodernism heralds the death of one particular version of the subject: 'the autonomous bourgeois monad or ego or individual' which existed in the period of 'classical capitalism and the nuclear family' has been dissolved 'in the world of organizational bureaucracy' (Jameson, 1991, 15). The result is that, in art, the kind of expression of anxiety which was typical of modernism ('alienation, anomie, solitude and social fragmentation and isolation'), and is represented by a modernist artwork such as Edvard Munch's *The Scream*, has been replaced by a more general reflection of 'intensities', feelings which besiege postmodern subjects and are 'free-floating and impersonal and tend to be dominated by a peculiar kind of euphoria' (Jameson, 1991, 16).

More than any other thinker Jameson is responsible for making the link between postmodernity and the third stage of capitalism, as is shown by the title of his influential book, *Postmodernism, or the Cultural Logic of Late Capitalism* (1991). Postmodernism, for Jameson, equates purely and simply to the effects of late capitalism on contemporary culture.

Central to his argument is his view that late capitalism has created a 'perpetual present' where time is dominated by the free-floating rhythms of the new electronic media. The result is that our apprehension of past and future is seriously weakened. Cultural production and consumption in postmodernity reveals that we are unable to place ourselves in a properly *historical* context. History has become simply a matter of 'styles' which can be pastiched in the latest retro clothes or 'theme pubs' or in 'nostalgia films' like Roman Polanski's *Chinatown* (1974) – a historical film which Jameson thinks bears no reliable traces of history (Jameson, 1991, 19–20). Postmodernism, for Jameson, is characterized by the 'random cannibalization of all the styles of the past, the play of random stylistic allusion' (18). In terms of aesthetic technique, it means a preference for pastiche over parody. Both are devices which mimic a 'peculiar or unique, idiosyncratic style'. But where parody has 'ulterior motives', namely a critical, satirical impulse, a commitment to making viewer or reader laugh, and retains the 'conviction that alongside the abnormal tongue you have momentarily borrowed, some healthy linguistic normality still exists', pastiche does not. It is simply 'blank parody, a statue with blind eyeballs' (Jameson, 1991, 18), a kind of reflex aping process devoid of any sense of critical distance.

This state of affairs does not simply pertain in popular culture but in the most serious art and literature. E. L. Doctorow's novel *Ragtime* (1975) is regarded by some (such as Linda Hutcheon) as an example of 'historiographic metafiction', a novel which powerfully interrogates our knowledge of the past. But for Jameson the novel is written in such a way as to 'short-circuit an older type of social–historical interpretation' (Jameson, 1991, 23) and ensure that its self-reflexive direction of the reader towards his or her own methods of knowing history prevents it from presenting its historical period with sufficient depth.

The problem is that postmodernism – or the cultural logic of late capitalism – has swallowed everything and it is impossible simply to ignore or extinguish it. This means that cultural production is unable to mount a critique of postmodernism because it inevitably conforms to its logic itself. From a Jamesonian perspective, Bret Easton Ellis's novel *American Psycho* (1991), is on the face of it a critique of late twentieth-century capitalism and its rampant commodification. But because its language so obsessively mimics the language of 1980s consumer culture and continually name-checks its products, all it can do ultimately is simply reflect the obsessions of the 1980s culture rather than comment meaningfully upon them (Annesley, 1998, 21–2).

For Jameson the only way 'out' of the postmodernist logic is through what he calls 'cognitive mapping', the identification and analysis of all its effects. Postmodernism has left us so disoriented, has so muddled up our sense of time and space, that we must construct maps to enable us to rediscover our spatial and historical location, to return us to a view of what he calls elsewhere 'the present as History' (Jameson, 1984, 65). This is what his own study aims to do, though he is aware of the paradox that if the logic of late capitalism envelops each discourse and cultural practice in postmodernity, then his *own* analysis is in danger of being contaminated by it.

Lyotard and the decline of the metanarrative

Jean-François Lyotard's idea of 'the postmodern condition' might seem the product of a similar impulse to that of Jameson's equation of postmodernism with mental 'disorder'. However Lyotard differs from the likes of Jameson and Baudrillard in depicting the condition of postmodernity as potentially more positive, even liberating.

His incisive analysis of postmodernism, *The Postmodern Condition* (1979), offers a variation on a thesis developed by the sociologist Daniel Bell (Bell, 1973) that the key consequence of the transition to a postindustrial, 'computerized' society is a change in the 'status of knowledge'. Lyotard agrees that where in modernity the assumption was that knowledge was universally applicable, now in postmodernity it is localized and partial. Unlike Bell's, Lyotard's quarrel in making this point is with the tradition of 'Enlightenment' thinking which dates back to the work of the eighteenth-century philosophers Immanuel Kant, G. W. F. Hegel, and Jean-Jacques Rousseau and, especially, their descendant and Lyotard's contemporary, Jürgen Habermas.

For Lyotard, Enlightenment thought is sustained by what he terms 'meta-narratives', grand stories which structure the discourses of modern religion, politics, philosophy, and science. Metanarratives are a form of ideology which function violently to suppress and control the individual subject by imposing a false sense of 'totality' and 'universality' on a set of disparate things, actions, and events. A metanarrative is like a literary narrative in that it is essentially a means of ordering discrete elements in a particular form and thus presenting a rhetorical case about the way things work or are connected, which legiti-mates political positions and courses of action. The metanarrative is at work in science, for example, in the tendency to legitimate a scientific discovery by recounting it in the form of 'epic' narrative. By this means science can sustain its powerful position in the social and political system. As Lyotard explains, '[t]he state spends large amounts of money to enable science to pass itself off as an epic: the State's own credibility is based on that epic' (Lyotard, 1984, 28).

But the characteristic feature of postmodernity, according to Lyotard, is that the power of the metanarrative as a legitimating, empowering force is on the wane. Postmodern subjects simply don't believe in metanarratives any more. They instinctively acknowledge instead the rhetorical function of narrative, and appreciate that alternative narratives could be fashioned from the same groups of events. Postmodernity, Lyotard argues, prefers 'little narratives' (*petit récits*), those which do not attempt to present an overarching 'Truth' but offer a qualified, limited 'truth', one relative to a particular situation.

Though he is a philosopher not a literary critic, Lyotard's assumption that narratives are never innocent nor natural but always partial, selective, and rhetorical, is entirely in keeping with the approach to narrative taken by post-modern writers and critics. One of the 'realist' conceits which postmodern writers reject is the impression that narrative somehow unfolds naturally with-out being shaped by an author, that the task of the narrator is simply to present the reader with a coherent narrative which s/he has come upon. Instead nar-rative is always the result of selection and interpretation. This is something demonstrated repeatedly by the self-reflexive techniques of the 'metafictional' writers (explored in Chapters 3 and 4).

Lyotard's critique of the metanarrative and his faith in the power of the *petit récit* also has powerful resonances with the way postmodern fiction eschews the modernist strategy of referring to a key intertext which enables the reader to make sense of the fiction by 'recuperating' its fragmented elements. The journey of Leopold Bloom in Joyce's *Ulysses*, divided into eighteen chapters, each written in a different style, can be – indeed must be, as Joyce directs the reader to do so through the title and also via extra-textual comments he made about the novel – set against the journey of the eponymous character who features in Homer's *Odyssey*. Postmodern novels, such as Angela Carter's *The Passion of New Eve* or Thomas Pynchon's *Gravity's Rainbow*, typically offer the reader a surfeit of intertextual references and allusions which seem, tantalizingly, to point to a single explanatory master-narrative but in the end lead us to nothing except an ironic recognition of how master-narratives function, and the value of individual, localized stories or temporarily useful interpretive constructions.

Irony and 'double-coding'

Lyotard's definition of postmodernism as 'incredulity towards metanarratives' implies that in his or her refusal to be duped by the legitimating ideology of the political system, the postmodern subject possesses a valuable critical awareness, a mindset more discerning and political than the portrait presented by Jameson. There is a parallel between this capacity and the attitude of *self-reflexivity* or ironic knowingness which other, more aesthetically oriented theorists have identified at the heart of postmodern culture. Their logic is that we may be the pawns of the political machine, we may be divorced from the real, but at least we *know* we are. More precisely, we know we can no longer take for granted (if we ever did) that 'reality' is something natural, something innocently 'given'. Rather, reality is always already manufactured, an ideological illusion sustained by the matrix of postindustrial capitalism and media culture. This awareness is suggestive of the attitude described as 'cynical reason' by the philosopher Peter Sloterdijk which embodies a different understanding of how ideology works to the old Marxist notion of 'false consciousness', where people were fooled into subscribing to the belief systems of the ruling classes. Now, according to Sloterdijk, instead of being seduced by ideology into acting in the way it wants us to act or believing what it wants us to believe, we know what we are doing is false, but we do it anyway (Sloterdijk, 1987, 5).

Another way of putting this is to argue that the postmodern attitude is predominantly *ironic*. Irony is a non-literal usage of language, where what is said is contradicted by what is meant (either deliberately or unwittingly) or what is said is subverted by the particular context in which it is said. It works because we are unconsciously aware that in language meanings are not fixed but contain other possible meanings. All words bear traces of previous and other potential uses, and their meaning changes depending on the tone of utterance or the particular context in which they are uttered. Irony is therefore not just cynical, not just a way of making fun of the world. It demonstrates a knowingness about how reality is ideologically constructed.

This ironic attitude is exhibited in works of popular culture which are seen as characteristically postmodern, such as *The Simpsons*, episodes of which continually allude to, parody, and imitate other TV programmes, films, and cultural events. Take the episode 'Homer the Moe' (2001) I quoted from at the beginning of this chapter. The website 'The Simpsons Archive' (www.snpp.com) identifies a host of cultural references in this show, from movies such as *Mad Max 2*, *Ironweed*, *The Awakening*, and *Coyote Ugly*, to TV series such as *CSI: Crime Scene Investigation*, *Happy Days*, *The Munsters*, H. G. Wells's novel *The Time Machine*, the death of Virginia Woolf, songs by R.E.M. and Joan Jett and the Blackhearts. This is entirely typical of *The Simpsons*, as even a cursory browse through such webpages suggest. While its intertextuality might be considered as simply one more source of comedy in a show designed to be funny, *The Simpsons*'s intertextual references and self-referentiality also serve to remind us how deeply enmeshed our lives are in the world of media representation.

The relentless energy of the humour in *The Simpsons* suggests that there is surely something more at stake than making people laugh (or, alternatively, we could acknowledge that making people laugh has nothing to do with triviality) and behind the incessant irony there is surely a serious point about how postmodernity imprisons us in a frame of cultural references. This idea has been wittily (but earnestly) expressed by the Italian novelist and cultural theorist Umberto Eco. When he set out to write his postmodern detective story *The Name of the Rose* – a departure for a critic because it meant putting himself on 'the opposite side of the barricade', actually telling a story rather than analysing how it is read – he wondered, 'Is it possible to say "It was a beautiful morning at the end of November" without feeling like Snoopy?' (Eco, 1985, 18). His theoretical exploration of his anxiety is one of the most persuasive theories of how and why irony functions in postmodernism.

For Eco postmodernism is not a style which is typical of a specific moment in cultural history, but an *attitude* which underlies cultural production in any period: 'We could say that every period has its own postmodernism' (Eco, 2002, 110). The postmodern, he argues, emerges at the point when whatever is 'modern' in a particular era (and he defines this as the 'avant-garde', those writers and artists who occupy the frontline in the battle against tradition, producing innovative, experimental work designed to push the boundaries) recognizes that it cannot go any further without lapsing into silence. They reach this point because in the pursuit of the new they have to 'destroy' the past. However, art must continue, and so the only solution for those who come after the moderns is to engage with the past once again. It is at this point that the postmodern comes into being. The renewed engagement with the past is made possible through the use of irony, paradoxically saying something new, but only by acknowledging that it has already been said.

To illustrate the point Eco transposes his 'Snoopy' remark into a more extensive and much-quoted comparison:

> I think of the postmodern attitude as that of a man who loves a very cultivated woman and knows he cannot say to her 'I love you madly', because he knows that she knows (and that she knows that he knows) that these words have already been written by Barbara Cartland. Still, there is a solution. He can say, 'as Barbara Cartland would put it, I love you madly'. At this point, having avoided false innocence, having said clearly that it is no longer possible to speak innocently, he will nevertheless have said what he wanted to say to the woman: that he loves her in an age of lost innocence. If the woman goes along with this, she will have received a declaration of love all the same. Neither of the two speakers will feel innocent, both will have accepted the challenge of the

past, of the already said, which cannot be eliminated; both will consciously and with pleasure play the game of irony . . . But both will have succeeded, once again, in speaking of love.   (Eco, 2002, 111)

For Eco this analogy encapsulates the difficulty faced by the postmodern writer who by virtue of his or her position in history must come after the innovations of modernism. A similar anxiety was also famously voiced by the American postmodern novelist John Barth in his essay 'The Literature of Exhaustion' (1967) which wonders how it is possible to continue to write in the face of the knowledge that all the forms of fiction had been 'used up' by the moderns. Barth turns to the fiction of Jorge Luis Borges as a model, since he gets over the impasse by ironically turning exhaustion into the very subject of his fiction.

Eco's argument is a powerful riposte to those Marxist critics (Jameson, 1991, Eagleton, 1997, or Žižek, 1999) who argue that the postmodern predisposition towards irony is nothing more than quietism, evidence of the complete lack of any political function in postmodernism. Eco demonstrates that irony is not necessarily an empty, cynical gesture, but a necessary negotiation, an essential strategy to avoid the inevitable silence to which avant-gardism leads.

Other theorists have also seen something powerful in postmodern irony, without agreeing with Eco's 'metahistorical' theory about the cycles of post-avant-gardism. The architectural critic Charles Jencks regards the defining element of postmodernism as the strategy he calls 'double coding'. Double coding in architecture means 'the combination of Modern techniques with something else (usually traditional building) in order for architecture to communicate with the public and . . . other architects'. In this way it is able to combine the élite with the popular and the old with the new. This bringing together of elements from two spheres, this practice of doing two things at the same time, is what makes it essentially an ironic technique.

Jencks is strict about the terms of his definition: a work of art must be double-coded for it to qualify as postmodernist rather than modernist or even what he calls 'late modernist', an intermediary form of aesthetic creation positioned between modernism and postmodernism. He argues that Lyotard, Baudrillard, and Jameson (among others) actually mistake 'late modernism' for postmodernism in their analyses. Late modernism, Jencks suggests, remains 'committed to the tradition of the new and does not have a complex relation to the past, or pluralism, or the transformation of western culture – a concern with meaning, continuity and symbolism' (Jencks, 1986, 33–4).

The notion of double-coding is also central to an important contribution to postmodern theory by the literary critic Linda Hutcheon. Developed in a productive burst in the late eighties, when she published three monographs on postmodern fiction (Hutcheon 1988a, 1988b, 1989 [2002]), Hutcheon argues that postmodernism is characterized by 'an inherently paradoxical structure' (Hutcheon, 1988a, 222). She insists that she does not mean postmodernism is oppositional or dialectical, but that it is *double* or contradictory, that is comfortable with doing two opposing things at the same time or representing both sides of an argument at once. Its approach is summed up by the linguistic conjunction 'both . . . and . . . ' rather than 'either . . . or . . . ' As such her theory provides a useful way of explaining why the debate about postmodernism has involved such radically polarized positions and also offers us a way of moving beyond such binaries. Rather than postmodernism being a continuation *or* a break with modernism, it is more accurate to see it as both. Rather than postmodern art being self-reflexive *or* referring to the real world, it does both.

For Eco, Jencks, and Hutcheon, then, postmodernism is principally an ironic mode, which simultaneously says or does one thing *and* another. Ironic strategies are frequently central to the examples of postmodern fiction discussed in this book. The most characteristic practice in postmodern fiction is *metafiction*, the technique by which a text highlights its own status as a fictional construct by referring to itself. Self-reference is the literary version of the postmodern ironic attitude, for it indicates – as I will show in the following chapter – that we cannot accept the 'reality' we are presented with in a novel at face value. Metafiction reminds us that the work of fiction we read *is* fiction; it is not a mirror-reflection of the world but a combination of words on a page that we must make sense of by relating them to other texts, not the external world. To state this seems superfluous, for even the least self-conscious reader of fiction knows that s/he is 'suspending his or her disbelief' as s/he reads. Yet the function of metafiction, as Patricia Waugh makes clear in her book *Metafiction* (1984), is to expose postmodernity for what it is: effectively just as constructed, mediated, and discursive as the reality we are presented with in the world of fiction.

Chapter 1

Postmodern fiction: theory and practice

Postmodern fiction can be considered as a response to the kind of socio-historical changes discussed in the previous chapter. Larry McCaffrey, for example, argues that with the assassination of President J. F. Kennedy on 22 November 1963, '[p]ostmodernism was officially ushered in – at least in the United States – since that was the day that symbolically signaled the end of a certain kind of optimism and naïvete in our collective unconsciousness, the end of certain verities and assurances that had helped shape our notion of what fiction should be' (McCaffrey, 1986, xii).

There can be no doubt that literary change works 'symptomatically', as a result of what occurs at a wider social and cultural level. But if there is any validity in the category 'postmodern fiction' it comes from using it for more than simply identifying particular related themes within a group of texts. Likewise, as well as being a symptom of wide-ranging cultural change, postmodern fiction needs to be understood in terms of specific currents within literary theory and practice. This means considering postmodern fiction in terms of form rather than context, assessing how social and cultural change might prompt changes in what fiction *does* and how it positions its readers to respond to it. This is the aim of this chapter, which is divided into three main sections. The first will consider the postmodern critique of 'mimesis' (the practice which informs realism), the second will set out the qualities that typify postmodern fiction as a result, and the third section will explore how all this relates to the key question of reading.

An incredulity towards realism

Realism and modernism

The extent to which postmodern fiction is post-modernist – in other words, the precise ways in which it might be judged as following on from modernist fiction – is, as I suggested in the introduction to this book, a complex issue. Throughout the postmodernism debate there have always been passionately expressed differences of opinion about whether postmodernism really amounts to a departure from modernism or whether it simply continues with concerns originally dealt with by modernist writers. The technical innovations of a writer like Beckett, for example, have been plausibly identified by various critics as both modernist and postmodernist, while modernist attitudes and techniques can be identified in contemporary writers who might otherwise be considered in tune with the postmodern (such as Jeanette Winterson, Ian McEwan, or James Kelman). Instead of becoming immersed in the debate about the relationship between modernist and postmodernist fiction, however, I think that it is more useful here to concentrate on one particular element which both movements share: a dissatisfaction with nineteenth-century realism. More precisely, the modernist approach to literary realism had profound consequences for how those writers who followed after modernism conceived of and wrote their own fiction.

Realism is a mode of production in literature, art and film which attempts to sustain the illusion that the fictional world we view or read about is a plausible version of the real one, replicating how it looks, how people in it behave, the kind of things which happen to them. A realist novel is often described as presenting us with a 'slice of life', as if the text has cut out a particular segment of reality – either in the past or the present – and served it to us so we can taste life as it is or was in some other place than our own. In particular, realism depends upon the practice of *mimesis*, the Greek term for 'imitation' (brought into literary theory by Aristotle), the idea that art and literature can reproduce aspects of the real world.

But as its suffix '-ism' suggests, realism is more than an aesthetic practice but a system of belief which revolves around the conviction that the work of art not only is capable of replicating the 'sensible' world (i.e. whatever we can experience through our senses), but has a duty to do so. Realist ideology asserts that art and literature should reflect life and the world soberly, in precise detail, so that we can learn from or analyse it rather than becoming swept up by idealistic and escapist flights of fancy.

Though realism has been a part of literature since Chaucer, it is especially associated with the novel, and in particular with the extraordinary pan-European production of rich and profound novels from the 1830s to the 1870s by the likes of Balzac and Flaubert in France, Tolstoy in Russia, and Dickens and George Eliot in England. This fiction demonstrated the realist philosophy to masterful effect. As such it became the principal object of critique for modernist novelists in the early part of the twentieth century. The key impulse behind modernist writing is encapsulated in the poet Ezra Pound's famous command that writers of the age 'make it new'. Rather than simply extending the possibilities for the novel in the name of producing something different, however, modernist novelists such as James Joyce, Virginia Woolf, and Joseph Conrad believed that subjectivity (the experience of being a human being, or social 'subject') ought to be rendered more accurately than it was in the nineteenth-century novel.

Their work consequently deploys techniques which convey how the conscious mind experiences reality not just as something that can be measured by universal norms, but as something deeply personal and particular. The 'stream of consciousness' technique, for example, perhaps the most famous modernist innovation in fiction, represents the contents of a character's conscious mind 'directly' without being mediated by a narrator. Its effect is typical of modernism in that it limits the traditional (realist) narrator's role as 'mediator', whose job is to present the fictional world to the reader by framing it and shaping our responses to it. Instead it plunges the reader directly into the fictional world with only limited guidance or bearings.

Postmodernism and the French nouveau roman

Although what is known as 'high' modernism, the literature which represents most consistently and confidently the values of the modernist era, was relatively shortlived (lasting from around 1890 to 1930), it had a profound effect on writers who came after. It 'destabilized' the widely held conception of the novel as the form geared up to presenting accurately the nature of the relationship between the individual and society, and prompted an increased self-consciousness amongst novelists about the practice of writing fiction, which often took the form of scepticism about the very function or possibility of realism. Even writers who were happy to continue in the footsteps of the great nineteenth-century realists felt that after modernism they were to some extent required to defend their values and techniques against the model developed by the modernist novel.

To adapt Lyotard's famous statement, we could define postmodern fiction as writing which is shaped in some way by an incredulity towards realism – a state of mind which does not necessarily conclude that representing the postmodern world accurately, *realistically*, is no longer desirable, but is convinced that the act of representation cannot be performed as unselfconsciously and wholeheartedly as it was in the nineteenth century.

This incredulity is articulated most powerfully by practitioners of the French *nouveau roman*, or 'New Novel', in the mid-1950s, whose approach to fiction was to prove highly influential on both British and American 'experimental' novelists in the 1960s and 1970s, and on literary and cultural theorists in

France and America in the same period (such as Roland Barthes and Susan Sontag, considered later in the chapter). In her seminal essay 'The Age of Suspicion' (1956) one of these writers, Nathalie Sarraute, argued that modernism was pivotal in what she considered a fundamental shift from confidence to suspicion – on the part of both writer and reader – which defined modern literature (Sarraute, 1963). The distinctive feature of the modernist novel, she suggests, referring mainly to the work of Joyce, Kafka, and Proust and its new approach to character and psychology, is that it amounts to a rejection of the pretence that the world depicted in a work of fiction, its characters and its story, is real. This is manifested mainly by the modernist attitude to character. Put simply, for Sarraute, the modern author no longer believes in his or her characters any more – and even if he or she does then the reader no longer will.

Sarraute suggests that the most distinctive features of modernist fiction are an anonymous first-person narrator/ protagonist who is somehow 'everything yet nothing', and secondary characters who are consequently 'deprived of their own existence' by this narrator (Sarraute, 1963, 58–9). The reader is therefore unable to conceive of these figures as recognizably human, still less to identify with them (in the kind of empathetic relationship which is central to the effect of nineteenth-century realism). The fictional world no longer seems to exist objectively, but comes to seem, as in Proust, wholly the creation of the narrator's ego. This results in a new relation between reader and author, as the reader is no longer able to rely on the author to guide him or her around the world of the novel. In fact, it seems as if the author himself is exploring this world for the first time. Rather than the world of the novel being presented to the reader as if fully created, ready to be inhabited, it is as if both novelist and reader are engaged in exploring fictional territory which is new to both. As a result the creation of the text is the result of a collaboration between author and reader rather than a kind of 'gift' presented from one to the other.

Unlike many critics and writers of the time, Sarraute regards this new difficult relationship between author and reader as a measure of the health of the novel rather than an indication of its imminent demise. The same applies to Alain Robbe-Grillet, besides Sarraute the other key figure in the *nouveau roman*. His collection of essays, *For a New Novel*, first published in 1955, was even more influential than Sarraute's following its English translation in 1963, and provides a complementary expression of the twentieth-century writer's disbelief in realism. In his essay 'Time and Description in Fiction Today' (1963), for example, he notes how nineteenth-century novels 'are crammed with houses, furnishings, costumes, exhaustively and scrupulously described, not to mention faces, bodies, etc.' But where the original function of all this description was 'to make the reader see', convince him or her 'of the objective existence – outside literature – of a world which the novelist seemed merely to reproduce, to copy, to transmit, as if one were dealing with a chronicle, a biography, a document of some kind', description does not work in the same way for the twentieth-century writer – or, he implies, reader. Description used to 'reproduce a pre-existing reality; it now asserts its creative function'. Where 'once it made us see things, now it seems to destroy them' (Robbe-Grillet, 1989b, 146–7).

For Robbe-Grillet, the function of the novel has changed in the twentieth century. Where the realists assumed the novel was a tool geared towards repro-ducing reality, he insists – in his 1955 essay 'From Realism to Reality' – that the novel is *not* a tool, not something 'conceived with a view to a task defined in advance'. Its purpose is not to 'translate' that which exists before or outside it, not to 'explain' or to 'express' reality, or to 'respect the truth' (Robbe-Grillet, 1989a, 160). The novel is not meant to inform us about reality but to *constitute* reality – in other words to create an aesthetic world which exists separately from the real world and does not necessarily correspond to it.

To illustrate this point, Robbe-Grillet gives the example of how he himself had succumbed to the temptations of what he calls 'the *realistic illusion*'. While writing his 1955 novel *The Voyeur* he was at one point struggling to describe exactly how seagulls fly and decided to use a trip to the coast of Brittany to refresh his memory: 'But from the first gull I saw, I understood my error: on the one hand, the gulls I now saw had only very confused relations with those I was describing in my book, and on the other it couldn't have mattered less to me whether they did or not. The only gulls that mattered to me at that moment were those which were inside my head' (Robbe-Grillet, 1989a, 161–2). Even though the gulls he was describing bore a relation to reality, they had taken on their *own* reality, or rather, they had become 'somehow more real *because* they were now imaginary' (162). So while it will always be natural for a novelist to try to make the world in his novel as real as possible – to guard against comments from readers such as 'a jealous husband doesn't behave like the one in [Robbe-Grillet's novel] *Jealousy*' or 'your soldier lost *In The Labyrinth* isn't wearing his military insignia in the right place' – at the same time his or her chief intention ought not to be to *transcribe* but to *construct* (Robbe-Grillet, 1989a, 162).

Where postmodern fiction begins

Readers of fiction will doubtless respond to such claims about a disbelief in realism in different ways, but in making them Robbe-Grillet and Sarraute figured as more than just apologists for the *nouveau roman*. In fact they were representative of a much more widespread anxiety amongst contemporary writers, not least British ones.

A similar disbelief in realism is the motivating force behind John Fowles's parody of nineteenth-century realism, *The French Lieutenant's Woman*, published in 1969 (and analysed in Chapter 4). It is expressed most directly in the extraordinary authorial outburst which constitutes the novel's notorious chapter 13. Having spent the previous twelve chapters portraying, in more or less faithful nineteenth-century realist style, a detailed world inhabited by characters the reader can identify with, Fowles suddenly interrupts the action to inform the reader that his story is 'all imagination', its characters 'never existed outside my own mind', and, because he lives 'in the age of Alain Robbe-Grillet and Roland Barthes', his novel cannot adhere to the traditional model (Fowles, 1996, 97).

Another example is B. S. Johnson, whose introduction to his collection *Aren't You Rather Young to be Writing Your Memoirs?* (1973) articulates his conviction that the realist tradition was fundamentally dishonest, not only in attempting to present a reality quite unlike the one that actually pertained in the late twentieth century, but in doing so pretending that there were 'real' people in the novel, and that all their actions could somehow be linked together. In his own fiction, he makes it clear that the only real character is himself, acknowledging all others bluntly as authorial puppets. He resists the temptations of a conventional plot, out of a certainty that '[t]elling stories really is telling lies' (Johnson, 1990, 153). A close parallel to Fowles's chapter 13 comes in Johnson's 1966 novel *Albert Angelo*. Just over ten pages before the end, a paragraph is begun in conventional narrative style – 'Albert lazed at his drawingboard before the great window. Nearly seven weeks' summer holiday lay ahead of him . . . ' – before the author abruptly intervenes: '–oh, fuck all this LYING!' The next chapter, appropriately titled 'Disintegration' continues where it left off, its jumbled language illustrative of the breakdown of the realist paradigm: '– fuck all this lying look what im really trying to write about is writing not all this stuff about architecture trying to say something about writing about my writing im my hero' (Johnson, 1964, 167–8).

Postmodern fiction, then, is rooted in the response of a range of writers and critics from the mid-1950s to the early 1970s to the way the modernist novel transformed the possibilities of fiction, most notably in their inability to conceive of realism without some degree of suspicion or disbelief. Fowles and Johnson are typical of these writers (as are British contemporaries such as Angela Carter and J. G. Ballard, and American writers like John Barth, Robert

Coover, William Gass, and Donald Barthelme) and the label 'postmodern' is applicable to them because of the way their own fiction is underpinned by a scepticism towards realism. By contrast, the actual novels produced by Sarraute, Robbe-Grillet, and the other *nouveau romanciers* have tended to be regarded by critics (for good reason, I think) as more a late-flowering of modernism than the beginnings of postmodernism 'proper'. Postmodern fiction tends to be marked by an ambivalence towards realism rather than a desire to reject it outright.

To put it differently, it would be a mistake to regard postmodernism as the 'opposite' of realism, or as the equivalent of 'experimentalism' in fiction. Andrzej Gasiorek has exposed the simplistic nature of such polarized classifications, noting, *à propos* the 'realism v. experiment' debate of the immediate post-war decades in British fiction, that even the most apparently experimental writers were actually engaged in reconceptualizing realism rather than destroying it and, conversely, the most apparently traditional writers were busily revitalizing an older form rather than simply imitating it (Gasiorek, 1995).

In any case, as Robbe-Grillet put it, '[a]ll novelists believe they are realists. None ever calls himself [*sic*] abstract, illusionistic, chimerical, fantastic, falsitical'. Realism, he suggests, is not 'a theory, defined without ambiguity' but an ideology 'brandished' by novelists against one another in order to champion their own efforts to depict 'the real'. '[I]t has always been the same', Robbe-Grillet writes: 'out of a concern for realism each new literary school has sought to destroy the one which preceded it' (Robbe-Grillet, 1989a, 157–8). This was true of modernism. For all their formal innovations it is clear that Joyce and Woolf were striving to depict everyday life in a manner more appropriate to their age than that of the nineteenth-century novel. In a different way it is true of postmodernism.

But one thing postmodern fiction is trying to be 'realistic' about, and grapples with at some level within its pages, is what fiction is and what its function should be. Postmodernism rests on the assumption that fiction – no matter how realist or experimental – is always, to use Robbe-Grillet's terms, a matter of 'constructing' rather than 'transcribing'. Transcription is in fact impossible because the act of representing something external to the text actually ensures that a separate, aesthetic version of it is created in the pages of the novel, and therefore in the minds of the writer and reader – as in the example of Robbe-Grillet's gulls. Postmodern writing recognizes, either implicitly or explicitly, that it is no longer possible to indulge in the kind of pretence about the possibility of 'transcription' which is central to realism.

A cautionary note is required here. For it is important not to assume that realism is a 'simplistic' kind of writing, nor a kind of naïve but necessary step on the way to the production of the 'perfect novel', nor that its authors were devious or manipulative ideologues. Nineteenth-century realist writers were the products of a particular worldview, just as postmodern writers are. In any case, if we look at it from the perspective of critics such as Robbe-Grillet or Sarraute, the achievement of the great realist writers is actually very difficult: making prose a kind of transparent window through which we can view the represented world of fiction is actually far *less* natural than producing fiction which foregrounds its own existence as text. The richness and symbolic potential of language means that it is hard for language *not* to draw attention to itself, whether through an unusual metaphor, a complex formulation, or an unusual choice of word.

We must also be careful not to conclude that the reader of a realist text is naïve or gullible for swallowing the realist illusion wholesale. Of course every reader of a realist text knows that the world they 'enter' as they read is not 'real'. Realism works because of a tacit contract established between reader and author: the reader agrees to 'suspend disbelief' and play the game that what he or she is presented with is 'real', on condition that the author makes the illusion as convincing as possible.

In fact it is this contract, this game, which postmodernism spoils. More precisely postmodernism objects to *two* key pretences which sustain the realist text:

(1) that the fictional world it creates exists in its entirety, is analogous to the real world, and that writing is, consequently, 'referential';
(2) that the story it tells is 'natural' and 'singular', a matter of the narrator simply *mediating* an 'existing' story.

My view is that postmodern writing does not reject these pretences on ideological grounds (though many postmodern writers are suspicious of the ideology behind realism), as did late-1970s critics like Catherine Belsey and Colin MacCabe who objected to the way 'classic realism' falsified the reality of the relationship between the individual human being and society (Belsey, 1980; MacCabe, 1974). Rather it opposed them on what we might call theoretical or aesthetic grounds. What I mean by this is that postmodern writers seem to assume that there is something fundamentally illogical and untenable about the way the story is transmitted to the reader in realism. To suggest why, we can now consider in more depth the theoretical problems with these two realist pretences.

The fictional world is not like ours

Writing fiction – any fiction, no matter if it is realist, modernist, or postmodernist – is, by definition, an act of creating a world. The world of a realist novel is to be imagined as analogous to our own. Although fictional, it is peopled by characters who might just as well exist in our world, in settings and amidst objects which we could plausibly find there, and who are subject to events and situations which could justifiably occur in ours – even though they tend to be more dramatic or symbolic than in our world.

Yet of course this fictional world is not the real world; it is 'heterocosmic', a 'world in itself, independent, complete, autonomous' (Bradley, 1926, 5). Indeed the very nature of the author's and reader's 'contract' is in fact an implicit admission that there is a difference between the two. Somewhat paradoxically, *mimesis* emphasizes the distinction between real and fictional worlds as much as it points to the similarity. As the postmodern theorist Brian McHale puts it, 'For the real world to be reflected in the mirror of literary mimesis, the imitation must be distinguishable from the imitated . . . A mimetic relation is one of similarity, not *identity*, and similarity implies difference' (McHale, 1987, 28).

In fact McHale's theory shows that the relationship between the heterocosmic world and the real world is more complex than this, for the heterocosm is not as autonomous as it might seem. It has in fact, he says, citing the narrative theorist Hrushovski, a 'dual referential allegiance' (McHale, 1987, 29). For it to appear realistic, to 'work' in the same way as our world, the fictional world is a continuum, with a consistent internal field of reference, meaning that things in the world – from objects to the causal links between events – relate plausibly to each other. But at the same time sustaining the realist illusion requires that it also point outside this to an *external* field of reference, namely our world – 'the objective world, the body of historical fact or scientific theory, an ideology or philosophy, other texts, and so on' (29). This dual referential logic is easily demonstrated in the classic realist novel when the same elements exist in both the real and the heterocosmic world. The village of Middlemarch, in George Eliot's 1871 novel of that name, for example, is fictitious, though it is set in the Midlands, which is a real part of England. The region is thus part of both the internal and the external field of reference in each text.

The apparent autonomy of the fictional world is also compromised by the fact that, as the phenomenological literary theorist Roman Ingarden points out, it requires the consciousness of the reader to actually bring it into being through the act of imagining it. It both does and does not exist 'by itself'. Middlemarch, that is, only exists when the reader imagines it, but he or she cannot imagine it without Eliot's descriptions. The world presented in a novel is also unlike the real world in that its objects may be ambiguous, for example, if the sentences describing them are ambiguous. Objects can also be presented with what McHale terms 'an emotional "coloration"' making them more than simply objects amongst others in the fictional world, but privileged ones (McHale, 1987, 32). Furthermore, while the reader may reasonably assume that Middlemarch is a complete, independently functioning 'world' including places not actually described in the text as well as other inhabitants it doesn't mention, it is also strangely incomplete. Ingarden argues that the world fiction projects is not a complete and fully realized one but partially *indeterminate*. The elements which exist are only those which have been described in the language of the text so that '[i]t is always as if a beam of light were illuminating a part of a region, the remainder of which disappears in an indeterminate cloud but is still there in its indeterminacy' (McHale, 1987, 31). To illustrate Ingarden's point McHale uses an episode in Gilbert Sorrentino's postmodern novel, *Mulligan Stew* (1979), in which two characters explore the house their author has created for them and are disturbed to find that the rooms outside the living room are simply not there, and a staircase leads only into a kind of 'haziness'. '*All* houses in fiction are like this,' McHale points out, 'partly specified, partly left vague' (McHale, 1987, 32). Usually, however – in most realist fictions – the narrator and author of the text ensure that neither the reader nor the characters are aware of this. They remain silent about it.

Narrative is not 'natural'

Fictional worlds, then, are more complex than realist texts acknowledge. So is narrative. The established structuralist definition of narrative is that any narrative is divided into three parts: the *story* (a set of events), recounted in a *discourse* (a process of narration) in which the events of the story are selected and arranged in a particular order (the *plot*) (Chatman, 1978, Genette, 1980, Rimmon-Kenan, 1983). Narrative is really a two-way process of construction by which the writer assembles events into a particular order, and so does the reader. The logic is most obviously illustrated in the detective story, where the writer tells 'what really happened' – though not in a straightforward way, but by using artifice to disguise or omit crucial details, conversations, and events. The reader's job is to 'recuperate' the tantalizing fragments of the story, to piece it all together, but s/he must not be allowed to do so too easily or the suspense will be lost. Nor must the author obviously withhold crucial details from the reader or s/he will feel cheated. The fundamental rule of the detective story is that the truth must be concealed but must also be present in disguised form, to be 'fair' to the reader (Bayard, 2000). Consequently the author of the detective story must engage in a process of concealment and distraction in order to put up a smokescreen.

But analysing how detective fiction works underlines the fact that reading *all* fiction is to be subject to similar manipulation. All narrative constantly involves artifice: telling a story is not an innocent act, involving a natural sequence of events which are simply 'extracted' and recounted. Rather narrative involves selection, organization, and interpretation on the part of the narrator. Similarly, reading is not a simple matter of 'receiving' a narrative passively, but requires a certain degree of activity: for example, we respond to repetitive elements in the text, such as events and symbols.

Nothing is natural in a narrative. As Roland Barthes makes clear in his 1966 essay, 'Introduction to the Structural Analysis of Narratives', 'everything, down to the slightest detail, [has] a meaning... Even were a detail to appear irretrievably insignificant, resistant to all functionality, it would nonetheless end up with precisely the meaning of absurdity or uselessness: everything has a meaning, or nothing has' (Barthes, 1977a, 89). As well as the details in a narrative this total 'functionality' applies to the sequence of events. 'The mainspring of narrative', Barthes argues, is the confusion between 'consecution and consequence', where 'what comes *after*', in a temporal sense, is interpreted by the reader as being 'what is *caused by*' (Barthes, 1977a, 94). He remarks that if a telephone rings in a narrative – unlike in everyday life – then whether or not it is answered is significant in some way to the narrative. Every event, chance or otherwise, is *meaningful*. Even if it is just a chance wrong number (as happens in Paul Auster's postmodern detective story *City of Glass*) it will have causal effects. As Barthes says, 'what is noted is by definition notable' in narrative (Barthes, 1977a, 89). Narrative is a world in which nothing is 'natural', everything is significant either because it has been arranged that way by the author/narrator or because whatever has been arranged will create particular effects.

The overall functionality and partiality of narrative, the fact that the narrative process is always a matter of rhetoric, always subjective, is suppressed or disavowed by realism. Narrators select and interpret continually, deciding the order in which to place narrative events, how to describe them and the narrative world. No matter how objective a narrator claims to be, he or she is inevitably partial. But a consequence of this is that a narrator cannot recount every event which occurs during the time of a given narrative. Time simply contains too many events for this to be possible. Narrative, as Peter Brooks has said, is therefore always a *perspective* on a story rather than a record of every single event (Brooks, 1993, 105).

There is an important parallel here with McHale's insistence (via Ingarden) that the represented world is incomplete and unrealistic, and must therefore be responded to differently than the real world. There are elements of the story which are indeterminate, which may be filled in in the reader's act of 'concretizing' the text. This is demonstrated by Pierre Bayard's *Who Killed Roger Ackroyd?* (1998), a brilliantly eccentric re-reading of Agatha Christie's *The Murder of Roger Ackroyd*, which argues outrageously that Hercule Poirot actually gets it wrong in the case which makes up that novel and points to a new suspect. His analysis of one genre, detective fiction, shows how all narrative trades on the logic of the 'lie by omission', the principle that to preserve the mystery in a detective story, elements of the story have to be left out, and are only included at the end. This is why Sheppard, the famously unreliable narrator of *The Murder of Roger Ackroyd*, is able to fool us for so long. As Bayard says, he always tells the truth. It is just that he omits crucial details from his account – such as the murder itself. But the brilliance of Bayard's book is that it shows how because this is a property of all narrative, given that no narrative, however impartial or detailed, is able to contain every event that occurs, it means that every story is potentially opened up to the kind of self-confessedly 'deluded' reading Bayard performs on *The Murder of Roger Ackroyd*. Without necessarily going so far as Bayard, it follows that we can reasonably assume that just as there are parts of the house in Sorrentino's *Mulligan Stew* which remain undescribed but which can plausibly be assumed to exist, so there are elements of every story which are unnarrated but can plausibly be assumed to have taken place.

Modernism, referentiality, and the avant-garde

What are the implications of all this? The fact that the fictional world and the narrative are indeterminate and subject to potentially infinite expansion effectively mean that realism is unstable, incapable of doing what it claims. The critique is delivered succinctly in the following passage from Barthes's 'Introduction to the Structural Analysis of Narrative'. Though he is writing from the perspective of narrative theory rather than seeking to classify movements within literature, still less champion experimental or postmodern writing, Barthes's words make explicit the implied grounds for the postmodern incredulity towards realism:

> Claims regarding the 'realism' of narrative are therefore to be
> discounted. . . . The function of the narrative is not to 'represent', it is to
> constitute a spectacle still very enigmatic for us but in any case not of a

mimetic order. . . . Narrative does not show, does not imitate; the passion which may excite us in reading a novel is not that of a 'vision' (in actual fact, we do not 'see' anything). Rather it is that of meaning, that of a higher order of relation which also has its emotions, its hopes, its dangers, its triumphs. 'What takes place' in a narrative is from the referential (reality) point of view literally *nothing*; 'what happens' is language alone, the adventure of language, the unceasing celebration of its coming.   (Barthes, 1977a, 123–4)

Naturally, this 'truth' makes itself felt in postmodern fiction through aesthetic practice rather than carefully prepared theoretical critique. The best example is the work of Samuel Beckett, whose fiction in many ways represents the beginning of postmodernism in literature. His *Trilogy* of 1951–7 (*Molloy, Malone Dies, The Unnamable*) is preoccupied by the efforts of a narrator to retain control of the world of his narrative. As a result each novel repeatedly reminds its reader that the fictional world is not equivalent to the real world. At one point in *Molloy*, for example, the narrator tries to explain in precise detail – in the manner of realist narration – what happened when Molloy deals the charcoal burner 'a good dint on the skull' with one of his crutches:

> This is how I went about it. I carefully chose the most favourable position, a few paces from my body, with my back of course turned to it. Then, nicely balanced on my crutches, I began to swing, backwards, forwards, feet pressed together, or rather legs pressed together, for how could I press my feet together, with my legs in the state they were? But how could I press my legs together, in the state they were? I pressed them together, that's all I can tell you. Take it or leave it. Or I didn't press them together. What can that possibly matter? I swung, that's all that matters . . .   (Beckett, 1994a, 84)

It is a passage that comically and powerfully questions the need for narrative to adhere to the details of the real world. The narrator's words force us simultaneously to imagine the fictional world he is presenting and thus affirm its existence while also to question his reliability in describing it. If, as it is logical to assume, there exist elements of a world and a narrative about which we are not directly informed, then the potential for interpreting the fictional world and story becomes infinite and beyond the author's control.

We must remember here that it is not only postmodern writing that is driven by the flaws in realist assumptions about its fictional world. Modernist fiction frequently problematizes the referential, producing language which refers to itself as much as to any fictional world. A prime example would be *Finnegan's Wake*, the last work by the greatest modernist writer, James Joyce, a profound influence on Beckett. This novel forsakes the referential almost completely as it is written in a private language, a code which has to be cracked in order to understand it. The complexity of *Finnegan's Wake*'s language means that even though there is a fictional world, characters and a kind of discernible plot, its words refer directly only to other words. The reader is continually conscious of this as s/he reads because s/he must translate or decode the private language in order to get to the represented world and narrative.

Finnegan's Wake thus offers one response to the pretences of realism: abandoning altogether the illusion that a novel's language refers to anything other than itself. But there is a danger here, and this is one reason why *Finnegan's Wake* can be regarded as the apex of fictional experimentation in the novel: after it there is nowhere to go. Joyce's novel would seem to conform to Eco's theory about the pattern replayed throughout literary history by which the avant-garde fights back against the way the past 'conditions us, harries us, blackmails us' (Eco, 2002, 111) by destroying or cancelling it. It is the culmination of modernism's destruction of the realist model of George Eliot or Balzac, problematizing the referential function taken for granted by the previous generation of novelists until 'it has produced a metalanguage that speaks of its impossible texts' (111). As an impossible text *Finnegan's Wake* heralds, in Eco's terms (though he doesn't mention Joyce's novel), the limit-point of the avant-garde cancellation of the past.

Postmodern fiction – which in Eco's theory is the solution to the avant-garde impasse, not the moment of impasse itself – subscribes as much as *Finnegan's Wake* to the critique of realism summarized by the passage from Barthes quoted above. However, because it must keep producing art rather than lapse into silence, and also because postmodernism has a strong desire to analyse contemporary reality (which in one way all the postmodern authors featured in this book do) it does not abandon the referential function but preserves it ironically, as Eco suggests, interrogating it while continuing to use it, continually examining the complex nature of the represented world and the narrative in fiction.

What postmodern fiction does

Without taking things as far as *Finnegan's Wake*, how does postmodernism remind us of the complexity and instability of the fictional world and the loaded functionality of narrative? To answer this question we need to consider in more detail what postmodern fiction actually does that distinguishes it from other kinds. This section, then, introduces 'metafiction', the most distinctive formal practice employed by postmodern writers (as demonstrated most persuasively by Patricia Waugh in her book *Metafiction: The Theory and Practice of Self-Conscious Fiction* [Waugh, 1984]), but first examines two different and very influential attempts to establish a 'poetics of postmodernism', by Linda Hutcheon and Brian McHale respectively, the two theorists who have made the most enduring impact on theories of postmodernism in fiction.

A poetics is the practice of breaking down a series of related texts into their constituent parts so that a taxonomy of features can be built up. These features can then be regarded as the *essential* properties of a particular genre or grouping of texts. While postmodern fiction is too diverse to be a genre, examples of it do, as I have been suggesting, share certain key features.

The value of both Hutcheon's and McHale's descriptions of how postmodern fiction works is that each preserves a flexibility which highlights what is distinctive about much of the fiction produced in the post-war period without suggesting that it is unique to this period. What distinguishes postmodern fiction is the *degree* to which these elements are present. Postmodernism does not do anything fiction has not done before; it is not innovative in this respect. It is rather, to return to the point about fiction's 'dominant' which I made in the Introduction (and which is drawn from McHale's appropriation of Jakobson's concept), a question of which elements are most obsessively considered.

Hutcheon and the 'double-coding' of postmodern fiction

Hutcheon's insistence about postmodernism's inherent doubleness (introduced in the Introduction), its adherence to the logic of 'both ... and ...' rather than 'either ... or ...' offers a useful way of conceiving of how the postmodern engages with realism and modernism. Postmodernism, she argues, is simultaneously 'intensively self-reflexive and parodic, yet it also attempts to root itself in that which both reflexivity and parody appear to short-circuit: the historical world' (1988a, x). It is an aesthetic practice which results from the paradox created at moments when 'modernist aesthetic autonomy and self-reflexivity come up against a counterforce in the form of a grounding in the historical, social, and political world' (1988a, ix).

She takes as her model for this postmodern architecture, explored by other theorists of 'double-coding' such as Charles Jencks and Paolo Portoghesi. Postmodern architecture, we recall from the previous chapter, is a kind of 'text' which those who look at or inhabit can 'read' as a kind of commentary on previous forms of architecture and aesthetic practice, while also being, much more practically, something which has to *function* in the real world at a particular point in history. Obviously, this latter point does not apply to fiction, whose 'function' is much more mysterious than architecture. Nevertheless, according to Hutcheon, postmodern fiction exhibits a similar need to engage in dialogue with past and present, the aesthetic and the political.

She is quick to point out that the doubleness she explores is not unique to the postmodern era, and can be found in *Don Quixote* or Shakespeare. However, she points to two significant differences between earlier times in which the self-reflexive and the historical combine in a similarly paradoxical way and the postmodern. First, postmodernism constantly treats this with a distinctive 'attendant irony' (Hutcheon, 1988a, x). Irony enables writers to continue working within particular discourses while simultaneously managing to contest them. Second, the presence of irony in contemporary art is 'obsessively recurring' (Hutcheon, 1988a, xi) – in other words postmodernism in fiction does what previous fiction has done, but at an extreme level.

For Hutcheon, postmodern fiction is both referential and self-reflexive; at the same time a preservation of some realist values and a shattering critique of them. Postmodern writing and art is frequently parodic and this is natural, given that parody is similarly double, 'for it paradoxically both incorporates and challenges that which it parodies' (Hutcheon, 1988a, 11). This doubleness relates to the position of the reader, who is invited to interpret the work freely, on the one hand, but on the other is required to adhere to the imposed logic of the writer's (political) agenda.

For Hutcheon one of the distinctive characteristics of the postmodern is its combination of theory and aesthetic practice. Postmodern fiction is undoubtedly art – that is, an aesthetic object which entertains and amuses us, makes us think, etc. – but at the same time engages in a form of theorizing. We might call this 'theory in practice', partly didactic, but also a form of writing which invites the reader to consider the theoretical questions it raises for themselves. How it goes about this is clearest when we examine (in Chapter 4) 'historiographic metafiction', the category of fiction Hutcheon regards as most representative of postmodernism.

Hutcheon's theory about the doubleness of postmodernism is a useful way of describing the relation between modernism and postmodernism. Rather than regarding postmodernism as an absolute break with modernism or realism we can argue that it *both* breaks with modernist conventions *and* continues with them. It certainly does not seek to put into practice a wholesale rejection of realism. Indeed she argues that 'the ideology of postmodernism is paradoxical, for it depends upon and draws its power from that which it contests. It is not truly radical; nor is it truly oppositional' (Hutcheon, 1988a, 120).

McHale's poetics of postmodernism

While Hutcheon's poetics of postmodernism is ambitious in its attempt to construct 'a flexible conceptual structure which could at once constitute and contain postmodern culture and our discourses about and adjacent to it' (Hutcheon, 1988a, ix), Brian McHale's is, on the face of it, more modest. He approaches postmodernism purely from the perspective of a literary historian, acknowledging that this means his system's 'explanatory scheme is entirely internal to the literary-historical dynamics and does not respond in any systematic way to larger historical developments' (McHale and Neagu, 2006, n.p.) His description of what postmodernism does is essentially that postmodern fiction foregrounds the problems or inconsistencies regarding the creation of a fictional world which we explored above – elements which are integral to every work of fiction but are passed over or suppressed in some, such as realist ones. To explain how, he sets up a useful comparison between modernism and postmodernism which is underpinned by Jakobson's idea of 'the dominant', 'the focusing component of a work of art', shifting through literary history which 'rules, determines, and transforms the remaining components and guarantees the "integrity" of the structure' (McHale, 1987, 6).

McHale's theory is that the 'dominant', or 'focusing component' of modernism is 'epistemological', or to do with knowing:

> [M]odernist fiction deploys strategies which engage and foreground questions such as . . . : 'How can I interpret this world of which I might be a part? And what am I in it?' . . . What is there to be known? Who knows it? How do they know it, and with what degree of certainty? How is knowledge transmitted from one knower to another, and with what degree of reliability? How does the object of knowledge change as it passes from knower to knower? What are the limits of the knowable? And so on.   (McHale, 1987, 9)

The dominant of postmodernism, by contrast, is 'ontological', to do with *being*:

> [P]ostmodernist fiction deploys strategies which engage and foreground questions like . . . : 'Which world is this? What is to be done in it? Which of my selves is to do it?' Other typical postmodernist questions bear either on the ontology of the literary text itself or on the ontology of the world which it projects, for instance: What is a world? What kinds of world are there, how are they constituted, and how do they differ? What happens when different kinds of world are placed in confrontation, or when boundaries between worlds are violated? What is the mode of existence of the world (or worlds) it projects? How is a projected world structured? And so on.   (McHale, 1987, 10)

McHale's choice of terms, the ontological and epistemological, can be slightly misleading, for if you 'google' them or look them up in a dictionary profound philosophical debates will be cited that do not seem to relate to the kind of things McHale is writing about. What is at issue in his theory is not really a matter of philosophical fundamentals, but the question of what we are invited to do as we read a text: what are the interpretive solutions available to us as we read particular examples of fiction? His answer is that some of these are to do with *knowing* (epistemological ones) and some are to do with *being* (ontological ones). More precisely, the key to understanding McHale's theory is to remember that the epistemological and ontological questions which various texts invite us to ask are to be asked of the fictional *world* – for example, raising questions about the fictionality of the work which creates this world.

McHale argues that detective fiction is 'the epistemological genre *par excellence*' (McHale, 1987, 9) because the detective story typically revolves around precisely the kind of questions he thinks are representative of modernism. Solving the mystery in a classic detective story is an epistemological task as detective and sidekick examine the evidence to determine what can be known about a particular crime. There is no doubt about the fact that a crime has occurred. A postmodern detective story, on the other hand (and there are plenty of examples of these, as I shall show in Chapter 7) is one in which the epistemological questions 'tip over' into ontological ones, and the detective is frequently left asking disturbing questions such as: *was* there a crime? If so, in which world did it occur?

For McHale the key genre which exemplifies the ontologically dominated text is science fiction. The reason for this is that science fiction stages ' "close encounters" between different worlds, placing them in confrontation' and, as a result, 'foregrounds their respective structures and disparities between them' (McHale, 1987, 60). Actually, McHale argues, confronting our *known* world with something which comes from outside or beyond that world is something that fiction does *by definition*. Every single work of fiction, no matter the genre, includes characters who did not exist and events which did not happen in the real world. This is of course even true (perhaps it is especially true) of realistic modes of fiction. Nineteenth-century realism, for example, for all its commitment to replicating the world we know, is really asking us to inhabit a parallel version of our world in which unreal yet plausible characters and events feature.

This leads McHale to make a persuasive parallel between the historical novel and sci-fi, because the former actually involves quite a radical 'violation of ontological boundaries'. It tends to fictionalize the lives of *real* people, such as Napoleon or Richard Nixon. Yet '[t]raditional historical novels strive to suppress these violations, to hide the ontological "seams" between fictional projections and real-world facts. They do so by tactfully avoiding contradictions between their versions of historical figures and the familiar facts of these figures's careers, and by making the background norms governing their projected worlds conform to accepted real-world norms' (McHale, 1987, 16–17). This is why sci-fi, according to McHale 'serves as a source of materials and models for postmodernist writers' and he mentions a number which we will cover in this book: Burroughs, Vonnegut, Pynchon, 'even Beckett and Nabokov' (McHale, 1987, 16).

Metafiction

Metafiction is the main technical device used in postmodern fiction. It may be defined as 'fiction about fiction' – fiction, that is, which is about itself or about fiction rather than anything else. John Barth described his novel *Giles Goat-Boy* (1966) as one of those 'novels which imitate the form of the Novel, by an author who imitates the role of Author' (Barth, 2002, 145). Metafiction is fiction (and other kinds of art such as film or visual art) which is 'self-conscious', that is, aware of itself *as* fiction (as if it has its own consciousness), or 'self-reflexive' or 'self-referential' fiction, that which reflects on or refers to itself as a work of fiction rather than pretending it is offering the reader an insight into the real world. More precisely we might define metafiction as fiction that in some way foregrounds its own status as artificial construct, especially by drawing attention to its form. The effect of metafiction is principally to draw attention to the *frames* involved in fiction, which are usually concealed by realism.

Patricia Waugh begins her discussion of frames in *Metafiction* by quoting from the OED definition of 'frame': a 'construction, constitution, building; established order, plan, system . . . underlying support or essential substructure of anything'. She goes on to claim that both modernism and postmodernism, 'begin with the view that both the historical world and works of art are organized and perceived through such structures or "frames". Both recognize further that the distinction between "framed" and "unframed" cannot in the end be made' (Waugh, 1984, 28). Waugh's statement makes the crucial link between postmodernism as a socio-cultural phenomenon – as discussed in the Introduction to this book – and postmodernism as an aesthetic practice. We suspect that our lives are 'framed', not necessarily in any sinister sense (though the connotations of paranoia do have a persistent relevance in postmodern fiction, as we shall see in due course) but because we experience the world as mediated through a range of discursive and narrative constructs, especially from culture, media and advertising.

The most obvious way of thinking of the 'frame' in a work of art is to consider the actual frame in a realist painting, a landscape for example. Its function is to show us what is represented in the picture. But it also provides the boundaries of what we can see of the pictured world. The implication, as with the fictional world created by any narrative, is that what we can see within the frame is not the totality of the represented world but only a small section of something much larger. The implication is that if we could peer through the frame and look to either side of the picture or above and below, we would see other aspects of the landscape, potentially in an unbroken continuum that accords with Euclidean laws of geometry. An equivalent of the frame in a painting would be the camera in a film or a TV programme. The 'natural' assumption here too – that is, the one proffered by realist forms of art, which still predominate in film and TV drama – would be similar, that the camera allows our gaze to roam around a fully realistic and natural world. But framing is not a natural nor an innocent act, and it is the job of the painter, those involved in the *mise-en-scène* in film or TV (director, cameraman, editor, etc.), or the author to decide which parts of the represented world to frame and how and when to do it. These visual examples make it easy to acknowledge that it is not possible to present any world or narrative *without* some degree of framing. This calls to mind a rather paranoid-sounding remark by the philosopher Friedrich Nietzsche: 'When we are confronted with any manifestation which someone has permitted us to see, we may ask: what is it meant to conceal? What is it meant to draw our attention from?' (Nietzsche, 1964, 358). Acknowledging the importance of framing in fiction means recognizing that anything we see in art is because we're *allowed* to see it by the author. What is more, in order to do this some kind of artificial device is used.

In fiction the frame is really the narration of the text – the element which takes place at the extra-diegetic level. Narrative framing is the means by which the fictional world is made accessible to the real world, and as such is a kind of portal, a viewing screen through which the reader can observe and 'enter' the fictional world – or at least the elements of it determined by the author – and experience what takes place there (the narrative).

Waugh identifies three main types of contemporary metafiction. The first is where a particular convention of the novel is upset, for example the way Fowles subverts nineteenth-century omniscient narration in *The French Lieutenant's Woman* (1969). The second type is where a text parodies a specific earlier text or recognizable fictional mode, such as John Barth's parody of the eighteenth-century novel in *The Sot-Weed Factor* (1960), while the third type is where a text, such as Richard Brautigan's *Trout Fishing in America* (1967), attempts in a more subtle manner to create alternative linguistic structures or evoke established forms by inviting the reader to draw on his or her knowledge of traditional literary conventions (Waugh, 1984, 4).

The effect of metafiction is often to foreground and problematize the act of 'framing' in both fiction and the real world. In Muriel Spark's 1953 novel *The Comforters*, for example, the young novelist Caroline becomes aware that she is a character in someone else's novel because she can hear noises from upstairs which turn out to be Spark tapping on the keys of her keyboard, writing Caroline's 'life'. Throughout Beckett's *Murphy* (1938) – which on the face of it preserves realist staples such as well-rounded characters and linear plot – there are a number of references to the practice of writing and reading which remind the reader that the world of *Murphy* is not real: for example, when the narrator comments 'All the puppets in this book whinge sooner or later, except Murphy, who is not a puppet' (Beckett, 1973, 71).

Other metafictional texts actively indulge in what the sociologist Erving Goffman calls 'frame-breaking', where the frames through which the fictional world is presented to the reader are actually dismantled or shattered. The most powerful way this is accomplished in metafiction is when the author of a fiction suddenly 'intrudes' into the fiction itself, seeming to move from the extradiegetic to the diegetic level (although technically this is an impossibility because the diegetic version of the author can be no more than an avatar, and the extradiegetic version remains during the intrusion). The phone call to a wrong number which starts it all in Paul Auster's *City of Glass* asks for a 'Mr Paul Auster, of the Auster Detective Agency' (Auster, 1988, 7). When reading this line, having been briefly immersed in a more or less realist, intriguing story, the reader of *City of Glass* is jolted into confusion, realizing that the author of the book has suddenly appeared within its pages. Depending upon how aware s/he is of the author Paul Auster the reader may quickly turn to the front cover to check the name.

Frame-breaking therefore involves foregrounding the machinery which perpetuates the illusion of fiction, 'baring the device' as the Russian Formalists called it, or to put it in less theoretical terms, creating the same effect as Toto the dog does in *The Wizard of Oz* when he pulls back the curtain to reveal the shabby 'wizard' creating an illusory world for his own pleasure. Its effect is 'ontological', in Brian McHale's terms, showing '[w]hat happens when different kinds of world are placed in confrontation, or when boundaries between worlds are violated' (McHale, 1987, 10).

Since, as Waugh is careful to state, frames are part of *all* fiction, it follows that the frame-breaking effect of metafiction is not simply 'postmodern'. In fact it can be found in numerous examples of modernist fiction and also the seventeenth- and eighteenth-centuries. In his discussion of novels which imitate the Novel by authors who imitate the role of Author, John Barth points out that 'this sort of thing' is 'about where the genre began, with *Quixote* imitating *Amadis of Gaul*, Cervantes pretending to be the Cid Hamete Benengeli (and Alonso Quijano pretending to be Don Quixote), or Fielding parodying Richardson' (Barth, 2002, 145).

This indicates that Ian Watt's familiar 'rise of the novel' thesis – that the novel was realist from its very inception in the eighteenth century because of the way social, economic, and cultural factors placed a new emphasis on collective experience (Watt, 1957) – is not as reliable as it may seem. Indeed there is a case to be made for the postmodern novel being, rather than a kind of mischievous destruction of the 'mainstream' realist tradition in the novel, an attempt to return the novel to its original course following a prolonged detour into realism. Two pre-nineteenth century novels in particular are worth considering for a moment because of the extent of their metafictional parody and their influence on some of the writers featured in this book.

The first is Miguel de Cervantes's *Don Quixote* (1605; 1615). Published a century before the first novels in the early eighteenth century, this novel seriously challenges Watt's 'rise of the novel' thesis, revealing it as partial and anglocentric. Besides its layering of authorial frames, the 'sort of thing' noted by Barth, it features narrative digressions, references to other works by Cervantes and to its own developing story, and discussions by characters about the rules of writing fiction, all of which draw attention to the narrative frames involved in presenting the story to the reader. The second example is Laurence Sterne's novel *The Life and Opinions of Tristram Shandy* (1759–67) which is apparently unable to tell its hero's story straightforwardly but disorders the sequence of events (his autobiography starts with the moment of his conception, and he does not actually get 'born' until Volume 4) and accompanies them with a range of typographical conceits, such as diagrams, blank pages, lines of asterisks and dashes, and variations in typeface.

Both texts parody the conventions of the new form, the novel – in Cervantes's case before it has even properly begun. In particular they draw attention, as do later postmodern excursions into metafiction, to the difficulties of presenting 'reality' in fiction, mocking the idea of narrative 'development', where one event leads 'naturally' to another.

If metafiction is not a new departure for the novel but one of its essential properties, the question is raised as to why it should begin to return so obsessively in postmodernity. Waugh's answer is a persuasive one. She argues that postmodern fiction, as theory-in-practice, seeks to demonstrate that reality as we experience it is always mediated through discursive frames. It thus complements the kinds of sociological and psychoanalytic theory we considered in the previous chapter. Metafiction reminds us that narration is a form of *media*. Narrative functions in a similar manner to the vast media apparatus which presents reality to us – TV and cinema, the internet, 24-hour news, newspapers, magazines, etc. Or, to turn it around, metafiction reminds us that the media relies upon the techniques and effects of narrative.

The political implications of this comparison are especially evident in the many examples of metafiction produced in the United States in the late 1960s and 1970s by the likes of Barth and Robert Coover (see Chapter 3). This was the age of the assassination of JFK and the Watergate scandal, and for all their playful 'fabulation', the work of these writers was underpinned by a serious commitment to exposing the fact that everyday American reality was manufactured, not by an author, but by the authorities (i.e. the government). As Malcolm Bradbury has put it, 'What distinguishes postmodern metafiction is its relation to the public and social fictions that surround it, and its attempt to find a mode of discovery and exploration within them' (Bradbury, 1992, 204).

The metafictional staging of a clash between real and represented worlds encourages us to pursue the implications to their logical conclusion: fiction is fictional, but no more so than reality. When it collapses the distinction between fiction and reality by causing the 'outside world' to seep into the world of the novel, metafiction is more subtly demonstrating that the obverse also happens, the fictional world intrudes into the real world. This might seem far-fetched until we consider the effect of having real historical personages feature in a work of fiction as they frequently do in postmodern writing. Jorge Luis Borges's short stories often set references to fictional authors alongside references to obscure real ones and confuse the reader as to whether the fictional ones are in fact real and the real ones fabrications. Similarly, the British author D. M. Thomas creates such a believable version of the psychoanalyst Sigmund Freud in his novel *The White Hotel* (1981), through a blend of quotations from his work and private letters and perfectly pitched counterfeit 'Freudian' documents, that it is difficult to read about the real Freud after reading Thomas's novel without confusing the two.

How to read postmodern fiction

What postmodern fiction does repeatedly is prevent us from passively entering the fictional world by constantly reminding us that it *is* a fictional world, that fictional worlds are complex, and that the way authors deal with fictional worlds might teach us something about the real world. It is clear from each of the theoretical perspectives summarized in the previous section that postmodern fiction continually challenges the reader. A postmodern text is one which – at some level at least – is aware of its own status as something we read, an aesthetic object. It doesn't pretend its world is the real world or its narrative is natural, and ensures that we cannot do the same, inviting us, indeed at times requiring us, to reconsider our relationship with the world of fiction and the story it tells. Self-conscious writing, in other words, produces self-conscious reading.

What this means is that postmodernism in fiction is not simply a matter of how authors write, but how readers read. One way in which we can conceive of postmodern literary theory and practice is as a clarion call not to writers but to readers to do things differently. Modernist literary innovation is often summed up through the poet Ezra Pound's command to writers to 'make it new'. Postmodernism might be characterized by a more implicit but just as insistent demand to 'read in a new way'.

Susan Sontag and the 'erotics' of reading

An important diagnosis of the changing conditions surrounding art in post-modernity (though she doesn't use the term) was put forward by the American cultural critic Susan Sontag in two essays written in the mid-sixties, 'Against Interpretation' (1964) and 'One Culture and the New Sensibility' (1965). The second essay in particular focuses usefully on the aesthetic consequences of major shifts in the late-twentieth-century way of life. Postmodernity, she argues, is characterized by the extreme growth of science and technology, a greater sense of 'extreme social and physical mobility', 'crowdedness', physical speed and speed of images, and the mass reproduction of art objects. This means that the function of art has consequently changed. Art is now less 'a technique for depicting and commenting on secular reality' and more 'an instrument for modifying consciousness and organizing new modes of sensibility' (Sontag, 2001, 296). In other words, in the late twentieth century, it is not so much what art is *about* that matters (i.e. not its subject nor ideas) but what it *does* and how this makes us respond to it. This also means a decline in the importance of the novel. When the function of art was to comment on secular reality, it was natural that the novel, a form which depicts the workings of social reality more powerfully than any other, perhaps even cinema, reigned supreme. Yet once the emphasis is placed on how things affect the consumer of art, it meant that fiction is superseded by modes such as cinema, visual art, and music, each of which can mirror the tumultuous late-twentieth-century social conditions in a way that impacts more powerfully and directly on the client.

Sontag nevertheless regards some writers as in tune with the new climate. She mentions Burroughs and Beckett, whose work is uninterested in offering rational commentary on social reality. But the examples she gives from visual art make her argument about what art 'does' rather than 'says' most clear. 'Yellow and Orange' by Mark Rothko, for example, a canvas upon which are simply two rectangular panels, one positioned above the other, the top one hazy yellow, the one below smudged orange, cannot be 'interpreted' in the manner of other modernist forms of visual art, such as work by Picasso. However obscure and challenging, Picasso can be explained. By contrast, it is difficult to say what Rothko's painting is 'about'. Rather it just *is*; it doesn't refer to anything – except the colours 'yellow' and 'orange'. So, if we wish to claim that 'Yellow and Orange' is 'about' anything we can only make the obvious claim that it is *about* yellow and orange.

A literary parallel might be B. S. Johnson's 1973 short story (though this label is unsatisfactory), 'A Few Selected Sentences'. It has no obvious narrative but presents us, as the title suggests, with twenty-seven short sections of prose, some no longer than a line or a word ('*Life.*') Confronted by such a text, skilled readers naturally start looking for patterns, such as the preoccupation throughout the sections with death and sex, or the repetition of the phrase 'Someone has to keep the records . . .', and conclude that these suggest that Johnson's text is a textual record of fundamental elements of *Life*: sex, death, etc. (Johnson, 1989, 285).

But it is impossible to go beyond this very general and unsatisfactory reading (every text could be said to be 'about life') without going outside the text and considering Johnson's own life (he committed suicide in the year this was published). Johnson's text seems to resist any effort to unify the disparate elements by establishing links between them or to impose an overall explanatory narrative. So in the terms of Sontag's theory it seems we really have to read the text precisely as its title tells us to, as simply 'a few selected sentences' which may or may not entertain or inform us, and which cause us to reflect on the story's form not content: for example, to think of the different kinds of texts in our culture, how they mediate our reality, how they interact together, even how Johnson 'selected' the sentences or whether he composed them himself.

Sontag's essay 'Against Interpretation' contends that the new emphasis in postmodern art is on *form* rather than content and explores further how we should respond to it. The consumption of art is about pleasure rather than 'edification', fun and wit rather than seriousness or morality. One of the happy consequences of this is that enjoying art becomes an egalitarian matter rather than something snobbish. Sontag's argument is in tune here with others by prominent cultural critics of the day, most notably Leslie Fiedler, who argued in 1972 that one of the defining features of postmodern art is that it 'closes the gap' between high and low culture (Fiedler, 2002), in other words incorporating the forms of pop culture into its work. Sontag insists that postmodernism is not a dropping of standards but a 'new way of looking at the world and at things in the world' (Sontag, 2001, 303).

But it is not a simple matter of suddenly learning to take pleasure in art instead of wasting our time worrying about how to interpret it. Central to Sontag's theory is the recognition that art is a challenge. It is not something that we can now just sit back and enjoy, like a fine wine, because part and parcel of this new approach to art is that art becomes formally more complex. This is how it creates its effects. Sontag acknowledges the difficulty of postmodern art by arguing:

> The commonest complaint about the narratives of Beckett or Burroughs is that they are hard to read, they are 'boring'. But the charge of boredom is really hypocritical. There is, in a sense, no such thing as boredom. Boredom is only another name for a certain species of frustration. And the new languages which the interesting art of our time speaks are frustrating to the sensibilities of most educated people.
>
> (Sontag, 2001, 303)

Realizing that one is not bored after all may not prove much consolation for those who do find reading Beckett or Burroughs something of a chore. But perhaps the key phrase in this provocative statement is 'the sensibilities of most educated people'. We are *educated* to think of fiction in a particular way – specifically, as if it were realist fiction, and to judge all fiction according to its standards. Readers of modernist or avant-garde fiction often express their boredom or frustration (which are of course the same thing, Sontag insists) by simply saying that it is not like a 'traditional' novel – a neutral statement on the face of it but one which, in this context, actually conveys a withering criticism.

However, Sontag's argument is directed not so much at everyday readers of fiction, educated or otherwise, but at that specific group of specialist readers known as literary critics. It follows, she suggests, that a new sensibility in art really needs a new approach to criticism. This means that criticism becomes a matter of analysing the form rather than the content of a work of fiction. Sontag explains this by calling at the end of 'Against Interpretation' for an *erotics* rather than a *hermeneutics* of fiction. By this she means that we concentrate on examining how fiction creates specific kinds of enjoyment in readers rather than trying to figure out a narrative, as if it is a matter of cracking a particular code and reading the hidden message (Sontag, 2001, 13).

Now we have to acknowledge that there is something very much of its time in this argument, something unmistakably '1960s' about the whole idea of art modifying consciousness and reading narrative being liberating and erotic. It happens that there is an odd 'sexual turn' around this time in theories of reading, most obvious and unconvincing in Robert Scholes's comparison of reading to the sexual act (Scholes, 1979). However, Sontag's use of the term 'erotic' is more complex, more Platonic, than Scholes's, and does not claim universality but only to be an analysis of contemporary art.

Roland Barthes and the 'writerly' text

Sontag's description of postmodern art and literature and her argument about how we ought to respond to it provides an interesting complement to the pronouncements by novelists at the time, such as Johnson, Ballard, and Carter, about how unsuited realism was to present-day reality. What she advocates also corresponds to the dynamic approach to reading championed by the poststructuralist theorist Roland Barthes in the late 1960s and 1970s, the 'goal' of which, *jouissance*, is the parallel to that of Sontag's 'erotics' of reading.

Even though Barthes never used the term 'postmodernism' and is not usually included in the list of postmodern thinkers, his approach to creatively reading fiction exemplifies the spirit of the postmodern version of 'making it new', especially in three works published in the late 1960s and early 1970s: 'The Death of the Author' (1968), *S/Z* (1970) and *The Pleasure of the Text* (1975).

The most important of them is his obsessive book *S/Z*, in which Barthes reads, line by line, an entire realist short story by Balzac, *Sarrasine* (1830). The result is a commentary over twice the length of the original text. Determined to dissolve the realistic text's illusion of unity, Barthes sets about 'disrupting' the Balzacian text, '*manhandling* [it], *interrupting* it' (Barthes, 1975, 15). This involves making the text 'plural' by 'cut[ting] it up' into 'a series of brief, contiguous fragments' which Barthes terms 'lexias', each of which is 'a stage or space in which we can observe meanings' (Barthes, 1975, 13). *S/Z* is a detailed account of how one reader (Barthes himself) interprets the meanings generated by the text, like a 'real-time' documentary about a reading (Barthes, 1990).

The violence Barthes does to *Sarrasine* is far from gratuitous. He doesn't seek to elevate criticism over literature out of vanity but, as in other of his works, is dedicated to showing how an apparently transparent and non-political act like reading can become part of an ethical movement geared towards unmasking the repressive ideology created by the capitalist system. His cutting-up of *Sarrasine* is supported by an ideology which is most polemically expressed in 'The Death of the Author'. Here Barthes argues that the idea of the author as the individual solely responsible for the meanings in the text is no longer tenable. The author is not the creator of his text but only a *mediator* – that is, someone who selects and organizes various discourses available in 'the general text' (in other words, language and literary convention) rather than producing anything 'original', in the conventional sense of this term. The outcome – as the famous last line of Barthes's essay has it – is that the birth of the reader must be at the cost of the death of the Author' (Barthes, 1977b, 148).

S/Z provides a more systematic account of how a reader is 'born'. Its supporting theory develops a binary model by which we can measure the level of activity which a particular work of fiction demands of its reader. The translated terms are a little confusing to us, but the concepts are useful when it comes to explaining how postmodern fiction works on its reader.

At one end of the pole is the *lisible* or 'readerly' text, so termed because it is a text which tries to confine the reader to a role *as* reader, one who is guided to interpretation by the narrative itself. At the other end – and this is the zone which brings Barthes himself most pleasure as a reader (as he expounds in *The Pleasure of the Text*, the work which is a follow-up of sorts to *S/Z*) – is the *scriptible* or 'writerly' text, one which does not have a single 'closed' meaning. Instead, with this text, readers are obliged to produce their own meanings from fragmentary or contradictory clues, thus effectively writing the text themselves (or at least co-producing its meanings). A 'readerly' text is a text which reads itself for us, as it were, meaning that its rhetoric guides us to respond to it passively, as consumers. A 'writerly' text, by contrast, is one in which the reader becomes 'co-writer'; it is he or she who is responsible for activating its meanings. The 'readerly' text is finite, whereas the writerly text 'exists nowhere', as what it 'is' depends upon how it is read at any one time. Put more simply, the 'writerly' text is one which is less conventional, less realist, and requires us to 'work' in order to make sense of what is going on within its pages.

A postmodern work of fiction is an example of a writerly text. However, it is important to understand that Barthes's definitions are really rhetorical models: the closest thing to 'readerly' texts are nineteenth-century realist narratives, such as those produced by George Eliot, Leo Tolstoy, and Honoré de Balzac. But in using a Balzacian short story as the way of putting his theory into practice, Barthes effectively demonstrates that *every* text is 'writerly'; it's just a question of degree. Similarly Pierre Bayard's reading of Christie demonstrates that a definitively *readerly* form of fiction, the classic detective story, can in fact be made writerly.

In his 1971 essay 'From Work to Text' Barthes sets up a similar binary based on two ways of conceiving of a work of fiction, in which the equivalent of the readerly text is the 'work' and the equivalent of the writerly one is 'text'. The shift of emphasis, though, is reminiscent of Sontag's point about how postmodern writing is 'frustrating to the sensibilities of most educated people' for it makes it clear that setting out to respond to a text in a 'writerly' rather than 'readerly' manner is not something that comes naturally because of the way we are taught to read.

The Work is something that is displayed, can be *seen* in bookshops, libraries, exam syllabi, etc. It is a finished product which is 'closed', finite and only '*moderately* symbolic (its symbolic runs out, comes to a halt)'. The Text, by contrast, is *demonstrated* rather than displayed; it exists only in the movement of discourse, is experienced only in an activity of production by its reader. It consequently 'goes to the limit of enunciation (rationality, readability, etc.)', challenges received opinions, is intertextual, and '*radically* symbolic' (Barthes, 1977c, 157–8).

Though it may seem like it (and there is perhaps some truth in this), Barthes is not trying to establish a canon of postmodern or avant-garde fiction by suggesting that some texts are 'better' (more open) than others. Rather he is concerned with how institutions, educational and legal, school us into a particular limited practice of reading. Where once we were taught rhetoric, and composition, since 'the coming of democracy' we have been taught in schools to *read* well – and reading here means consuming rather than *playing*. This institutionalized method of reading brings 'pleasure' but it is not the *jouissance* Barthes most values. Unlike simple 'pleasure', *jouissance* moves one away from their fixed subject position and all the ideological and authoritarian operations it involves. Pleasure merely confirms it (Barthes, 1975).

'Paranoid reading' and 'rhizomatic reading'

Sontag's and Barthes's arguments suggest that there is a case to be made for a text's identity as 'postmodern' being determined by the act of reading rather than writing. There is some value in this, though it would clearly be stretching things to call certain texts postmodern – like *Sarrasine*, for example – simply because of how we choose to read them. Nevertheless, for all their differences in form, postmodern texts generate a self-consciousness about how we read which is in tune with the ideas about reading put forward by Sontag and Barthes. To complement their insistence that postmodern fiction invites us to concentrate on form rather than content, we need to conclude this chapter by considering two other kinds of reading practice which are relevant to the postmodern fiction considered in this book.

The first of these is what some critics (Siegel, 1976; McHale, 1992) have termed 'paranoid reading'. This concept might usefully be considered in relation to Sarraute's notion of the 'age of suspicion', and also in terms of Paul Ricoeur's idea of the 'hermeneutic of suspicion', something that became dominant in the twentieth century – on a wider cultural level than simply literature – as a result of the influence of Marx, Nietzsche and Freud. These thinkers developed 'a method of interpretation which assumes that the literal or surface-level meaning of a text is an effort to conceal the political interests which are served by the text. The purpose of interpretation is to strip off the concealment, unmasking those interests' (Ricoeur, 1970, 33).

Similarly, when interpreting fiction we bring to texts a certain logic, one predicated on the idea of reading 'beneath the surface'. We assume that texts are *really* saying something different deep down, that the various patterns and repetitions are not coincidences, that symbols and images are not there just to please us but because they mean something. This is a kind of reading practice which does not allow for significance, which assumes that everything must mean something. Mark Siegel argues that paranoia 'is the condition under which most of modern literature comes to life: the author relies on the reader to find correspondences between names, colours, or the physical attributes of characters and other invisible qualities of those characters, places, and actions, while to do so in "real life" would clearly be an indication of paranoid behaviour' (Siegel, 1976, 50). Brian McHale has built upon Siegel's insight to provide a kind of historical context for this modern approach to reading, arguing that the approach to criticism is in fact instituted as a kind of critical orthodoxy during the era of modernism, namely through its academic counterpart 'practical criticism', a technique taught in university English departments (variations continue to be taught even now) which involves 'close reading' of the text and is governed by the assumption that what it presents us with directly is only a cipher for what it is *really* saying deep down. To really understand a modernist or postmodernist work of art, McHale argues, we have to work on this assumption.

Postmodern fiction displays a typically double-coded attitude to paranoid reading. Unlike modernism, where paranoid methods are 'rewarded', postmodern works of fiction are ambivalent about the practice. As we shall see in some of the readings which follow, postmodern texts frequently invite readers to interpret them in a paranoid manner – and this is undoubtedly part of their appeal – but some deliberately frustrate their attempts or demonstrate that determining a final meaning is more complex than it seems.

The second reading-practice relevant to postmodern fiction is more playful and accepting of open-ended interpretation than paranoid reading. Postmodern narrative involves us in a process of *conjecture*. This is a notion I have adapted from Umberto Eco's discussion of detective fiction in his short postscript to his own postmodern detective novel, *The Name of the Rose*. The appeal of detective fiction, he suggests in *Reflections on The Name of the Rose*, is not because of some morbid fascination with the corpse or even because the genre represents the victory of order over 'the disorder of evil'. Rather, he argues, the appeal is that of *conjecture*: a hypothesis formed through speculation (usually without hard evidence) that, moreover, works through narrative. The crime story presents us with a set of events which we conjecture (usually by following the lead of the detective, the reader's more enlightened avatar in the world of the text) have a logic to them, which can explain what happened and the criminal responsible.

Eco's model for how conjecture works is the labyrinth. Some labyrinths, he argues, are straightforward. The 'classical' version 'does not allow anyone to get lost: you go in, arrive at the center, and then from the center you reach the exit', while 'the mannerist maze' – the kind popular in theme parks and the gardens of stately homes – is a structure which, if unravelled, is 'a kind of tree, a structure with roots, with many blind alleys. There is only one exit, but you can get it wrong'. But the labyrinth Eco is most interested in is what he calls the 'rhizomatic' maze (Eco, 1985, 57).

The metaphor of the rhizome (a botanical term for a kind of plant stem) is used by the philosophers Gilles Deleuze and Félix Guattari in their book *A Thousand Plateaus: Capitalism and Schizophrenia* (1980) to enable us to picture the relation of things to other things in philosophy, language, the arts, and social sciences – according to principles of connection, heterogeneity, multiplicity, and rupture – in a way that provides an alternative to a straightforward linear 'surface–depth' model of interpretation which is central to paranoid reading. Unlike the roots of a tree 'which plots a point, fixes an order' the value of the rhizome is that 'any point . . . can be connected to anything other, and must be' (Deleuze and Guattari, 1987, 7).

They suggest that language works in this way. While it can be understood in 'tree-like' terms if we work with a basic Saussurian signifier–signified model, Deleuze and Guattari's point is that because language is a living phenomenon, there are always numerous other meanings suggested, other traces of usage which deepen the meaning. Interpreting a text can work the same way. We can look for one underlying meaning which can make sense of what is 'above' ground, or we can accept that any text is likely to generate a whole string of meanings which are only connected by the fact that they are triggered by the same element of the text. This explains the appeal of the metaphor for Eco's comparison of labyrinths: 'The rhizome is so constructed that every path can be connected with every other one. It has no center, no periphery, no exit, because it is potentially infinite' (Eco, 1985, 57). An obvious comparison now would be with the internet, which can be imagined as a labyrinth with a rhizomatic structure. The internet 'starts' and 'ends' nowhere, or rather you can enter and exit from anywhere and go from any one place to any other. The rhizome, according to this model, means that connections can be made between things which are otherwise unconnected.

Eco's analogy suggests that we can understand the process of interpreting different kinds of text according to the idea of being lost in a maze. The classic detective story – for example, Conan Doyle's Sherlock Holmes stories or Agatha Christie's 'clue-puzzle' version – can be regarded as 'mannerist mazes' which require us to arrive at the conclusion, to establish the final narrative, via a lengthy process of trial and error. Reading a detective story involves going through a process of entertaining various hypotheses regarding the crime. The process is made particularly vivid in TV/cinematic adaptations of Agatha Christie's novels, in the convention where, as the detective hypothesizes about a particular scenario or suspects claim to remember an event, the episodes their words conjure up are presented on screen as if they really happened. The televisual mechanism is particularly powerful here as it is able to present the conjecture as if indistinguishable from the real.

Realist fiction and classic detective fiction typically closes down the conjectural possibilities at a certain point in the narrative – certainly by the conclusion, when the true narrative becomes apparent and replaces all the other potential versions of the truth. Postmodern detective fiction, on the other hand, has shown a fondness for keeping the possibilities open – in the manner of Borges's story 'The Garden of Forking Paths' (considered in the next chapter). Once activated they are not closed down. This is also the logic of Bayard's *Who Killed Roger Ackroyd?*, in which he refuses to accept that the paths opened up throughout Christie's novel have to remain closed once Poirot privileges one of them over the other.

Beyond detective fiction, however, I think the parallel Eco draws between conjecture in narrative and the rhizome has a much wider significance. As we shall see, postmodernist narrative frequently works according to this model. The classic example is Nabokov's *Pale Fire* (see Chapter 3), a text which opens a number of conjectural possibilities and leaves it impossible for us to close any of them down. Texts like this suggest that the ideal reader of postmodern fiction is less a detective and more of a traveller in space, ready to encounter different, co-existent, worlds.

Chapter 2

Early postmodern fiction: Beckett, Borges, and Burroughs

While modernist fiction can be seen as the response to Ezra Pound's command to 'make it new', the major question for the early postmodern writers of the 1960s and 1970s – though they share the modernist conviction that realism as a fictional mode is largely invalid in the twentieth century – is simply how to keep on *writing* in the face of developments in newer artistic forms such as cinema and television, the increasingly 'fictional' quality of contemporary life, and also the strong sense that the novel is effectively exhausted as a literary form.

Exhaustion is the term used by the American postmodern novelist John Barth in one of the most important contributions to the postmodern debate, 'The Literature of Exhaustion' (1967), which views the contemporary novel as in decline. What he means by exhaustion is not some kind of 'physical, moral, or intellectual decadence' but simply the growing sense that 'certain forms or . . . certain possibilities' in fiction are 'used up' (Barth, 2002, 138).

Barth here is voicing an anxiety that beset a number of 1960s and 1970s writers: that it is impossible to say or do anything new in the novel following the achievements of modernism. The problem, he writes, is not a general weariness towards all-too familiar traditional art forms, for this could simply be overcome by producing gimmicky novels made up of other kinds of documents such as 'Somebody-or-other's unbound, unpaginated, randomly assembled novel-in-a-box' (a curious prediction of B. S. Johnson's experiment in his novel *The Unfortunates*, published two years after Barth's essay) or 'printing *Finnegan's Wake* on a very long roller-towel' (Barth, 2002, 139). Rather, the problem is how to produce something new which is still a 'proper' novel, one which manages to be 'technically up-to-date' while also being able 'nonetheless to speak eloquently and memorably to our still-human hearts and conditions, as the great artists have always done' (Barth, 2002, 140).

Three novelists who fulfil this exacting task, to Barth's mind, are Samuel Beckett, Jorge Luis Borges, and Vladimir Nabokov, precisely because their work confronts the possibility of exhaustion head on. Their value is that 'in an age of ultimacies and "final solutions" – at least *felt* ultimacies, in everything from weaponry to theology, the celebrated dehumanization of society, and the history of the novel – their work in separate ways reflects and deals with ultimacy, both technically and thematically' (Barth, 2002, 141). Barth's point is that these authors do not just write novels *about* ultimacy (the sense that everything, from theology to society to the novel itself, is about to end), but their fiction *performs* it by making their texts deal with the issue formally rather than at the level of content. As a result, reading them, we are invited to consider the function and value of literature.

Barth mentions Nabokov only scarcely, does not refer to Burroughs, and makes it clear that he prefers Borges's way of building ultimacy into his work to Beckett's (more on why below). But leaving Barth's particular thesis aside I think we can affirm that the three writers dealt with in this chapter – Beckett, Borges, and Burroughs – are each influential on postmodern writing because they suggest solutions to the two questions which prompted Barth's essay: how to remain in tune with significant developments in the modern world, and how to continue writing despite the apparent exhaustion of a literary form. Their ability to deal with ultimacy directly is part of this, as Barth explains, but each writer also develops formal innovations in his work – defying the view that the possibilities for new departures in fiction are exhausted – which have proven especially influential. These writers are anti-realist to the core: their work seldom resembles realist fiction. In particular they explode the staple realist values of maintaining consistent, reliable narration, and establishing a stable imaginary world, analogous to the real one.

Each of these writers might be regarded as key transitional figures in the passage from modernism to postmodernism. Beckett's prose writings began in the late 1930s, Borges's in the 1940s, while Beckett and Burroughs each produced especially pioneering fiction in the 1950s – the decade which might consequently be regarded as the period of gestation for postmodern fiction, before it emerged fully in the 1960s. It is in this decade that the influence of each of these writers really makes itself felt. In the case of Burroughs this was due to the impact of late 1950s' and early 1960s' works, while Beckett's and Borges's influence increased because of landmark events in the world of letters at the turn of the decade, namely the publication in English and in one volume of Beckett's Trilogy in 1959, the award of the 1961 'Formenter' International Publishers' Prize to both authors jointly (an event described by Barth as 'a happy exception' to the rule that literary awards are insignificant in literary history [Barth, 2002, 140]), and the publication of Borges's *Ficciones* in English translation in 1962.

The fiction produced by these writers exemplifies Brian McHale's definition of postmodernism as a form of writing preoccupied with *ontological* questions.

They remind their readers that fiction does not – even if it pretends to – refer to some outside reality (the 'level' at which the reader exists) but inside to its own imagined world. Perhaps this is the most interesting effect of their work: that it focuses the reader's attention on the question of *reading* rather than writing – that is, specifically how to read the challenging fiction they produce, but also how and why we read *all* fiction.

Beckett, Borges, and Burroughs occupy a somewhat liminal position with regard to the two most significant movements in twentieth-century fiction: not modernist yet not postmodernist, even though their work is the foundation upon which postmodernist writing rests. McHale uses the term 'limit-modernism' for writers like Beckett who take modernism as far as it can go (McHale, 1987, 13). Or, to turn again to Umberto Eco's theory of postmodernism expressed in *Reflections on The Name of the Rose*, we might suggest that these writers are working in the immediate aftermath of the avant-garde – in the wake of *Finnegan's Wake*, as it were – when art realizes it has to turn back, or end up unable to express itself at all. Referring to one of these writers, Eco suggests that if writing continued in the same vein all we would have is 'the destruction of the flow of discourse, the Burroughs-like collage, silence, the white page' (Eco, 1985, 67). It may also explain why it is that although Beckett is the figure most cited as an influence by postmodern writers, very few could be regarded as trying to imitate him or even to extend his achievements. The fiction that follows the dying embers of the avant-garde has to be postmodernism, according to Eco's theory, a mode defined by its self-reflexivity. We shall consider postmodern writing 'proper' as it develops in the 1960s in the next chapter, but here we can consider in more depth the innovations of the three writers it repeatedly echoes.

Samuel Beckett

Samuel Beckett is one of the most distinctive and important of twentieth-century writers. Thanks to photographs of him in his later years, with his deep wrinkles and bold gaze, he is also one of the most iconic, his face visual shorthand for 'The Twentieth Century Artist', someone writing in a bleak era, an age, indeed, of 'felt ultimacies'. Beckett is often considered the supreme embodiment of the 'existentialist' artist, that is, a writer whose plays, such as his most famous work *Waiting for Godot* (1953), and fiction seem to dramatize the concerns deemed central to the philosophies associated with the existentialist tradition in philosophy (Kierkegaard, Nietzsche, Heidegger, and Sartre) which insist that the human being, once stripped of his or her value systems, is left to face existence without recourse to accepted judgements of right or wrong.

There are two reasons why Beckett's fiction is central to postmodernism. First, it is regarded as being so distinctive, so different from what preceded it, despite or perhaps because of the necessity to follow on from modernism (as Barth's essay suggests), that Beckett himself amounts to a kind of 'existentialist hero', one who stands for what can be done in the face of exhaustion if one tries. This accounts for his appeal to writers such as Robert Coover or B. S. Johnson. The second reason is more precise, and that is the way that Beckett's fiction deals with the problem of how language relates to the real world. His novels are concerned more than anything else – more, that is, than telling a story or mounting any kind of social critique – with their own process of construction. On the face of it this exemplifies the practice of metafiction, and explains why metafictionists like Coover and Johnson are so indebted to Beckett. Yet, while Beckett's writing is continually very witty and funny, reading it is a more alienating experience than the kind of writing usually classified as postmodern metafiction.

Beckett's iconic status as the exemplary Serious Modern Writer is perfectly accurate. Specifically, he was concerned, from the outset, with the peculiar paradox of fiction. It was the job of literature, he thought, to reflect the meaninglessness of existence. Yet the paradox is that it must do this via language, which is endlessly (in his view) *meaningful.* So his writing attempts the impossible task of conveying meaninglessness through meaning, of trying to convey nothingness through something, or silence through words.

In a way, Beckett's writing is the counterpart of the abstract visual art of the painter Mark Rothko, who exemplifies Susan Sontag's new postmodern sensibility in art (summarized in the previous chapter), and whose paintings defy any viewer to say plausibly what they are 'about' other than what the title tells us. Beckett's prose does something equivalent, though of course language cannot be as abstract as colour and his fiction still features peoples, places, and situations which can be taken as corresponding to those in the outside world. Nevertheless his prose writing is dedicated to the idea of upholding the notion that fiction is not 'about' anything, does not 'refer' to anything outside itself.

Amongst Beckett's huge body of work, critics agree that there are six 'major' novels: *Murphy* (1938), *Watt* (written in 1942–5 but not published until 1953) the Trilogy: *Molloy, Malone Dies, The Unnamable* (published from 1951–7), and *Comment C'est / How It Is* (1961). As a sequence Beckett's novels take us about as far as one could get from the realist paradigm of reliable narration which functions as a transparent medium through which we can access the imagined world of the novel. Each of his fictions is a prolonged and increasingly more bleak and alienating exercise in questioning the status of the represented world of fiction and its relationship to the real world.

This is true of *Murphy*, even though it remains the most accessible and widely read of Beckett's prose works. It tells the story of the eponymous central character, an Irishman living in drab 1930s London who, through some unspecified philosophical conviction, is determined to exist only in his mind and to reject, where possible, the world of the body, but is gradually forced by his lover, Celia Kelly, to engage with the real world. This he does, finding a version of the peace he has been seeking by taking a job in a mental hospital, until he dies suddenly when an unknown person clicks on a faulty switch in the WC downstairs which results in his room being flooded with gas.

It is a captivating story, a witty combination of the picaresque and the philosophical, yet readers often find it difficult to determine what is actually going on. Some readers even realize they have missed Murphy's death. This is because the prose is so mannered – recalling Eco's speculation that postmodernism is really just our age's 'mannerism', an obsessively stylized form of art (Eco, 2002, 110–11) – that the narration gets in the way of what is being depicted. Although *Murphy*'s story is linear, features a number of characters and a realistically drawn social world, the language of the novel is not a transparent medium for conveying the imagined world to the reader. The narrator pursues puns and flights of fancy continually; the dialogue, though witty, makes no attempt to mimic real speech.

The narrator's partiality is clear from the first sentence: 'The sun shone, having no alternative, on the nothing new' (Beckett, 1973, 5), which subtly parodies Ecclesiastes I.v ('What has been is what will be / and what has been done is what will be done; / there is nothing new under the sun'). Why is he making this parallel? This continues throughout the novel, with other idiosyncratic ways of setting the scene: 'The moon, by a striking coincidence full and at perigee, was 29,000 miles nearer the earth than it had been for four years' (Beckett, 1973, 19), or ironic comments such as 'Let us now take Time that old fornicator, bald though he be behind, by such few sad short hairs as he has, back to Monday, October the 7th (Beckett, 1973, 67), or referring to the reader as 'gentle skimmer' (Beckett, 1980, 51). It is clear that this is a parody of realism, the mode 'borrowed' by Beckett to convey this set of ideas. As well as narratorial objectivity and reliability, the other key staple of realist fiction, character, is parodied, too. The narrator compares the novel at one point to a puppet show rather than fiction, reminding us of how characters, unlike the free, independent versions of 'real' people they are supposed to be in the realist novel, are always subject to the whim of their author. Some of them – Endon ('peace' in Greek), or Neary (an acronym of Yearn) – are given emblematic names.

Chapter 2 begins with a list of features belonging, it seems, to Celia (though there is no indication of who compiled the list: the narrator? Murphy, her lover? Herself?). It describes her head ('small and round') and eyes ('Green'), and goes on to note, as well as her height and weight, bizarrely, the precise measurements of her neck, arms, wrists, bust, waist, 'Hips, etc.', thigh, knee, calf, ankle – though her age and the instep for some reason is listed as 'Unimportant' (Beckett, 1973, 10). This seems like an ironic version of the signature feature of realism, its descriptive precision, a parody which gives the reader no help whatsoever in visualizing the character more clearly, as key indicators such as its age and even gender are missed out.

From the outset, alert readers ought to be deeply suspicious of the narrator's desire or ability to render the fictional world accurately. The second paragraph of the novel describes Murphy's 'recreation' of tying himself up in his rocking chair to meditate, stating that 'Seven scarves held him in position. Two fastened his shins to the rockers, one his thighs to the seat, two his breast and belly to the back, one his wrists to the strut behind' (Beckett, 1980, 5). The description is authoritative, yet only accounts for six of the scarves. This leads to the obvious question: where is the seventh? More pertinently, it leads to questions about the narrator. Why is he not telling us where the seventh scarf is? Has he forgotten, does he not know, or is he deliberately playing games with us? These questions each lead to further questions regarding his motives. But of course they really subvert the entire realist enterprise of narrator presenting reader with a faithfully drawn imagined world. If *Murphy*'s narrator is capable of lying or being mistaken about what he is telling us, how can we trust any other aspect of the imagined world? Despite its engaging central character and plot, the only thing we can ultimately be *sure* about the narration in *Murphy* is that it refers us to itself, as an exercise in fiction.

Beckett's later novels obscure the reader's view of any reality they represent even more powerfully by increasing the complexity of the narrator's relation to the imagined world and making the language more impenetrable still. *Watt* is a novel in which, at the conventional level of plot, nothing happens, except for the most mundane events. The eponymous character waits for a train and travels to begin work as a servant for a Mr Knott. There he performs a series of elaborate, though routine, tasks before being replaced by another servant and taking the train to the 'end of the line', ending up at the 'manor', a house which resembles a mental hospital.

It is a scenario which seems typically 'Beckettian' to those who know his plays, featuring solitary figures performing repetitive tasks and a 'plot' that amounts to a prolonged journey to the void, or death. As such it seems to demand an allegorical reading, especially given the fact that the names of these characters seem to be obvious ciphers: Watt (what?) is the questing figure, only for his quest to meet a negative (a not). Watt is unable to determine anything about Knott, who never speaks. However, the novel ends with a famously enigmatic statement which seems a kind of warning to the reader: 'no symbols where none intended' (Beckett, 1994b, 254). If *Watt* is not symbolic, it means we must take the text *literally*, as it is, that is, as a story which someone is telling us, or, even more literally, 'simply' a piece of writing.

It asks more directly the question implied in *Murphy*: why should we assume that literature should signify something at a deeper level? In the third part of *Watt* the process of narration is made clearer as it is revealed that Watt is telling his story to 'Sam', a figure who of course seems to signify Beckett himself. This further compromises the sense of reliability of the story. Sam informs us that the period when Watt was working for Knott didn't really happen, and is really an illusion. According to Watt, however, it is the first and fourth sections of the story (the journey to and from Knott's house) which are illusory. Who can we trust? There is no external perspective by which we can judge what the truth is. The only conclusion is that the novel is not referential. Beckett's novel – like all novels – is really just 'whatnot', pieces of prose composed by an artist about, literally, Nothing.

Beckett's Trilogy, completed in the post-war years 1947–1950, before *Watt* was published, is one of the bleakest, most disturbing yet brilliant prose achievements of the twentieth century. The three novels complicate the idea of the narrated world still further. Rather than the kind of parodic realist narrator we have in *Murphy* and *Watt*, untrustworthy, inconsistent and unidentifiable, the Trilogy presents us with a series of narrators, this time recounting rambling, faltering, fragmented, contradictory stories in the first person each in an effort to make sense of his own existence. In fact it is the act of narration that constitutes their existence, a way of passing the time. They long for silence, yet are seemingly unable to stop narrating.

Molloy combines the stories of Molloy, who sets out – on crutches and a bicycle – to find his mother and writes his story from her bedroom, and Moran, who searches for Molloy but fails and writes a report about it. A note of indeterminacy is sustained, though, because throughout Moran's quest he seems to lose his identity and become Molloy's double (complete with crutches), so that the distinction between characters is unclear and the story's temporality and plausibility becomes endlessly complicated (is Molloy searching for himself?)

The opening of *Malone Dies*, the second novel in the Trilogy, further complicates the ontological status of the world represented in *Molloy* when the eponymous narrator claims both Molloy and Moran as his inventions. His narrative in this volume revolves around a figure called Macmann, whom he refers to as Scaposcat. Yet his narrative suddenly breaks off and we are left to infer (from the title) that this is because Malone has died. We are then faced with a further indeterminacy about the status of the imagined worlds in the Trilogy: do we believe in the world that Malone inhabits, narrating his stories in between eating and defecating, or in the world which he tells us about, that is, the world of Molloy, Moran, and Scaposcat/Macmann?

This complex structure is complicated still further at the beginning of *The Unnamable*, where the disembodied voice which is the eponymous narrator claims to have created not only Molloy, Moran, and Malone but *Murphy* and *Watt* as well. The Trilogy thus creates a potentially infinite regress of ontological levels. The obvious assumption is that this all stops at Beckett 'himself', 'the unnamable', who exists at a level *outside* the fictional ones. Yet Beckett, like any author, only 'exists' in fiction. While *The Unnamable* contains stories about another pairing of beings (this time barely human: Mahood, nothing more than a limbless torso and head in a jar, and Worm, an even less human creature), it is really about the narrator's desperate, paradoxical recognition that he only exists in the text, as there is no correspondence whatsoever between the real world and the world of the fiction:

> there was never anyone, anyone but me, anything but me, talking to me of me, impossible to stop, impossible to go on, but I must go on, I'll go on, without anyone, without anything, but me, but my voice, that is to say I'll stop, I'll end, it's the end already, shortlived, what is it, a little hole, you go down into it, into the silence, it's worse than the noise, you listen, it's worse than talking, no, not worse, no worse, you wait, in anguish, have they forgotten me, no, yes, no, someone calls me, I crawl out again, what is it, a little hole, in the wilderness.
>
> (Beckett, 1994a, 395)

Beckett's Trilogy demonstrates powerfully, harrowingly, that fiction can only be about itself. Any attempt to refer to a world outside the imagined world of the novel is always already fictional because the description becomes incorporated into the imaginary world.

This is what Patricia Waugh calls the 'creation/description' paradox of metafiction: the law that when you try to describe something, what you really do is *create* it. The point at the heart of the Trilogy is illustrated most directly perhaps in *Molloy*. Moran tries to begin his report in the referential mode of realism: 'It is midnight. The rain is beating on the windows'. His efforts to write an objective report, however, break down as he is unable to find Molloy and his prose starts to ramble like Molloy's. In the end he finishes his 'report' with the line 'It was not midnight. It was not raining' (Beckett, 1994a, 176). The world of fiction is a world with its own laws which only correspond to the laws of the real world if that is what the author decides (and if the reader agrees to interpret the novel in this way). It can be no more than analogous to the real world. It is the logic of the surrealist painter Magritte's 'Ceci n'est pas une pipe'. A painting depicting a pipe and labelling it a pipe can still never *be* a pipe, only a representation of one.

Jorge Luis Borges

Borges's writing consists only of short, sometimes very short (only a paragraph) 'fictions', to use the title of his most famous and influential volume of texts published in 1944. Though prolific, he never wrote anything remotely of novel length. Indeed he disliked long fiction and considered the full-length novel so tediously prolonged as to be practically unreadable. This was true even of Kafka, whom he admired, but felt his novels ought to have been condensed into short stories because it was immediately obvious at the beginning how they were going to end (Borges, 1982).

To call Borges's texts 'fictions' is not just a quirk of translation but perfectly appropriate. This label has fewer of the connotations of narrative which alternatives like 'short stories' or tales have. Borges's fictions are a long way from the established genre of the short story practised by American writers like Raymond Carver. Even though there is often a clear narrative sketched out within them, they are not chiefly concerned with recounting it. Instead they tend to deal with the idea of how fiction creates an imagined world quite independent of the real world, though it may be analogous to it. As such they are the model for the kind of short playful metafictional texts produced by North American descendents such as Robert Coover, John Barth, and Donald Barthelme (see Chapter 3).

Barth admires Borges because he demonstrates 'how an artist may paradoxically turn the felt ultimacies of our time into material and means for his work – *paradoxically* because by doing so he transcends what had appeared to be his refutation' (Barth, 2002, 144). He does this by making literary history the context for much of his writing – not in the way favoured by those practitioners of what Linda Hutcheon was to call 'historiographic metafiction', by choosing specific canonical intertexts and embedding them systematically in an otherwise realist narrative (see Chapter 4), but by producing 'fictions' which either take as their subject books themselves or are set in a bibliographic context.

This tendency has an obviously biographical significance, as Borges worked as a librarian for most of his life. Indeed placing books and bookish heroes at the centre of works of fiction might be regarded as the sedentary academic's fantasy of action. His bookishness is suggested by his fondness for titles which sound like academic studies: 'The Library of Babel', 'A Survey of the Works of Herbert Quain', 'A Biography of Tadeo Isidoro Cruz (1829–1874)', and his use of a typically 'academic' narrator, whose style is learned, erudite, cautious, even pedantic.

One of the exemplary Borgesian 'bookish' texts is the 1939 story 'Pierre Menard, Author of the *Quixote*'. It masquerades as an introduction to a forgotten great writer, the early twentieth-century writer Pierre Menard, written by an unnamed academic, writer, or librarian. It begins by listing the items in his body of work, with academic precision: poems, translations and monographs, etc. Yet the narrator claims that these are only his *visible* works, implying that there is a hidden body of work, too. We then realize the real purpose behind this introduction to Menard. Menard devoted his life, the narrator claims, to writing *Don Quixote*. He is quick to point out that this means not another contemporary *version* of *Don Quixote* nor that Menard mechanically transcribed the original. He insists Menard's *Don Quixote* is *not* a copy but in fact 'a number of pages which coincided – word for word and line for line' (Borges, 1998a, 91) – with those of Miguel de Cervantes.

The reader is thus faced with an apparently impossible conundrum: how can one 'write' a text that has already been written without reimagining or simply copying it? The narrator's analysis of this new *Don Quixote* does not resolve the paradox but deepens it. He argues that 'The Cervantes text and the Menard text are verbally identical, but the second is almost infinitely richer' and goes on to compare passages from the two to prove his case:

> It is a revelation to compare the *Don Quixote* of Pierre Menard with that of Miguel de Cervantes. Cervantes, for example, wrote the following (Part I, Chapter IX):
>
>> . . . truth, whose mother is history, rival of time, depository of deeds, witness of the past, exemplar and adviser to the present, and the future's counselor.
>
> This catalog of attributes, written in the seventeenth century, and written by the 'ingenious layman' Miguel de Cervantes, is mere rhetorical praise of history. Menard, on the other hand, writes:
>
>> . . . truth, whose mother is history, rival of time, depository of deeds, witness of the past, exemplar and adviser to the present, and the future's counselor.

> History, the *mother* of truth! – the idea is staggering. Menard, a
> contemporary of William James, defines history not as a *delving into*
> reality but as the very *fount* of reality.   (Borges, 1998a, 94)

On first reading this seems an elaborate joke. As Barth notes, however, the idea
of 'writing' a previous work is actually 'intellectually serious' (Barth, 2002,
142). It is how Borges surmounts the problem of the exhaustion of fiction by
making this exhaustion the very subject of the work. Borges does not attribute
Don Quixote to himself nor recompose it in the way his Menard does. Rather
'he writes a remarkable and original work of literature, the implicit theme of
which is the difficulty, perhaps the unnecessity, of writing original works of
literature' (Barth, 2002, 142).

  Beyond Barth's particular reasons for admiring the story, 'Pierre Menard,
Author of the *Quixote*' indicates Borges's value for postmodern writing. We
could effectively turn Barth's argument around and say that rather than how
it is possible to still *write* once the possibilities for fiction have been exhausted,
what 'Pierre Menard' illustrates is how fiction is radically altered by its context
because it depends upon the way it is *read*. Besides pastiche which functions as
homage – Jamesons's pointless 'blank parody' – a more aggressive strategy of
appropriation or outright copyright *does* operate in postmodern art. Authors
who deliberately plagiarize, such as William Burroughs, Kathy Acker, D. M.
Thomas, and the visual artist Sherrie Levine are the real-life counterparts of
Pierre Menard. The effect of their work is radically to question values we take
for granted, such as originality, and to emphasize in a new way the significance
of historical context in making sense of a work.

  This view of 'Pierre Menard' had been offered by another theorist-
practitioner of contemporary fiction a few years before Barth's essay on Borges
appeared. In *For a New Novel* (1965) French novelist Alain Robbe-Grillet argues
that it would be a mistake to consider the scenario set out in 'Pierre Menard'
as somehow paradoxical. In his view the story makes an entirely logical point:

> To praise a young writer in 1965 because he 'writes like Stendhal' is
> doubly disingenuous. On the one hand there would be nothing
> admirable about such a feat . . . ; on the other, the thing itself is quite
> impossible: in the first place, to write like Stendhal one would first of all
> have to be writing in 1830. A writer who produces a pastiche skillful
> enough to contain pages Stendhal might have signed at the time would
> in no way have the value he would still possess today had he written
> those same pages under Charles X. It is no paradox that Borges
> elaborates in *Ficciones*: the twentieth-century novelist who reproduces
> *Don Quixote* word for word writes a totally different work from that of
> Cervantes.   (Robbe-Grillet, 1989a, 10)

Robbe-Grillet's remarks indicate that there is actually a strong point of concordance between Fredric Jameson's arguments against pastiche and those of postmodern writers, such as Barth, Robbe-Grillet, and B. S. Johnson, who regard the determination of many of their contemporaries to maintain previous literary traditions, notably the realist novel, as an inappropriate, perverse kind of pastiche, which their own work must fight against.

Menard's rewriting of *Don Quixote* also relates neatly to an idea introduced into literary theory at around the same time as Barth's 'The Literature of Exhaustion', in Roland Barthes's polemical essay 'The Death of the Author' (1968). Barthes contends that literary composition is not and never has been an 'original' activity, but a matter of the author rearranging previous literary and linguistic conventions rather than creating something completely new. Menard's act of appropriation emphasizes Barthes's view that the idea of the author as the stable guarantor of the meanings we take from a work of literature is no longer tenable; rather the reader functions as 'co-writer' of a text, free to derive from it the meanings he or she desires (Barthes, 1977b).

Like Beckett, one of the effects of Borges's writing is to ensure the reader becomes critically aware of his or her own process of reading. It is impossible to read the passage quoted above from 'Pierre Menard, Author of the *Quixote*' without doing so self-consciously. We are compelled to re-read the extracts from Cervantes and Menard carefully to verify our suspicion that they are exactly the same. This is one of the characteristic effects of metafiction generally, to prevent us from simply 'consuming' fiction passively in the way classic realist works invite us to, but making us into active co-creators of meaning, aware of the author's process of construction and our own role as 'receivers' of the messages he or she generates.

The effect Borges's fiction has on its readers is clear from one of his strangest but most characteristic fictions, 'Tlön, Uqbar, Orbis Tertius'. Most of the story purports to be an article written in 1940 detailing the research of an anonymous narrator-academic and a colleague who pursue a reference to somewhere named Uqbar and realize they have uncovered a mysterious hidden world called Tlön. Based on their research, they introduce the reader to the history, properties, and customs of the strange, fantastic world, from its 'transparent tigers' and 'towers of blood' to its philosophy, language, and literature.

But the 'article' has a 'Postscript' written in 1947 (a date in the near future when Borges's story was first published, in 1941) which reveals that Tlön is the invention of a secret society of scholars who have set out every detail of the world in the entries which make up a vast forty-volume encyclopaedia named *A First Encyclopaedia of Tlön*, and who were planning to compose an even more exhaustive work about another secret world, *Orbis Tertius*. The postscript also includes disturbing evidence to suggest that the fantastic world of Tlön is gradually intruding into and taking the place of the 'real' world (i.e. ours), beginning with the discovery of two strange Tlönian objects and followed by insidious changes to our society such as Tlönian history replacing the history taught in schools, the reformation of academic disciplines such as pharmacology and archaeology along Tlönian lines, and the Tlönian language being spoken. When *A First Encyclopaedia of Tlön* was found in a Memphis library in 1944, the narrator notes, some of the more unbelievable features of Tlön were curiously 'eliminated or muted', presumably 'to obey the intent to set forth a world that is not *too* incompatible with the real world' (Borges, 1998c, 80). But he speculates that in a hundred years time *A Second Encyclopaedia of Tlön* will be found. This, the implication goes, will present a world indistinguishable from the thoroughly transformed world ours has by that time become, and its Tlönian takeover will be complete. The sinister implications are emphasized by a subtle reference to Nazism, still in its prime in Europe when Borges wrote the story, as the narrator notes how susceptible mankind is to 'any system with an appearance of order', like that of Tlön.

As with 'Pierre Menard', reading this story is not simply a matter of following a narrative and taking it at face value, but of tracing the implications and even trying to solve the puzzle it presents us with. Is it possible for fiction to become part of reality? Just as Tlön is a parallel universe that reflects upon our own, so Borges's story encourages us to reflect on our own world, in particular how the apparent naming or cataloguing of its elements – by books such as encyclopaediae – can actually *influence* the world rather than simply describing it. The story would seem to demonstrate Jean Baudrillard's point, central to understanding postmodern aesthetics, about the paradox of representation, that any copy actually creates a separate entity with equal status to the original, resulting in a collapsed distinction between 'real' and 'copy' (Baudrillard, 1994b). This would seem to be what has occurred with *A First Encyclopaedia of Tlön*, as its virtual references become actual. Tlön is a hyperreal world, just as Pierre Menard's *Quixote* is a hyperreal document.

Both stories demonstrate Brian McHale's point about the 'ontological confusion' generated by postmodern writing, most obviously through their practice of citing real and fictional names with deadpan academic authority. Tlön is obviously fake, but the authors the narrator mentions – Bioy Casares and Enrique Amorim – are real. Similarly, Cervantes is clearly a 'real' historical personage, as are many of the others whom Pierre Menard's 'visible' work concerns: the French poet Paul Valéry, the philosophers Descartes, Leibniz, the Spanish literary critic and poet Francisco de Quevedo. However, some of the names mentioned are difficult to verify as having existed. If we 'google' the name Carolus Hourcade, a lithographer, for a catalogue of whose works Pierre

Menard apparently wrote the foreword, nothing is returned – except references to Borges's story. Reading the story is a continual process of judging which element of the story is real, and which a fabrication. It is natural to wonder at points whether Pierre Menard *was* actually real or which of the obscure real writers are in fact fake. Borges's speciality is to sketch in a parallel universe, another world which co-exists alongside ours, but which is emphatically *not* our world.

'Tlön, Uqbar, Orbis Tertius' is actually *about* this process of one world disturbingly coming to overlap with another. The narrator notes in his 'Postscript' that once the *First Encyclopaedia* was found numerous '[h]andbooks, anthologies, surveys, "literal translations" filled the world and still do', with the result that '[a]lmost immediately, reality "caved in" at more than one point'. Juxtaposed with our real world the elements of Tlön make our conventions and customs seem fictional: 'Contact with Tlön, the habit of Tlön, has disintegrated this world' (Borges, 1998c, 81).

Like 'Pierre Menard' the story causes the reader to reflect upon the process of reading. More than a tale simply about Tlön's capacity to intrude into the real world it is about one person's *reading* of this event. On one level it affirms the value of scholarly reading as a kind of intervention, as it is the narrator who has seemingly uncovered this conspiracy. But on another it points to the dangers of 'paranoid reading'. All we have to vouch for the existence of Tlön or the secret conspiracy to ensure it takes over our world is the narrator's word. Is he interpreting what he reads correctly? He acknowledges that through 'unsettling coincidence' he is the person who happens to have witnessed *both* of the intrusions of objects from Tlön in the real world. Perhaps the whole world of Tlön, and its explanatory literature, is simply the narrator's delusion or part of his own sinister plot?

Borges loved adventure stories and detective fiction, stating his admiration for Poe and Stevenson, and frequently deploys the conventions of popular thriller genres through the prism of the learned narrator. One of his most important stories, 'The Garden of Forking Paths' (1941), masquerades as a First World War spy story in order to explore further fiction's capacity to create imagined worlds. The academic protagonist of this story, Yu Tsun, a Chinese former English professor, is trying to pass information about a planned British offensive to his German paymasters, and is being pursued by his adversary, Captain Richard Madden. Tsun finds his way to the house of a British spy Dr Stephen Albert, who informs him that the house had formerly belonged to Tsun's great-grandfather Ts'ui Pen, an esteemed and learned man who spent the last thirteen years of his life in solitude writing an 'inexhaustible' and 'infinite' novel entitled *The Garden of Forking Paths*.

The conceit behind Ts'ui Pen's novel is that where 'ordinarily' in a work of fiction 'each time a man meets diverse alternatives, he chooses one and eliminates the others', in this one

> the character chooses – simultaneously – all of them. He *creates*, thereby, 'several futures', several *times*, which themselves proliferate and fork. . . . Fang, let us say, has a secret; a stranger knocks at his door; Fang decides to kill him. Naturally, there are various possible outcomes – Fang can kill the intruder, the intruder can kill Fang, they can both live, they can both be killed, and so on. In Ts'ui Pen's novels, *all* the outcomes in fact occur; each is the starting-point for further bifurcations.
>
> (Borges, 1998b, 125)

This is a fascinating conceit for a story – but it is also an insightful view of narrative, one which to a point, as Brian McHale notes, anticipates the ideas about narrative advanced by structuralist theorists thirty years later (McHale, 1987, 106). But it also presents a more radical view of narrative as working on other levels than linear and causal ones. In Ts'ui Pen's labyrinth one choice does not mean the other remains hypothetical, as it does in real life and in conventional narrative. Both are activated together with the cumulative result of all the resulting bifurcations being a truly vast labyrinthine virtual model where the various paths collide and overlap.

This story is representative of one of the characteristic effects of postmodern storytelling: the universe is replaced by parallel universes, or what we might call a *multiverse*, a term which emerges in 1960s British science-fiction (e.g. Michael Moorcock, Brian Aldiss, and J. G. Ballard) and which is defined by the OED as 'hypothetical space or realm of being consisting of a number of universes, of which our own universe is only one'. It suggests that the space of all fiction, not just the postmodern variety, is 'virtual reality' – and this has been operational long before computer technology produced its more limited version. The 'technology' employed is an old one, the pages of a book, but in its interface with the imagination of its user (the reader) virtual spaces are opened up and can be inhabited by fictional characters and the reader. Postmodern fiction merely emphasizes this special capacity rather than choosing to adhere to the ideology of realism.

'The Garden of Forking Paths' ends with Tsun's realization that Stephen Albert devoted his time to creating a real version of Ts'ui Pen's fictional labyrinth in his own garden, and this multi-dimensional model of reality, the Garden of Forking Paths, is what Tsun has entered. 'I sensed that the dew-drenched garden that surrounded the house was saturated, infinitely, with invisible persons. Those persons were Albert and myself – secret, busily at work, multiform – in other dimensions of time' (Borges, 1998b, 127). At this point we are returned to the spy story as Madden, the agent who has been in deadly pursuit of Tsun, suddenly arrives on the scene – except of course that he also does not appear. The story at the end acknowledges that the multi-dimensional logic which governs the garden means that further suspenseful plotting, indeed plotting itself, is pointless: 'The rest is unreal, insignificant' (Borges, 1998b, 127).

William Burroughs

William S. Burroughs is significant to postmodernism not just as a literary influence but as an iconic cultural figure. He was associated with the pop culture of the 1960s and 1970s (Bob Dylan invited him on his Rolling Thunder tour, and his work inspired band names such as Steely Dan and Soft Machine), has featured on a hip hop record (Material's 'Seven Souls' in 1989), is celebrated for predicting the internet, and is responsible for some terms in the pop culture lexicon, such as 'heavy metal' and 'interzone'. Not surprisingly, his status as cultural icon is not just because of his ideas and writing but because of his anti-establishment credentials. Burroughs was the most prominent member of an experimental strain within twentieth-century US writing, which included expatriate bohemians like Henry Miller (who wrote his most important fiction in the 1930s) and the 1950s' 'Beat Generation', lead by Jack Kerouac. He was a drug addict and a homosexual, once deliberately injured his trigger finger to get out of joining the army, and notoriously shot his wife during an ill-fated reconstruction of William Tell. In sharp contrast to the sedentary, cerebral Borges, Burroughs is a writer who lived his art.

From his first publications the most distinctive feature of Burroughs's fiction was its combination of different kinds of texts: autobiographical, fictional narrative, texts by other writers. A Burroughs 'novel' (though this label seems even less appropriate for his work than Beckett's) is a patchwork of different texts: streams of consciousness, dreams, and hallucinations rub shoulders with passages from essays, history books, official documents, or propaganda. The effect is disorienting for the reader, who finds him or herself suddenly trans-ported, often in the middle of a sentence, into a different place and situation without warning. Often a section will be inserted which is irrelevant to the plot as it seems to be unfolding. But this implicitly invites the reader to reconsider how he or she reads the text, and to trace meanings in other directions.

The Naked Lunch, Burroughs's second, most influential and still most pop-ular novel, is ostensibly a first-person narrative by a junkie recounting his experiences at the hands of the doctors and scientists who 'treat' him. It is accompanied by his 'Habit Notes' and 'Detoxification Notes', but interspersed with these are hallucinatory episodes detailing extreme sadistic sexual behaviour. The novel does not have chapters in the conventional linear sense, one leading on to another, but are organized into sections with titles such as 'Doctors and Scientists' and 'Eros and Thanatos'. So disorienting is the experience of reading the text that following its plot or logic is impossible, and instead it becomes a matter of becoming attuned to the various themes which run through them all. Without replicating the kind of measured rational academic discourse its chapter titles suggest, the text has the effect of exposing the way that human behaviour is determined by our bodily urges and unconscious desires (e.g. for power and sexual gratification). This illuminates the strange title, as Burroughs claims in the Introduction: 'The title means exactly what the words say: NAKED Lunch – a frozen moment when everyone sees what is on the end of every fork' (Burroughs, 2008, 42).

The disorienting effect of *Naked Lunch* is the result of Burroughs's use of free association as a method of composition. But it was also the result of a more literal kind of accident if we believe Brion Gysin, Burroughs's friend and an artist with whom he collaborated on such works as *Exterminator!* (1973) and *The Third Mind* (1979). Gysin noted that the shape of the rat-gnawed typescript of *The Naked Lunch* was determined by the random order in which its sections happened to fall into place as the final draft went to the printer. For subsequent works, Burroughs sought a more radical way of injecting such randomness into the process of composition – and thus opening up its potential meanings and the number of situations we 'experience' as we read it.

The result was what he called the 'cut-up' technique. This involved literally cutting up pages of text – his own or whatever he happened to be reading at the time – so that 'new combinations of word and image' (Burroughs, 1982, 279) result. This, and the related 'fold-in' technique, where a page of text 'is folded down the middle and placed on another page [and] [t]he composite text is then read across half one text and half the other' (279), made reading fiction into a multi-dimensional, sensual experience like listening to music, watching film or looking at a collage of images. The effect is indeed extremely distinctive and unsettling, as the piece 'Astronaut's Return' from *Exterminator!* (1973) shows.

The title of 'Astronaut's Return' evokes the familiar science-fiction device of having an astronaut return to planet Earth (Burroughs was fascinated by science-fiction and many of his works, such as *The Ticket That Exploded* [1962] and *Nova Express* [1964] use sci-fi motifs). The fiction can thus defamiliarize our existence by providing an alternative and rather disturbing history of the Western world. 'Astronaut's Return' begins with Peter, a teenager who we assume must be the astronaut of the title (though there is no other evidence), returning home and apparently remembering scenes from his past, such as walking with his father in the town where he grew up. He then starts to shave in front of the bathroom mirror which appears to have been 'partially melted'. Without warning, the next paragraph plunges readers into a strange piece of pseudo-history, informing them that following a nuclear explosion in the Gobi desert 30,000 years ago, the only survivors, slaves, became albinos as a result of radiation and settled in 'the caves of Europe', where they contracted a dangerous virus which still infects the current inhabitants of the United States and western Europe, the descendents of these cave-dwelling slaves. The virus makes them 'a hideous threat to life on this planet'. Mid-paragraph we are returned to the shaving scene:

> At Hiroshima all was lost. The metal sickness dormant 30,000 years stirring now in the blood and bones and bleached flesh. He cut himself shaving looked around for styptic pencil couldn't find one dabbed at his face with a towel remembering the smell and taste of burning metal in the tarnished mirror a teen-aged face crisscrossed with scar tissue pale grey eyes that seemed to be looking at something far away and long ago white white white as far as the eye can see ahead a blinding flash of white the cabin reeks of exploded star white lies the long denial from Christ to Hiroshima white voices always denying excusing the endless white papers why we dropped the atom bomb on Hiroshima how colonial peoples have benefited from our rule why look at all those schools and hospitals overgrown with weeds and vines windows melted dead hand frayed scar tissue lifted on a windy street lying white voices from the Congo to Newark the ancient mineral like bleached flesh false human voices slow poison of rotting metal lies denials white papers *The Warren Report* he picked up a shirt white wash flapping in the cold spring wind Oppenheimer wipes a tear from one eye with one long finger.
>
> (Burroughs, 1974, 24–5)

The text then pitches us into a dialogue between another father and son, a blind 'Nigger killing sheriff' who asks the boy to bring him his gun because he likes the feel of it, and then reminisces (apparently) about the 'systematic' brutal killing of 15,000,000 black men in the Congo by white hunters. Snippets of racist dialogue between the hunters follows before the piece modulates into reports of violent news items from sixties America: an oblique reference to the Kennedy assassination in 1963 is accompanied by references to the 'Algiers Motel' incident in 1967, when three young black men were murdered by Detroit police, and the 1968 Kerner Report set up to investigate urban riots.

Like all the pieces in *Exterminator!* – although Burroughs classified the work as 'a novel' – 'Astronaut's Return' is a series of sketches melded roughly together, observing no unity of time, place or character. It swings without warning from one fictional world to another, combining various types of discourse – historiography, characters' reflections, dialogue, news reports, and, finally, snippets of poetry or sloganeering ('Go out and get the pictures. Get all the pictures of / DEATH DEATH DEATH' [Burroughs, 1974, 27]) – so that there is none of the stability we normally experience in fiction, no central character, and no sense of reliable temporal perspective: it is not clear whether Peter or the racist sheriff *are* in fact remembering things or whether the content of the memories are glimpses into other narrative worlds. Rather than narrative being perceived as a temporal entity which works causally and chronologically and unfolds event by event, in a text like this it comes to seem *spatial* – as in the Borgesian 'Forking Paths Principle' – where different narrative worlds exist simultaneously.

The progression from the collective to the individual which we can see in this passage is typical of Burroughs, and is typically effected by the crude juxtaposition of pseudo-rational academic-essay discourse with demotic, uneducated patois. The non-grammatical sentences, and the sudden switches of scene – where the perspective moves from the external position of the historian to the episodes involving Peter looking into the 'tarnished' mirror as he shaves, and the 'nigger-killing' sheriff and the sadistic bounty hunter – is evidence of Burroughs's cut-up and fold-in technique. It means, though, that while it does not observe the unities of realist narrative, it sustains through its associations, from Hiroshima to colonial violence to the Kennedy assassination, a disturbing emphasis on the dominance and brutality of the white Euro-American race which has dominated the modern world and which is truly, in a more directly relevant way than the sci-fi idea of the deadly virus, 'a hideous threat to life on this planet' (24).

Burroughs was deeply pessimistic, viewing contemporary First World society as essentially fascist. His fiction explores unflinchingly the sadistic and cruel elements integral to the white American characters but which he thought the civilized American mind had repressed – especially hatred towards minorities such as homosexuals, black people, and Jews. Although on one level his experiments in composition seem like a retreat into the esoteric province of avant-gardism, his methodology enables him to foreground cruelty and violence especially powerfully and directly. Burroughs's 'cut up' and 'fold in' techniques remove the kind of 'protection' a reader might normally have in fiction, in the form of the first- or third-person narrator who 'frames' the diegesis, from the sudden encounter with disturbing racist views or sadistic fantasies.

The Third Mind (1979) records the collaboration of Burroughs and Gysin in the 1950s and 1960s, and functions as a manifesto for the theory of the 'cut-up'. It makes clear that the technique was influenced by surrealism, citing in particular Tristan Tzara's appearance at a 1920s surrealist rally where he created a poem on the spot by drawing words out of a hat. It reveals that Burroughs would typically type out selections from writers both living and dead and incorporate them in his own work. In one piece Burroughs tries retrospectively to identify the cut-ups in *Nova Express* and says that 'Joyce is in there. Shakespeare, Rimbaud, some writers that people haven't heard about, someone named Jack Stern. There's Kerouac. I don't know, when you start making these fold-ins and cut-ups you lose track'. He claims that one of his methods was, when travelling, to keep a journal with its pages divided into three columns, the first recording a straightforward account of the events on the trip, the second detailing the memories and thoughts he was undergoing at the time, and the third, the 'reading column', including quotations from the books he was reading at the time (Burroughs, 1982, 266).

Burroughs was seeking a way of unlocking the creative potential of the mind which could bypass what he saw as the restrictive 'Aristotelian construct', a supremely rational process of understanding the world and expressing oneself, which had its impact on literature in urging that drama observe the 'three unities' of time, place and action. Aristotelianism was, for Burroughs, 'one of the great shackles of Western civilization', and cut-ups 'a movement towards breaking this down' (265). Burroughs's writing clearly disrupts the 'three unities' but also works by directing itself to the unconscious, triggering off sensations and ideas, so that reading Burroughs is a sensual experience as much as a rational process – even though his work is fascinated by ideas.

The cut-up and fold-in techniques challenge the association between artistic creation and property law which underpins modern attitudes to artistic creation. Cutting up the words of other writers and including their work uncredited obviously invites charges of plagiarism, and inevitably Burroughs faced these on many occasions, though he was never put formally on trial for literary theft – perhaps because the results of the cut-up method were so intricate that it was difficult to trace. But his writing powerfully makes the point that writing is inherently intertextual, that it is impossible to write without being aware of the literary context in which one operates. His method figures as a practical rehearsal of the Barthesian thesis about the author's demise, Burroughs claiming unequivocally that '[a]ll writing is in fact cut-ups. A collage of words read heard overheard' (Burroughs, 1982, 269). This is because when composing a piece of work, '[w]hat does any writer do but choose, edit and rearrange material at his disposal?' (Burroughs, 1982, 262).

Burroughs's work has proved hugely influential on postmodern authors who want to challenge conventional realist approaches to composing fiction and associated values such as originality. While we could see his cut-up techniques as prefiguring the use of sampling or 'mash-ups' in popular music today, Burroughs's techniques were really geared toward bringing writing up to date in the twentieth century and enabling it to extend the sensual appeal of fiction by producing effects which parallel those already possible in visual forms such as art and cinema. Burroughs confessed that he couldn't understand the fear of technology amongst writers, the fear of 'tape recorders and the idea of using any mechanical means for literary purposes' (Burroughs, 1982, 263). Aside from his influence on the general approach to literary appropriation, explicit traces of his influence are abundant among postmodern novelists. Kathy Acker, for example, employs identical cut-up techniques and, like Burroughs, blends them with science-fiction and pornographic motifs. B. S. Johnson's famous 1969 novel-in-a-box, *The Unfortunates*, which enables readers to shuffle its contents and read them in the order he or she desires, undoubtedly owes something to Burroughs (even though Johnson did not mention him). J. G. Ballard, who called Burroughs 'the linear successor to James Joyce', was not influenced by Burroughs stylistically so much as thematically – using science-fiction conventions to comment on the bewildering nature of postmodern reality.

Perhaps the most significant implication of the cut-up/fold-in process is that essentially it is not about writing but reading – perhaps even a new way of experiencing the world. Burroughs claimed, with justification, that the 'cut-up' technique was actually a form of realism especially suited to reflecting the nature of modern reality than any kind of 'representational' art. He insisted it is closer to the very nature of perception than realism: 'Take a walk down a city street and put down what you have just seen on canvas. You have seen a person cut in two by a car, bits and pieces of street signs and advertisements, reflections from shop windows – a montage of fragments' (Burroughs, 1993, 61). As Burroughs put it, consciousness *itself* is a cut up, constantly being modified by random factors generated by what a person is thinking, doing and seeing at any one moment. His writing was thus an alternative to 'the representational straitjacket of the novel' and it is also particularly suited to conveying the real nature of late twentieth- and, we might speculate, twenty-first century existence.

This explained why Burroughs could regard his own 'Sickness' (to use the term used in the Introduction to *The Naked Lunch*), his drug abuse, as the equivalent of the cut-up technique, in a rather romantic affirmation of the confluence of art and life. One of Burroughs's key terms was 'junk' (his first novel, written under the pseudonym William Lee, was called *Junkie*). Junk signifies in his writing, as Malcolm Bradbury has said, in 'two senses: junk as drugs (especially heroin, from addiction to which Burroughs was releasing himself), and junk as cultural rubbish, randomly collected' (Bradbury, 1992, 190). The parallel which Burroughs was keen to impress upon his readers was that the experience of living in modern America was akin to living under the influence of drugs, that is, being subject to a constant flow of random images and discourses which mingle with the hallucinatory mix of memories and feelings conjured up from within one's own mind.

This might sound suspiciously like the kind of self-deceptive justification indulged in by all addicts. There is also the sense – the more one reads Burroughs's discourses on the cut-up and the fold-in – that the technique actually comes to seem quite the opposite of randomness, and instead figures as a kind of 'magical thinking' or example of what Freud called 'the omnipotence of thought', when thoughts from inside an individual's mind appear to have uncanny causal effects on the world outside (such as thinking of a friend and then immediately seeing her come around the corner). This is clear from Burroughs's expressions of wonder at the synchronicity between his real-life experiences and his reading:

> I'm in a boat or a train and I'm reading *The Quiet American*; I look around and see if there's a quiet American aboard. Sure enough, there's a quiet sort of American with a crew cut, drinking a bottle of beer. It's extraordinary, if you really keep your eyes open. I was reading Raymond Chandler, and one of his characters was an albino gunman. My God, if there wasn't an albino in the room. He wasn't a gunman.
>
> (Burroughs, 1982, 266)

This somewhat paranoid dimension of Burroughs's theory coincides with one of the major preoccupations within his writing: the way the population is controlled by the government and other figures of authority (doctors, scientists, etc.) Burroughs's fiction is an example of the paranoid conspiracy-thinking which has dominated US culture and which bears a pivotal relation to the postmodern approach to narrative.

Chapter 3

US metafiction: Coover, Barth, Nabokov, Vonnegut, Pynchon

It is generally agreed that writing in the United States went through an extraordinary period of regeneration in the 1960s because of a combination of political and social factors. The decade began with the election to president of John F. Kennedy, ushering in a very short-lived period of hope. Kennedy was of course assassinated in 1963, one year after the Cuban Missile Crisis almost plunged the world into nuclear war. During the presidencies of his successors, Lyndon B. Johnson and Richard Nixon, there was the war in Vietnam and widespread protests against it, the advent of the civil rights movement, the rise of black power, and an alarming increase in violent murder and gun crime throughout the decade.

All this contributed in various ways to a growing 'counter-culture', which had begun with the Beat generation in the 1950s, but now expanded to take in the 'hippy' movement, drug culture, bop and jazz events, 'happenings', and left-wing political rallies, and expressed a general suspicion about authority and official power, and a faith in the values of youth and spontaneity.

The spirit of the counter-culture is reflected in popular culture of the time such as music (e.g. *The Beatles*, Woodstock) and film (e.g. *Easy Rider*), but also pulses through 'serious' art, including literature. However, here we come to one of the odd things about this moment in US culture. US fiction of the 1960s and 1970s was more concerned than ever with history and politics, yet tended to express this concern – unlike British fiction of the time which reaffirmed its faith in 'social realism' – through non-realist modes. Whereas British writers, for the most part, thought social reality could only be accurately represented through the rational clarity of realism, American novelists tended to conceive of the realist novel as the literary equivalent of official structures of power and oppressive social convention.

Although a new documentary kind of realism did underpin some notable departures in the novel, such as the works of 'faction' produced by Truman Capote and Norman Mailer in the 1960s, the task of commenting on the social world – though quite indirectly – was chiefly taken on by experimental writing. In particular, the sixties in the United States saw the coming to prominence of a generation of writers who produced a radical brand of metafiction, influenced heavily by the pioneering forebears we considered in the previous chapter: Beckett, Burroughs, and Borges. Other labels for this kind of fiction were current at the time, such as 'fabulation' (Robert Scholes) and 'surfiction' (Raymond Federman), but it was 'metafiction' that stuck, perhaps because of its similarity to related terms such as 'metapolitics', 'metarhetoric', 'metatheatre' and 'metanarratives', which, as Patricia Waugh has pointed out, are symptomatic of the contemporary 'cultural interest in the problem of how human beings reflect, construct and mediate their experiences of the world' (Waugh 1984, 2).

Prominent figures like William H. Gass (who coined the term 'metafiction' in a 1970 collection of essays entitled *Fiction and the Figures of Life*), Robert Coover, John Barth, and Donald Barthelme, produced fiction which was primarily about fiction itself. The kind of texts they wrote were endlessly inventive, taken as a whole giving an overwhelming impression of relentless storytelling, with endless tales within tales and parallel versions of the same tale. Their work repeatedly draws attention to the process of constructing fiction. Gass's *Willie Master's Lonesome Wife* (1968), for example, has no pagination but only sections with differently coloured pages (reflecting the changing state of mind of the eponymous character). This kind of fiction also frequently concerns itself with what we might call the 'philosophical' dimension of writing – what it means *existentially* to compose fiction. Barth's 1979 novel *Letters* consists of letters written to him by characters from his own previous fiction.

The stories draw frequently on fairy tale and myth, as a way of emphasizing how our experience of the world is 'literary'. Barthelme's *Snow White*, for example, a self-conscious use of the fairytale form to explore contemporary social issues such as the liberation of woman, is interrupted at one point by a 'Quiz' asking the reader such questions as: 'Does Snow White resemble the Snow White you remember? Yes ( ) No ( )' and 'Are the seven men, in your view, adequately characterized as individuals? Yes ( ) No ( )'.

The work of these writers is profoundly intertextual, constantly referring directly or indirectly to other texts and genres, obsessively indulging in parody and pastiche. Barth's 1960 novel, *The Sot-Weed Factor*, for example, is a version of the eighteenth-century form originally practised by Sterne and Smollett, filled with narratorial digressions and anecdotes which divert from the main tale. It might be regarded as Barth's own attempt to achieve what he so admired in Borges: a way of getting beyond the impasse of the 'used-up' nature of literary forms by revisiting past forms ironically. Although its hero Ebenezer Cook really existed (1672–1732), and was the author of the poem about a tobacco merchant that gives the novel its title, the work is really *about* the eighteenth-century novel itself rather than a serious attempt at reconstructing a plausible version of the past. Its 'history' of Maryland is too fantastic to be accurate.

Critics of the time often remarked upon the sheer playfulness of the work of the metafictionists and indeed sought to classify it under such general labels as 'black humour', or 'absurdist' or 'humorous' fiction (Schultz 1973; Hauck 1971). Re-read now, however, it seems obvious that there is a deadly seriousness about this writing. This surely comes from the conviction, as articulated by Robert Coover in the dedication to Cervantes that begins his sequence 'Seven Exemplary Fictions' from *Pricksongs and Descants*, that contemporary writers were really, in the 1960s, 'standing at the end of one age and on the threshold of another': 'We seem to have moved from an open-ended, anthropocentric, humanistic, naturalistic, even – to the extent that man may be thought of as making his own universe – optimistic starting point, to one that is closed, cosmic, eternal, supernatural (in its soberest sense), and pessimistic' (Coover, 1973, 61–2). Coover delivers his dedication in a reverential style, reminiscent of the seventeenth-century convention of addressing superior personages, but is so overblown that it seems ironic. But then this is precisely the irony which Umberto Eco thinks postmodern writers depend upon: irreverent and humorous, yes, but essential for the very survival of post-avant-garde fiction.

United States' Literature of the 1960s and 1970s conveys the sense that everyday existence in America was a matter of being confronted by events that were so bizarre, incredible, or absurd that they eclipsed anything even the most imaginative writer of fiction could produce. In his 1961 essay 'Writing American Fiction', the novelist Philip Roth surveys the 'fixes, the scandals, the insanity, the idiocy, the piety, the lies' (Roth, 1990, 30) which make up the daily diet offered up by the newspapers, and the fact that real public figures such as Richard Nixon seemed more like 'satiric literary creations' than real people. He concludes that 'the American writer in the middle of the twentieth century has his hands full in trying to understand, describe, and then make *credible* much of American reality. It stupifies, it sickens, it infuriates, and finally it is even a kind of embarrassment to one's own meagre imagination' (Roth, 1990, 29). Similarly, the pervasiveness of corruption, violence, scandal, and cover-up in American politics, exemplified by the assassinations of John Kennedy, and his brother Robert and the civil rights campaigner Martin Luther King, and the Watergate scandal which brought down the by-then President Nixon in 1973, convinced cultural figures in America that reality, even history, was not transparent, but a kind of 'front' for the *real* story which was unfolding behind the scenes.

The determination to explore fictionality in the 1960s, then, was motivated by a sense that everday reality was always already fictionalized, either because of its sheer absurdity, or by the power of the media in shaping it and presenting it to the viewer, or because it was being actively manipulated by unseen hands. Much of 'reality' is indeed mediated via communications technology, the meta-narratives and myths proffered by politics, and the conventions and genres of popular culture. This is important to acknowledge, because the American 'metafictionists' are often assumed to have been concerned purely with playing with the possibilities of self-conscious fiction for its own sake – or in order to comment only on the history of the *novel* rather than history itself. But it makes sense to see the turn to innovative non-realist techniques as the result not of a kind of private domestic battle kept within the family of literature but the literary contribution – albeit a rather displaced, esoteric, one – to the widespread counter-cultural conviction that social reality was becoming disturbingly fictional.

A more direct political function in metafiction of the period is visible in Coover's 1977 novel *The Public Burning*, which many critics would see as his best. This novel is a fictionalized version of a shocking episode in post-war history when, in 1953, at the height of the anti-communist 'witch hunts' led by Senator Joseph McCarthy, two left-wing Jewish activists, the couple Ethel and Julius Rosenberg, were tried and executed for stealing the 'secret' of the atomic bomb and giving it to the Russians. Coover's novel imagines the actual execution as a public spectacle, set in Times Square and filmed by Cecil B. DeMille. It thus comments on the intense media hysteria of the original case by making it more explicit and drawing the parallel with a more medieval kind of punishment. His novel combines analysis of the real newspaper coverage of the case with fictionalized devices such as having Richard Nixon (featuring again because of his apparently fictional quality), who was involved in the trial, narrate part of the novel and introducing the mythical American figure, Uncle Sam, to explain events. These elements of critique draw attention to the textuality of the novel but *also* demonstrate powerfully how far the real case depended upon the fiction of a plot by the Rosenbergs in order to garner public support for foreign policy and the appeal to pervasive cultural myths about communism and Jews.

Barth's *Funhouse* and Coover's *Descants*

In the mid to late sixties in the United States, a series of important full-length metafictions were published, including Coover's *The Origin of the Brunists*

(1965) and *The Universal Baseball Association, Inc., J. Henry Waugh, Prop* (1968); Barth's *Giles Goat-Boy* (1966); William H. Gass's *Omensetter's Luck* (1966); John Hawkes's *The Second Skin* (1964); Jerzy Kosinski's *The Painted Bird* (1965); Richard Brautigan's *Trout Fishing in America* (1967); Donald Barthelme's *Snow White* (1967). However, the spirit, achievement, and literary aims of the 1960s American 'metafictionists' is perhaps best encapsulated by two collections of short stories which appeared at the end of the decade, and are still read or discussed now: John Barth's *Lost in the Funhouse* (1968) and Robert Coover's *Pricksongs and Descants* (1969).

Both collections are distinguished by their exuberant invention, extreme playfulness, and by their appropriation of myth, fairytale and fantasy. Their stories are stories in the process of being constructed, which flit restlessly between different tales-within-tales but also repeatedly interrupt this process as we are shown how and why the fictions are being generated. The distinction between author and narrator, though always *technically* preserved because of the way writing functions as a separate realm from the real world (the real 'flesh-and-blood' author automatically becomes a literary construct once he appears in the fiction) is at the closest it can be to being broken down here. In each collection the narrator is to be imagined as the textual mouthpiece for Barth or Coover. These texts might therefore be thought of as 'confessional' in an unusual way. Both present us with authors being honest about their roles as creator – even if this is rather disturbing at times, particularly in the moments of casual sexual brutality towards women in some of Coover's stories.

Both books, too, invoke the oral or even musical storytelling tradition, Barth's stories being subtitled 'Fiction for Print, Tape, Live Voice' and Coover's title denoting two different kinds of musical composition. Indeed, both collections work along the lines of the musical idea of 'variations on a theme' (one definition of 'descant'), their stories reworking similar ideas about the existential implications of authoring, the process of composition, and the relationship between author and reader. As Barth explains in the 'Author's Note' which begins his book, the fourteen texts are to be thought of as a 'series . . . meant to be received "all at once" and as here arranged' (Barth, 1981, vii).

John Barth's contribution to the postmodern debate is significant, we recall, because of his 1967 essay 'The Literature of Exhaustion'. This is one of postmodernism's most important statements of 'belatedness', a meditation on the difficulty of writing something new – even writing at all – in the wake of modernism. But 'The Literature of Exhaustion' can also be read as a kind of commentary on his own *Lost in the Funhouse*, which was in progress while he wrote the essay, and even Coover's *Pricksongs and Descants*. In fact Coover's collection refers explicitly to Barth's essay in its own equivalent to *Lost in the*

Funhouse's 'Author's Note', the lengthy dedication to Cervantes which begins 'Seven Exemplary Fictions': 'We, too [like Cervantes], suffer from a "literature of exhaustion"'. This indicates that Cervantes plays the same role in Coover's aesthetic to Borges in Barth's, in that he shows how to respond to 'adolescent thought-modes and exhausted art forms . . . with new complexities' (Coover, 1973, 60).

Barth's eponymous funhouse (a kind of fairground house of mirrors with 'labyrinthine corridors' [Barth, 1981, 92]) clearly functions as an analogy for the fictional text, on one level his equivalent of Borges's 'labyrinth': a space where the search for meaning takes his protagonist and us on a journey through twisting paths of meaning and significance, at once progressing towards enlightenment and doubling back on ourselves, frustrating our efforts to interpret. The most obvious image for this process comes in the brief opening text in the collection: 'Frame-Tale', which invites the reader literally to cut a strip off the page which on one side reads 'ONCE UPON A TIME THERE' and on the reverse 'WAS A STORY THAT BEGAN' and join the ends together as directed. This will create a Möbius strip of infinite tales within tales: 'Once upon a time there was a story that began "Once upon a time there was a story that began ""Once upon a time there was a story that began"" . . . ' etc. This logic is actually applied in the story 'Menelaid' which represents a Chinese-box of tales within tales, each of the seven narrative levels requiring a different configuration of speech marks, leading to the point where Helen of Troy cries: "" ' " ' " ' " "Love!" ' " ' " ' " '" (150).

Unlike a circle, the Möbius strip is distinctive for the twist along its surface which means that as one proceeds around it one alternates between the 'outside' and the 'inside' edge. This logic applies to the fictions in *Lost in the Funhouse*: at times we appear to be 'outside', namely in an imagined world created by Barth, only to suddenly find ourselves on the 'inside' of the fictional apparatus itself, watching the machine generating the fiction, as it were. The title story, for example, blends together the tale of a thirteen-year-old boy called Ambrose and his momentous visit to a 'real' funhouse with a didactic guide to writing fiction and a commentary on the narrative as it goes on, the two elements coming together in the same paragraphs without warning:

> Under the boardwalk, matchbook covers, grainy other things. What is the story's theme? Ambrose is ill. He perspires in the dark passages; candied apples-on-a-stick, delicious looking, disappointing to eat. Funhouses need men's and ladies' rooms at intervals. Others perhaps have also vomited in corners and corridors; may even have had bowel movements liable to be stepped in in the dark. The word *fuck* suggests suction and/or and/or flatulence.   (Barth, 1981, 76)

The impression is of the cut-up technique, as if Barth is inserting lines almost at random, grouping them together associatively. It is not a question of literal Burroughs-style cutting-and-pasting, however, but of demonstrating how the creative mind works associatively (as Burroughs also noted) on a number of different levels at the same time.

But Barth's story also highlights the difference between Borges's labyrinth and his own funhouse. The Borgesian labyrinth is primarily one in which the *reader* gets lost while the author, Borges 'himself', remains detached, a godlike creator of mazes. But Barth's funhouse is primarily a place where he himself, as writer and indeed as person, gets lost. Ambrose is clearly a version of Barth as adolescent, and his wanderings around the funhouse, in which he 'rehears[es] to himself the unadventurous story of his life, narrated from the third-person point of view' (Barth, 1981, 92) and imagines his future, is an exercise in concealed autobiography. Moreover the funhouse is not just 'labyrinthine', it is a 'mirror-maze' which endlessly reflects the venturer's image: Ambrose 'saw once again, more clearly than ever, how readily he deceived himself into supposing he was a person. He even foresaw, wincing at his dreadful self-knowledge, that he would repeat the deception at ever rarer intervals, all his wretched life' (Barth, 1981, 89–90).

Writing fiction, this story suggests, is a question of dramatizing reflections of oneself until one realizes that the self is not the unified, autonomous entity it is presented as in realist fiction, but something that continually changes. As the French literary philosopher Maurice Blanchot has argued, the 'space of literature' is one in which the author relinquishes his extra-literary identity and takes on an alternative which he inhabits purely in the world of the fiction. It is at the very least a significant coincidence that *Lost in the Funhouse* shares its publication date, 1968, with his near namesake Roland Barthes's famous polemical essay 'The Death of the Author'. Barth's collection is entirely in keeping with that essay's logic that the author is no longer the godlike genius but a person constructed in his own text by the reader, who is really a co-author.

So the term 'self-conscious' applies to Barth's fictions not just in a metaphorical sense, as if the texts themselves are aware of their own status as fiction, but more literally, too, as they are about Barth's own self-exploration, in particular his own experience of being an author. Authorship, they suggest, is a continual journey of self-discovery and the division of self into other fictional selves.

'Life-Story' is about an author writing a story in the manner of realist 'biographical' narrative: that is, descriptive, chronological, objective, full of detail:

He happened at the time ∗ to be in his study attempting to draft the opening pages of a new short story.
  ∗9:00 A.M., Monday, June 20, 1966.   (Barth, 1981, 113)

This author comes to suspect that he may be a character in someone else's fiction (which of course he is). In 'Autobiography', a tale intended to be recorded by Barth and then played during live performance as he stood 'visible but silent' (Barth, 1981, vii) beside the tape player, he comments 'I must compose myself' (33), referring not only to the discomfort of appearing exposed before his 'readers' but to the fact that it is only in the act of writing that an author comes into being. This story, in being addressed directly to us, the readers of the work, is typical of American metafiction in the 1960s, always reminding us of how indispensible the reader is to the process of creation.

The role of the reader as co-creator of a text (in the Barthesian sense) is also central to Coover's *Pricksongs and Descants*, especially the collection's masterpiece, 'The Magic Poker'. On one level this is a fairytale about an exotic island inhabited by two apparently modern-day girls, a civilized 'tall man' and a brutish Calibanesque caretaker's son. As with other tales in the collection, such as 'The Door' and 'The Gingerbread House', here Coover's strategy is to turn the subtle erotic undercurrents which operate in fairytales – the chopping of wood, the relationship between beauty and beast – into overt, obscenely sexualized elements. 'The Door' suggests a cruder meaning of the collection's title, when Granny imagines the Wolf telling Red Riding Hood 'his old death-cunt-and-prick songs' (Coover, 1973, 11), the pun indicating that these are stories about death and sex.

The eponymous object in 'The Magic Poker' parodies the traditional fairy-tale's deployment of magic, fetishized objects such as magic beans. On three occasions one of the sisters picks up the magic poker, 'kisses its ornate handle, its long rusted shaft' (Coover, 1973, 19), and twice a prince appears. But the comedy of using such a mundane object as magical fairytale device also functions as a gesture towards the exhaustion with used-up forms noted by Barth, or the need for the author, as Coover puts it in the dedication to Cervantes, to 'struggle against the unconscious mythic residue in human life'. Recycling 'mythic or historical forms' is actually a way of 'conduct[ing] the reader . . . to the real' (61). How do contemporary attitudes to sex differ from those which underpin the fairytale?

But what makes 'The Magic Poker' especially notable is the overt presence of the author in the act of composing it as he goes along – and who comes across as more the sex-hungry wolf than the benign bard. The story's first line declares: 'I wander the island, inventing it' (14), making our manipulation at the hands of the author clear from the outset. He 'arranges' the guest cabin and puts a wrought-iron poker outside, brings the two sisters to the island, making it clear that he will 'send them home again', just as easily as he has 'dressed them and may well choose to undress them' (18). The author's godlike power – and his ability to use this power however he will, certainly not just for benign aims – is thus asserted.

But from the outset, too, he informs us that even though it is he who invents the island and everything on it, still, 'anything can happen' (14). Sure enough, soon things apparently begin to go out of control. He apparently loses track of the caretaker's son, who then turns up at the guest cabin and smashes it up, defecating in a kettle, which he thinks of as 'a love letter'. This leads the narrator to comment: 'A love letter! Wait a minute, this is getting out of hand! What happened to that poker, I was doing much better with that poker, I had something going there, archetypal and maybe even beautiful' (22). From this point Coover's story begins to pile inconsistency on inconsistency. The characters begin to act increasingly brutally towards each other and their surroundings, destroying any sense of a progressive, plausible narrative, and, towards the end, new characters and scenes suddenly intrude.

The end of 'The Magic Poker' is distinguished by a succession of what seem to be openings to new stories, separate sections which each seem to juggle around with the main elements of the story explored up until this point, and each begin with the conventional fairytale opening:

> 'Once upon a time, a family of wealthy Minnesotans bought an island on Rainy Lake up on the Canadian border . . . ' (31)
> 'Once upon a time there was an island visited by ruin and inhabited by strange woodland creatures . . . ' (31)
> 'Once upon a time, two sisters visited a desolate island . . . ' (32)
> 'Once upon a time there was a beautiful young Princess in tight gold pants . . . ' (32)

All this may plausibly be seen as another variation on the Burroughs 'cut-up' technique, as the sections of Coover's story could be ordered and re-ordered and still work in more or less the same way. A more persuasive reading of the story, however, is that it is 'baring the device' of literary composition, showing us what normally remains hidden in the creative process. It might thus be considered the literary equivalent of the Lloyds Bank building or the Pompidou Centre, postmodern buildings which expose architectural and engineering workings which normally remain hidden.

This means that 'The Magic Poker' is not a finished story but a story in process. What we have before us is like a set of working drafts for a story entitled 'The Magic Poker', a range of narrative possibilities considered by the author before he decides upon the final version. This explains the story's fragmented layout, which consists of blocks of prose each separated by a line of asterisks. It also makes sense of other oddities in the story such as why only one sister is given a name and why the characters and actions keep changing. The *real* story 'The Magic Poker' – which can of course only remain imaginary – is left to us, the readers and 'co-writers', to construct from the pointers which Coover gives us. In any case, the assumption that any story ought to adhere consistently to the parameters established by its earliest events and characters is purely part of *realist* convention and is not to be mistaken for a rule of writing fiction (if such a thing could exist).

The logic of Borges's 'The Garden of Forking Paths' informs 'The Magic Poker'. This, we recall, is a work of fiction in which every choice of event takes place simultaneously, until eventually a vast, infinite, inexhaustible set of realized possibilities is left. It was typical of Borges simply to tantalizingly sketch out the possibility of this vast novel and leave it at that. 'The Magic Poker' goes further down this line, as its fragmented form means that none of the storylines it begins are actually closed off but continue to exist simultaneously. In fact, similar scenarios are presented in other stories in *Pricksongs and Descants*, such as 'The Elevator', 'The Babysitter' (which presents us, Jerome Klinkowitz once said, with 'not only what "does happen" . . . but all the things which *could* happen' [Klinkowitz, 1975, 17]), and, most of all, 'Quenby and Ola, Swede and Carl'.

This last story might be seen as an attempt to actually write the kind of story only imagined in 'The Garden of Forking Paths', one in which a series of contradictory events involving combinations of the four eponymous characters remain 'active'. Carl sleeps with Swede's wife Quenby or his daughter Ola – and simultaneously does not sleep with either of them but just fantasizes about it in detail. If it is true, then Swede both knows about it and decides to take murderous revenge on a boat on the desolate lake, *and* remains unaware.

The 'forking paths principle' also operates in Barth's 'Lost in the Funhouse' which contains the apparently impossible lines: 'Naturally he didn't have nerve enough to ask Magda to go through the funhouse with him. With incredible nerve and to everyone's surprise he invited Magda, quietly and politely, to go through the funhouse with him' (Barth, 1981, 86). In both stories, rather than sort between likely possibilities like a kind of literary detective, the reader has to accept that all possibilities do actually occur – and simultaneously do not. To use the terms of Deleuze and Guattari, introduced in Chapter 1, the narrative structures of these stories are rhizomatic rather than arborescent, and continually invite us to conjecture rather than to interpret.

Vladimir Nabokov, *Pale Fire*

Barth and Coover expand upon Borges's sketched-out 'forking paths principle' to powerful effect. Yet the most brilliant and expansive example of this approach to keeping the conjectural possibilities open is undoubtedly Vladimir Nabokov's novel *Pale Fire*, published in 1962. Nabokov was an important influence on the US metafictionists, in many ways as significant as the other non-Americans Beckett and Borges. He was a Russian *émigré* who, after publishing a number of novels in his native language, settled in America where he taught literature at Cornell University (the young Thomas Pynchon claimed to have been in one of his classes there, but Nabokov could not remember him) and wrote fiction in English.

Although Nabokov can plausibly be regarded as a 'late modernist', his writing is ultimately more about fictionality than consciousness or psychology. He is most famous – notorious, in fact – as the author of *Lolita*, his 1955 novel detailing the narrator's obsession with the eponymous prepubescent girl, which has recently taken on a new significance given the late twentieth- and early twenty-first-century fears about paedophilia. While this novel conforms to the classic modernist form of the retrospective narrative composed by an unreliable artist-*manqué* narrator and seems to present a consistent and knowable imagined reality, because of the first-person narration it is never clear how much of the story represents Humbert Humbert's fantasies and how much reality. At least one critic has suggested that Humbert never meets Lolita at all (Tekiner, 1979).

Due to its formal complexity, *Pale Fire* – one of three remarkable metafictional works, along with *Ada* and *Look at the Harlequins*, produced by Nabokov in the 1960s – magnifies vastly the effects of *Lolita*'s unreliable narrator. The convention of the 'unreliable narrator' is when an account is demonstrably erroneous or biased, not necessarily because the narrator is *lying* (though some narrators, like Sheppard in Agatha Christie's *The Murder of Roger Ackroyd*, do lie) but because something – such as age, vanity, spite, questionable sanity, etc. – causes his or her presentation of 'the facts' to be distorted. What makes it a modernist rather than postmodernist convention, according to Brian McHale, besides the fact that modernist writers like Ford Madox Ford, André Gide, or William Faulkner favour it, is that 'we can determine *in what ways* and *the degree to which* a narrator is being unreliable' (McHale, 2002, 291). The unreliable narration in *Pale Fire*, by contrast, is much more destabilizing, for we cannot be sure of either. In the end our only option is to accept that a number of possibilities have *equal* validity.

The first impression on encountering *Pale Fire* is not of being immersed in a fully realized world, but that we must come to this world through a collection of different texts. The main text, a poem by John Shade entitled *Pale Fire*, is framed by texts written by the critic, Charles Kinbote. Both writers are employed by Wye College in Appalachia and are nextdoor neighbours. The starting-point of the plot is that Shade has been killed by a man named Jack Grey, just after he has finished his manuscript for *Pale Fire*. Kinbote has managed to get hold of this document and has taken it to the southern states of the US to edit it, apparently with Shade's widow Sybil's permission, so he can keep it safe from Professors 'H' and 'C', both of whom are rival 'Shadeans' and would love to get their hands on it. The poem is prefaced by a Foreword and then followed by a Commentary, which is by far the most extensive part of the book and as such resembles what Barthes would produce eight years later in *S/Z*: a line by line, sometimes word by word, analysis of the poem. The volume concludes with an Index. All three of these texts are written by Kinbote.

The structure of *Pale Fire* can be illuminated by Gérard Genette's theory of 'paratexts', his term for the various kinds of texts which supplement a 'main' text. There are two kinds of paratext: a *peritext* is a text like the title, the dedication, the preface or postscript, etc. which occupies the same space as the main text (i.e. in the same volume), while the *epitext* is a contributory text which exists outside the space of the main text (i.e. not in the same volume), such as an interview with the author, letters or diaries by the author. The value of this theory – as with Barthes's opposition between readerly and writerly texts and 'work' and 'text' – is that it enables us to recognize fiction as a battle for meaning between author and reader. Paratexts function in different ways to *control* the readings which may be taken from a text: an introduction, for example, sets the scene and alerts the reader to what s/he must look out for, sets out the background to the work and the intentions behind it.

The function of Charles Kinbote's paratexts conforms to Genette's theory, only more obviously so – their explicitness about their purpose expressing what most 'real' paratexts keep implicit. Kinbote is trying deliberately to steer the reader towards a particular reading of the poem. In his Foreword he writes: 'Let me state that without my notes Shade's text simply has no reality at all since the human reality of such a poem as his . . . has to depend entirely on the reality of its author and his surroundings, attachments and so forth, a reality that only my notes can provide' (Nabokov, 2000, 25). 'For better or worse', the

Foreword concludes, 'it is the commentator who has the last word' (Nabokov, 2000, 25).

Read on its own – and some students, well-versed in the practice of reading scholarly editions of canonical texts, will automatically skip the Foreword and turn to the poem first – *Pale Fire*, the poem, appears to be a personal meditation on Shade's life, a kind of updating of an introspective romantic poem such as Wordsworth's *The Prelude*. However, from the outset, Kinbote's commentary argues forcefully that the poem is *really* about something entirely different. He insists that it is a meditation on the land of Zembla, where he himself comes from. More precisely he claims his own friendship with Shade and his tales of the exiled king of Zembla 'Charles the Beloved' have inspired the poet to write a veiled tribute to the King. Given that Zembla nor Charles are never mentioned directly in the poem, swallowing this reading takes some persuasion. In his efforts to persuade, Kinbote's reading of specific images and lines stretch credibility. The words 'that crystal land', for example, are interpreted by Kinbote as being 'Perhaps an allusion to Zembla, my fair country'. But peeking through this hidden story appears to be another, even more 'shady' one. It appears that Kinbote is not only from Zembla but is none other than the exiled king of that country himself, having been forced to flee and adopt a disguise. He has been pursued to the United States by a gunman working for the Zemblan secret police, Jakob Gradus. Gradus intended to assassinate Kinbote, but killed Shade instead.

But, of course, so outlandish and far removed from the poem is *this* story, that there emerges with it yet another possibility for what the real story behind *Pale Fire* is, and which Kinbote inadvertently supports by reporting comments others have made about him. It is possible that Kinbote is quite mad. He is really a Russian *émigré* named Botkin who harbours a delusion that he is the king of Zembla. In this narrative, the criminal Grey is precisely who he claims he is and in fact has done just what he said he'd tried to: he was originally intending to kill the landlord of Botkin's house, a judge named 'Goldsworth', in revenge for once committing him to an asylum, but mistakenly killed Shade instead.

In 'A Bolt From the Blue: An Introductory Essay' written to accompany the publication of the book in 1962 (an example of a peritext, incidentally), the novelist Mary McCarthy argued that one way of thinking of the three narratives is as a stately house. The point behind the analogy is to emphasize that these are *not* the 'levels of meaning', typical of modernism, but 'planes in a fictive space' (McCarthy, 2000, v). Like rooms in a house they can be inhabited at different times; once you leave one room it continues to exist. On the ground floor is the first and most obvious story, the one in which Shade is murdered by Jack

Grey and Kinbote takes the manuscript of his poem into hiding to edit it. But 'above' this, on the first floor, the 'real' story is continuing, in which the poet is killed in a botched attempt at regicide. Beneath both these floors, however, is what McCarthy calls the 'real, real story', in which Kinbote is really an insane refugee academic named Botkin who believes he's the king of Zembla and is pitied by everyone in the college, including Shade.

Rather than being a set of hierarchies which obliterate another each time a more plausible scenario becomes possible, each story, each reading of the text, is potentially as valid as the other. Not even the 'real, real story', 'the plane of ordinary sanity and common sense' can be considered final. This means that even Kinbote's 'Zemblan' reading of the poem does have a certain validity, even though it appears untenable because there are no direct references to the country anywhere. For Shade's poem does seem, particularly at the end, to detail the creeping up of the killer. Lines 997–9 read:

> A man, unheedful of the butterfly –
> Some neighbor's gardener, I guess – goes by
> Trundling an empty barrow up the lane.
>
> (Nabokov, 2000, 58)

The poem has been written in rhyming couplets all the way through, and it seems very odd for it to end without completing the final couplet, which would also bring the total number of lines to a round 1000. Moreover, the opening line of the poem 'I was the shadow of the waxwing slain' (Nabokov, 2000, 29) *would* complete the couplet, suggesting that the poem is urging us, as a way of accusing the killer, to start at the beginning again. But surely this is impossible, if the author of these lines dies at line 999? Unless someone else is responsible for revising or even writing the poem . . .

The interpretive gymnastics *Pale Fire* invites is a way of asking us not to solve the mysteries of the text so much as to consider what a legitimate reading of a text is. Can we read the line 'that crystal land' in a poem and assert confidently that it is about a particular country without any evidence? More precisely, what *Pale Fire* also does is invite us to consider the status, not just of reading, but academic reading, literary criticism. What is the function of this kind of professional reading? Should criticism 'reflect' the truth of a work? Or does it end up remaking it?

Kinbote's narration is undoubtedly partial. In the third paragraph of the foreword he suddenly abandons his measured academic contextualizing of the poem by noting that 'There is a very loud amusement park right in front of my present lodgings' (Nabokov, 2000, 13). Coming at the beginning of the Foreword this bizarre inclusion signals right away that the discussion is anything but detached, and is possibly even deluded, for only a mad person will write, or more properly keep, such a line in the finished volume. But in doing so it suggests, hyperbolically, that all academic criticism is partial.

This is what accounts for the postmodernism of *Pale Fire*: the novel exposes the partiality of *all* narration. Once we acknowledge the possibility that Kinbote is deluded, it means that nothing in the text is reliable any more: does Shade exist, in the world of the story? If he does, did he write the poem 'Pale Fire', or is this Kinbote's fabrication? In exposing the subjective nature of narration it also rejects the referential function of narrative, implying that a work of literature can only point to other texts. This is what McCarthy means by describing *Pale Fire* as 'a book of mirrors'. Every reference is reflected in another. The name Zembla, for example, recalls 'semblance', and also features in Alexander Pope's *An Essay on Man* to signify 'the Lord knows where'.

Where postmodern fiction typically asks us to reflect on the act of reading, few texts force us to do so to the degree where we become aware of physically cross-checking pieces of text and turning from one page to another, reading backwards and forwards as we go through the story, as we do in *Pale Fire*. This process is, once again, rhizomatic, not only because we can enter the text at any point and then proceed to any other from there, but because we have to think of the narrative possibilities as spatial and of equivalent value rather than linear and hierarchical. Each of our interpretations of *Pale Fire* are potentially as valid as the other. Rather than sorting through the evidence like a literary detective, our job is to accept that they can and must co-exist.

Kurt Vonnegut, *Slaughterhouse-Five*

As I have suggested, the challenge to orthodox views of reading we find in the metafiction of Coover, Barth, and Nabokov may be seen, by virtue of its historical context, as a parallel to the challenge to other forms of authority in the real world. However, a more directly political edge to metafiction is demonstrated by a novel published, like Barth's and Coover's collections of stories, at the tail-end of the 1960s, Kurt Vonnegut's *Slaughterhouse-Five*.

Before Coover's *The Public Burning* this novel pointed to a link between the more radical metafictional tradition in the 1960s and 1970s and the tradition of absurdist US fiction which emerged at the same time, and which is powerfully underpinned by a distrust of politics and authority. The most celebrated novel of this type was Joseph Heller's blackly comic *Catch-22* (1961) which presents us with a 'looking-glass' world where the sane is regarded as mad and the collective madness of war and the military approach to it appears sane.

Like *Catch-22*, *Slaughterhouse-Five* is a war novel, though one with a much more complicated structure. Its hero, Billy Pilgrim, an optometrist from New York working as a chaplain's assistant during the Second World War, is captured by the Germans and witnesses at first hand a real historical atrocity: the largest massacre in European history, the fire-bombing by the Allied forces of the city of Dresden – a cultural centre and beautiful city, with no military significance, and up until this point untouched by the war. The attacks resulted in the deaths of 135,000 people (though historians now place the figure much higher). The dead included huge numbers of refugees, as well as women and children, and they were killed by the simultaneous launch of a massive tonnage of bombs, causing the temperature in the city to reach 1600 degrees centigrade. Billy is taken with other American prisoners of war to be incarcerated in an abattoir in Dresden (this explains the title of the novel) where he only manages to survive by chance, happening to be down in the meat locker when the bombs fall.

The fire-bombing of Dresden was a horrific event, one to compare with the Holocaust itself, though one that is not often told. Indeed *Slaughterhouse-Five* became significant – despite its innovative, non-realist form – as a piece of rare eye-witness testimony. From the very outset the book makes it clear that Pilgrim's experience is based on Vonnegut's own. Beneath the author's name on the title page is a note informing readers that he is 'A fourth-generation German-American now living in easy circumstances on Cape Cod (and smoking too much), who, as an American infantry scout *hors de combat*, as a prisoner of war, witnessed the fire-bombing of Dresden, Germany, "The Florence of the Elbe," a long time ago, and survived to tell the tale.' But while much of the book is clearly drawn from Vonnegut's real memories of his time in Germany, only lightly fictionalized and given to Billy Pilgrim, the tale is not presented in a linear, realist manner. It consists of fragmented paragraphs which place beside the Dresden episodes scenes from a range of different periods after the war. Its 'realist' element – the account of the war and the thinly disguised authorial substitute's attempt to live his life in the shadow of the terrible events – is accompanied by an audacious science-fiction plot. On his wedding night Billy is kidnapped by a flying saucer from the planet Tralfamadore and taken aboard their flying saucer to a simulated version of America, where he lives in a furnished apartment complete with stereo and broken television, and experiences flashbacks from his past.

This seems to make sense of the moments in the narrative when Billy suddenly finds that he has come 'unstuck in time', and is able to flit in and out of scenes from his own life but which – due to the time-travel process – are made strange to him, so they are less like memories of events he has experienced, but alternative realities in which he happens to be the protagonist. In fact, it is quite possible that this might not be time travel after all. It might just be Billy hallucinating. The effect is certainly disorienting for the reader, who is unclear which of the narrative scenarios are to be taken as 'real', that is, as having happened in the past, and which are hallucinatory. An unresolvable uncertainty reigns regarding the novel's present: is Billy captured by the Germans and then 'travels' through time, or is being captured itself a time-travel flashback? (Or both?)

The form of the novel is more than just a way of packaging all the various narratives which have been triggered in the author's mind after his experience in Dresden: autobiography, sci-fi or war novels, etc. Rather *Slaughterhouse-Five* is about the impossibility of narrating such a traumatic event at all. This is made clear in the novel's first chapter, which is an autobiographical introduction to Vonnegut himself and his reasons for writing the novel. He explains that he has been trying for twenty-three years to write about Dresden, but has always been unable to. Now, finally, he has hit upon a way of doing it, by producing the fragmented text we have before us. As he explains to his editor:

> It is so short and jumbled and jangled, Sam, because there is nothing intelligent to say about a massacre. Everybody is supposed to be dead, to never say anything or want anything ever again. Everything is supposed to be very quiet after a massacre, and it always is, except for the birds.
> And what do the birds say? All there is to say about a massacre, things like '*Poo-tee-weet?*'.   (Vonnegut, 2000, 14)

This suggests that a linear, rationalist realist account of the massacre is inappropriate. The novel has its own name for its fragmentary form, as the note on the title page declares: 'This is a novel somewhat in the telegraphic schizophrenic manner of tales of the planet Tralfamadore, where the flying saucers come from'. This obscure methodology becomes clearer when Billy is captured by the Tralfamadorians. He learns that Tralfamadorian books are not linear ones in the manner of 'Earthling' ones, but a collection of 'telegraphic' clusters of symbols which make up 'a brief, urgent message – describing a situation, a scene' which Tralfamadorians read 'all at once, not one after the other'. The individual clusters do not relate to each other in any particular way but 'when seen all at once, they produce an image of life that is beautiful and surprising and deep' (Vonnegut, 2000, 64). This is similar to the organization of *Slaughterhouse-Five* and the effect of its strategy of grouping together situations and scenes.

The opening note and its later explanation, in other words, effectively tell us how to read the novel. Reading *Slaughterhouse-Five* should not be a systematic rational approach of explaining how episodes relate to one another – however tempting that may be (e.g. to note patterns and parallels, such as Billy being captured by two different peoples, the Germans and the Tralfamadorians, who seem to beg comparison, as many commentators have noted, with the lifestyle and attitudes of contemporary Americans), but a matter of trying to look at its different episodes, its various time periods, 'all at once'. If we try this we do indeed, as promised, find something surprising, shocking and perhaps even beautiful.

It should be clear by now that the 'telegraphic schizophrenic' method is another variation on the metafictional logic of 'The Garden of Forking Paths'. In Tralfamadore 'when a person dies he only *appears to* die. He is still very much alive in the past, so it is very silly for people to cry at his funeral. All moments, past, present, and future, always have existed, always will exist' (Vonnegut, 2000, 19). So the fact that *Slaughterhouse-Five*'s narrative is not linear but a collection of events means that the events are all simultaneously present. One poignant consequence of this is that the constant presence of past events is typical of a traumatized state of mind. There is no sense in the mind of Billy (and Vonnegut, it seems) that the events of Dresden can ever be properly 'past', they are always painfully present. For this reason, a conventional narrative approach to this event – narrative being a particular organization of events in time – is unsuited to the task. The form of *Slaughterhouse-Five* implies that it is impossible, or perhaps simply pointless, to *narrativize* a series of horrific and unbearable events.

The opening autobiographical chapter means that the device of fictionalizing the past is not disguised as it might be in a more realist version of the same novel, but is always foregrounded and means that we have to read everything which follows in its light. This results, movingly, in our realization that the novel is an example of what psychoanalysis would call a 'displacement exercise', a way of confronting something traumatic in an indirect way which protects the psyche from unbearable material. An example is the refrain 'So it goes' which crops up continually in the narrator's discourse. On one level he is simply following Tralfamadorian custom, which requires the phrase to be uttered every time a dead person is mentioned (and reflects the overall indifference of the Tralfamadorians towards death). But in the light of the Author's Note it seems more like a neurotic ritual designed to ward off the pain associated with death. The indirectness of *Slaughterhouse-Five*'s convoluted metafictional form thus packs a profound emotional punch.

Thomas Pynchon

It is often remarked that Thomas Pynchon is to postmodernism what James Joyce is to modernism, a figure whose writing is unprecedented yet somehow entirely representative of the fiction of a particular age. Like Joyce Pynchon's output is at once rather sparse and hugely ambitious. Joyce famously boasted that his *Finnegan's Wake* would 'keep the critics busy for 300 years', and Pynchon's work, too, especially *Gravity's Rainbow*, has spawned a vast industry of interpreters and devoted students, determined to pursue every lead in the text and decode every reference. Homages range from Steven Weisenburger's academic labour-of-love *A Gravity's Rainbow Companion: Sources and Contexts for Pynchon's Novel* (1988) to the artist Zak Smith's extraordinary *Pictures Showing What Happens on Each Page of Thomas Pynchon's Novel Gravity's Rainbow* (2006).

To pursue the Joyce comparison we might note how Pynchon's career involves a similar commitment to authorial impersonality, as he has done his best to make himself 'disappear' as a biographical persona (no mean feat in the era of mass media) in order to speak only through his art. But the most valid parallel with Joyce is the sheer 'heteroglossia' of Pynchon's writing. Heteroglossia, a complex term usually translated as 'different-speechness' or 'multilanguagedness', is used by the literary philosopher Mikhail Bakhtin to refer both to the very condition of the world (we are surrounded by different forms of language, both spoken and written) and the specific form of the novel. For Bakhtin the novel is defined simply by the very fact that it contains different types of speech and therefore mirrors the society which produces it. Its value is consequently that it is naturally a *social* form, not because it depicts society in a realistic manner, but because it contains different voices which interact with each other in a work of continuous prose. Each discourse which features within its pages complements, counters, and modifies the discourses of others. As the different speech types are each representative of a different point of view on the world, it means a range of viewpoints enter into dialogue with each other. For Bakhtin, meaning cannot be stable or singular so long as it is expressed in language (which means it never can be).

Pynchon's work revels in the juxtaposition of different voices. Weisenburger's *A Gravity's Rainbow Companion* lists the 'formal discourses' we encounter in *Gravity's Rainbow*: Hebrew, German, Kazakh, Russian, Spanish, French, Japanese and Herero, languages which are in each case represented by 'specialized jargon' such as Kabbalistic writing (Hebrew), bureaucratic acronyms (Russian) or conversational puns (French). But Pynchon's prose also, Weisenburger shows, mixes together such 'informal discourses' as 'popular slang' (jokes, song lyrics, street speech), 'ethnic usage' (black English), 'underworld cant' (black-marketeering in drugs), 'regional dialects' (British, American) military 'service slang', 'esoteric cant' (astrology, black magic, freemasonry, etc.), 'folk usage' (folktales, children's games, etc.) and 'professional jargon' (cinematography, chemistry, psychology, etc.) (Weisen-burger, 1988, 5–6).

Reading Pynchon, then, is a matter of being immersed in a constant stream of different voices, an impression deepened by his characteristic long, rhythmical, parenthetical sentences. If we stick to the Bakhtinian definition of the novel – perhaps the most sensible one there is – Pynchon's fiction is perhaps as close to a pure example of the form as there is. As such it underlines the implicit challenge in Bakhtin's theory to the ideology which has dominated literary criticism – that the novel is by definition inseparable from realism (Holquist, 1990, xxvii). While his work is packed with a multitude of different 'social speech types' it would be stretching things to claim that Pynchon's novels provide the reader with any representative portrait of 'society'. Nevertheless, as commentators have remarked, one of the special abilities of Pynchon's fiction is to help us conceive of the interconnected webs of science, technology, politics, and history, and the events they produce (e.g. wars, the cold war, the space race) which drive post-war American society.

Pynchon's fiction also eschews the realist staple of convincing, rounded characters. There are many *people* in Pynchon's novels – vast numbers of them in fact, over 400 in *Gravity's Rainbow*, for example – but they could never be mistaken for the autonomous, 'rounded' people we find in George Eliot or Leo Tolstoy. They have been referred to as 'figures' (Tanner, 1971, 164), 'interchangeable ciphers' (Aldridge, 1983, 54) or even 'cartoon characters' (Lauzen, 1986, 101) – a fitting description, as one of Pynchon's key influences is the comic strip. Their names immediately suggest their status as ciphers: some comically evoke the 1960s drug-addled counter-culture, like Zoyd Wheeler or Weed Atman (*Vineland*), some are Dickensian emblematic names, like Tyrone Slothrop and Pirate Prentice (*Gravity's Rainbow*) or Herbert Stencil (*V.*) and some are outright parodies, such as the psychiatrist Dr Hilario (*The Crying of Lot 49*). Although they behave most of the time in plausible ways (i.e. like the characters of realism) they are also given to sudden more or less unexplained changes in behaviour, such as when the previously socially conscious Frenesi Gates betrays the resistance movement in *Vineland*.

But to regard Pynchon as some kind of paradigmatic novelist makes it problematic to try to associate him with one particular moment in the novel's history, as is the case if we label him postmodern. So what makes Pynchon postmodern?

One obvious factor is that he exemplifies Leslie Fiedler's theory that post-modern fiction 'crosses the border, closes the gap' between high and low culture (Fiedler, 2002, 168). The seriousness of his representations of the grip of the military–industrial complex on American culture is accompanied by references to pop-cultural ephemera: for example, *Vineland*'s continual *Star Trek* references and allusions to *Godzilla* or *The Smurfs*. In this respect it seems entirely appropriate that the notoriously reclusive Pynchon's only deliberate emergence into the public world (aside from his publications) was his 2004 'appearance' in *The Simpsons* episode 'Diatribe of a Mad Housewife', where he stood outside his house with a paper bag over his head with holes cut out for the eyes, before a flashing neon sign declaring 'Thomas Pynchon's House – Come on In' (Season 15, episode 10).

But the most important postmodern element is Pynchon's approach to narrative. Reading *V.*, *Gravity's Rainbow*, or *Against the Day* is on one level akin to reading a sprawling nineteenth-century 'yarn', given the panoramic cast of figures and their stories. Yet the narrative does not involve an accumulation of clear suspense-inducing events. Rather it depicts characters who are themselves trying to discern what is going on around them. The reader is faced with a similar problem because of Pynchon's preference for focalizing the narrative through the minds of his central characters. The absence of a reliable external perspective can make Pynchon's fiction extraordinarily difficult to follow at the basic level of plot. What events occur can only be discerned through characters' reactions. Readers of *Gravity's Rainbow* commonly comment on the challenging experience of reading the novel. It is a novel one has to 'complete', as in finishing a task, rather than reading for pleasure.

For all the excess of character, event and detail, Pynchon's major novels effectively each boil down to a complex quest-narrative played out on two levels: one in the plot, conducted by a central character, and the second undertaken by the reader, whose efforts to decode what he or she is presented with in the novel mirror the frustrated efforts of the questing character. This is what happens in Pynchon's first masterpiece, *V.* (1963; the other being *Gravity's Rainbow*). *V.*'s questor is Herbert Stencil, a scholarly figure who attempts to understand the world he inhabits through a process of investigation and hypothesis. He is set against a counterpart Benny Profane (one of Pynchon's favoured ways of organizing his narratives is to divide it between two almost binarily opposed male characters, one of whom represents order and the mind, the other who represents chaos and the body), who drifts through the bohemian underground world of the book.

The names, again typically for Pynchon, give us a clue here. Stencil is trying to inscribe a pattern which applies to the world around him. And if his co-protagonist is 'profane' then it suggests that Stencil's task is akin to searching for some kind of sacred scripture. More precisely, his quest is for a mysterious woman known only as 'V.' Since happening upon an enigmatic entry in his late father's diary – 'Florence, April, 1899 . . . There is more behind and inside V. than any of us had suspected. Not who, but what: what is she' – Stencil has been searching for this woman since 1945, travelling the world and interviewing anyone he can find who has been connected with her. He has come to suspect that she is part of 'one of those grand conspiracies or foretastes of Armageddon which seemed to have captivated all diplomatic sensibilities in the years preceding the Great War' (Pynchon, 1991, 161).

Like all the great literary questor-figures – from Oedipus on – the quest promises to have even more personal ramifications for Stencil too, as it is possible that V. is his own mother. The novel documents his attempts to construct a coherent narrative biography of V. – what he calls a 'Real Text' – from the isolated fragments he is able to unearth. Sure enough his enquiries seem to suggest that V. has somehow been involved in a number of key historical events, from the crisis in Fashoda to the Second World War siege of Malta. But the various possibilities are so multiple and interconnected yet so far apart that Stencil's quest is doomed to failure. The world he inhabits is one in which there is too much significance rather than not enough.

There are two obvious parallels here. The first is with the 'information overload' of postmodern culture, the comparison suggested by Pynchon's depiction of the details of contemporary existence. The second is with the act of interpreting a novel – and *this* novel in particular. The reader of course shadows Stencil on his quest and registers all the different potential meanings of V. that he provides us with. The letter V. figures in this novel as an example of a master-signifier to which a vast array of signifieds can potentially be attached. V is Valletta, capital of Malta, the symbols of the Virgin or Venus, the shadowy underworld of Vheissu; the Void, 'God v. Caesar', 'Fausto V' of Malta, the 'voiding' of human history by the increased modern significance of science and technology.

Stencil's experience in a world of overloaded signification is repeated in Pynchon's next novel, his shortest but still his most read and studied, *The Crying of Lot 49* (1966). In this novel, the 'drifting' character has been removed, or more properly the characteristic binary opposition of characters is effectively distilled into one person, its heroine Oedipa Maas. Like Stencil, Oedipa embarks upon – or is 'despatched' in the manner of the fairytale hero/heroine – upon a quest for knowledge. But this quest leads her to encounter a kind of internal chaos which leaves her in limbo.

Pynchon did not much care for *The Crying of Lot 49*, feeling that in it he had 'forgotten most of what I thought I'd learned up till then' (Pynchon, 1995b, 22). It has tended to be seen by some critics as either a pale follow-up to *V.*, or as a prelude or 'key' to *Gravity's Rainbow*, rather than an important work in its own right. Yet, because of its brevity and structure, it serves even more powerfully than *V.* to illustrate the archetypal Pynchonian 'double movement' whereby the frustrated quest for narrative certainty depicted within the pages of a novel is paralleled by the reader's attempt to interpret it.

The novel may be considered a kind of 'reverse' detective story – not in the sense that it begins with an investigation and ends with a murder, but in the way the signs which confront its investigator-figure proliferate rather than reduce as her quest continues. Detective fiction typically presents us with a mystery which leads to other mysteries as the investigation gets underway: Who is the killer? Why was a suspect behaving so oddly that evening? Why did the victim happen to be in that particular location that night? etc. Gradually, though, the investigator's detective-work ensures that the different conjectural possibilities are in fact progressively closed off, as it emerges that there is in fact one sole narrative which explains all the mysterious events and clues.

The Crying of Lot 49 works the opposite way. Its heroine, Oedipa Maas, is presented with a relatively straightforward task at the beginning of the novel – to co-execute the will of her lover Pierce Inverarity, a 'California real estate mogul' – but this task becomes more and more complex until it seems that in trying to understand Inverarity's life she has stumbled upon a vast global conspiracy – 'the Tristero' or 'Trystero' – which seeks to undermine Western society and politics, and has been operating behind history from the end of the sixteenth century. Pynchon's protagonist's name most obviously implies that she is a female equivalent of Oedipus, arguably the first literary detective. But a gendered reading of the novel is unconvincing, beyond the general idea, as Patrick O'Donnell puts it, that she inhabits a masculine world, 'searching for truth, community, significance in the interconnected realms of the phallocratic military-industrial complex and the narcissistic leisure world of southern California' (O'Donnell, 1991, 9). A more plausible interpretation of her name is that it casts *The Crying of Lot 49* as an inversion of the Oedipus story. Where Oedipus is able to solve a riddle and discover a hidden truth, Oedipa is patently unable to do either. Her quest is a failure. Like Stencil, she wanders through the city of San Narciso (on the surface an obvious version of bohemian 1960s San Francisco but also a cipher for the over-signified world of postmodernity), and everywhere she finds signs which seem to verify her suspicions about the secret system: garbage cans on the streets, children's songs, everywhere the word WASTE (We Await Silent Tristero's Empire) and Tristero's symbol of the Horn. At this point Oedipa's role as surrogate detective is clear:

> Where was the Oedipa who'd driven so bravely up here from San Narciso? That optimistic baby had come on so like the private eye in any long-ago radio drama, believing all you needed was grit, resourcefulness, exemption from hidebound cops' rules, to solve any great mystery.

> But the private eye sooner or later has to get beat up on. This night's profusion of post horns, this malignant, deliberate replication, was their way of beating up. (Pynchon, 1998, 85)

Her problem is not that some vital information is hidden or profoundly encoded – as is the case in private-eye stories – but, as in *V.*, that there is a surfeit of information. As in the earlier novel, too, the reader is engaged in a similar quest. And, at the end, just as the truth promises to be revealed in an auction for some valuable stamps (labelled by the auctioneers 'lot 49'), the novel is cut short. This means that the novel apparently stops one paragraph short of full revelation, and ensures that its title is a suspended chord: we will always await the crying of Lot 49 just as we wait for Beckett's Godot.

Oedipa begins to wonder if she is going mad, and realizes towards the end of the novel that there are four alternatives for making sense of what is happening to her: (1) she has really discovered a secret network; (2) this discovery is simply a delusion; (3) a vast conspiracy has been mounted to fool her into *thinking* she has discovered a secret network; or (4) she's imagining such a conspiracy. She is unable to determine which one is the truth.

This 'void' (118), this huge space of endless possibility, is one we might recognize from reading other postmodern writers, most notably Jorge Luis Borges, whose economical, refined, geometrical style is otherwise the polar opposite of Pynchon's chaotic, parenthetical, jumble of prose. But both writers, as Debra A. Castillo has said, specialize in 'a desperate comedy of inaccessibility' (Castillo, 1991, 22). The suspended chord at the end of *The Crying of Lot 49* really signals that the reader's task is not to choose between the four alternatives, for each is equally plausible. As in 'The Garden of Forking Paths', *Pale Fire*, and certain stories by Barth and Coover, the world of *The Crying of Lot 49* is one in which four potential plots are to be imagined as unfolding *simultaneously*. It is, again, Umberto Eco's logic of conjecture which then deepens throughout the story (Eco, 1985, 57).

Pynchon is not a 'metafictionist' in the way fellow 1960s and 1970s writers such as Coover, Barth or Vonnegut are, because his work does not involve the continual frame-breaking or autobiographical enquiry which is central to theirs. Nevertheless his work shares their obsession with the quest for meaning – both in terms of literary meaning, but also in the way that the quest for meaning in life operates like fiction. *The Crying of Lot 49* is metafictional in a subtle, extensive way, as it serves as an implicit comment on the whole activity of reading, the practice of making connections between signs. It demonstrates that 'the activity of connecting [is] *the* characteristic human endeavour, whether it be in writing and reading literary works, or in articulating ourselves – our identities – as historical beings' (O'Donnell, 1991, 1).

More precisely, Pynchon extends the metafictionists' interest in the political implications of fictionality exemplified in *The Public Burning* and *Slaughterhouse-Five* to take in the specific extra-literary connotations of the term *plot*. As well as a particular organization of the events of a story, 'plot' denotes a conspiracy. The 'paranoid' approach to reading exemplified in works such as *V.* and *The Crying of Lot 49*, where every signifier is potentially connected with any other, is instrumental to 'conspiracy thinking' – a dominant pattern within US culture. Pynchon is usually seen as the key figure in a paranoid tradition in contemporary American fiction, which also includes William Gaddis, William Gass, Joseph McElroy, and Don DeLillo. It is no coincidence that this tradition emerges in American writing in the same decade as traumatic cultural events which trigger conspiracy-thinking, such as the assassination of John F. Kennedy. On a wider level, too, we might suggest that Lyotard's diagnosis of a decline in the belief in 'metanarratives' is paralleled by a rise in conspiracy narratives, alternative metanarratives in which disparate and apparently unconnected events can be linked together.

The novel which explores the idea of paranoia most directly is *Gravity's Rainbow* (1973), commonly regarded as Pynchon's masterpiece and one of the most important novels of the twentieth century. If Pynchon is postmodernism's Joyce then *Gravity's Rainbow* is his *Ulysses*. His novel certainly resembles *Ulysses* in ambition. Where Joyce's novel concentrated on a representative day in the life of a modern Everyman, Leopold Bloom, Pynchon's story focuses on a period of critical importance in modern history: the Second World War and the implication that thereafter the world began to slide into chaos.

The novel is organized around the conviction that the Second World War represents a system which is the point of constellation for various patterns within history, society, and individual identity. This idea is explored chiefly through the novel's governing metaphor, of the V2 bomb (another V, mentioned in the earlier novel). The V2 (or *Vergeltungswaffe 2* – Retaliation Weapon 2) was a rocket-propelled bomb, the first ballistic missile, which weighed 13 tons, travelled at 3,000 miles an hour and at an altitude of up to 50 miles. It represented a key moment in the development of ballistic missiles as it could not be effectively stopped once launched. Thus it stands symbolically for another 'v': vengeance.

Joyce's conceit was to underpin Bloom's story with that of Ulysses, the hero of Homer's *Odyssey*, one of the foundational texts of Western culture (hence the title of the novel). Each of the eighteen chapters, which concentrates on a period in Bloom's day, is written in a different style, mirroring an appropriate discourse (Catholic catechism and women's romance novel, for example), and corresponds directly to a parallel episode in Homer. This gives the novel an added dimension of meaning as it invites the reader to consider how we can take the ironic parallel between Bloom as a modern-day equivalent of the epic questor.

But *Gravity's Rainbow* complicates the idea of such a clear correspondence between character and external world and text and intertext. Up to a point it works along the same lines. The novel's questing hero, Tyrone Slothrop, has been 'programmed' in childhood by a Harvard scientist named Lazlo Jamf and eventually attached to the British forces during the war. Once the German V2 bombs begin to fall on London it appears that they land precisely on all the places where Slothrop has had sex. This comic conceit invites us to treat it as evidence of a hidden plot, and to make associations between the phallic connotations of rockets and Slothrop's sexual encounters, considering the interconnection between sex and aggression, Eros and Thanatos. But, equally, it might just be random, and – as with *V.* and *The Crying of Lot 49* – the novel continually plays with the possibilities that everything is either deeply significant or entirely meaningless.

The structure of *Gravity's Rainbow* emphasizes its central point about paranoia, 'the onset, the leading edge, of the discovery that *everything is connected*' (Pynchon, 1995a, 703). But although Slothrop is a descendent of the questing protagonists in *V.* and *The Crying of Lot 49*, he is not the principal questor in this text: the reader is. Rather than simply shadowing the labyrinthine and ultimately frustrated investigations of a central character, as we do with Stencil and Oedipa, in this one we are left on our own. Slothrop actually disappears from the novel (the narrator commenting in an oddly poignant passage, 'There ought to be a punchline, but there isn't. The plans went wrong. He is being broken down instead, and scattered' [Pynchon, 1995a, 738]). And we have no option other than to indulge in an ultimately frustrated process of paranoid reading, linking together different elements in the narrative, connecting symbols, dates, and times.

Pynchon's fiction, however, also requires its reader to approach it in a 'rhizomatic' way. *Gravity's Rainbow* is often compared to an encyclopaedia or a database, a vast network of potential symmetries and correspondences. Although these promise a kind of coherence, the attempt to determine it is ultimately frustrated, for the texts are literal equivalents of the kind of oversignified world inhabited by Herbert Stencil or Oedipa Maas. More productive is to recognize that Pynchon's writing invites us to make connections at both a temporal and a *spatial* level.

Central here is the way Pynchon deals with time in his novels. *V.*, for example, begins in 1956 when Stencil comes into contact with the other main character in the novel, Benny Profane. From there the narrative does not proceed in a linear fashion, but alternates continuously between a range of periods stretching from 1898 to 1944. Because of the rejection of chronology, the effect is that time becomes less a matter of linearity, a causal and chronological passage from a point in the past to the present, and more a question of space – literally the pages of the novel, in fact, as if all events in the sixty-year span of the novel are potentially accessible at once. The narrative thus operates in the rhizomatic manner: history is envisioned not as an 'arborescent' or tree-like structure where the branches lead back down to the roots, but as a network where any one point in time can potentially lead to any other.

Pynchon's novels are packed with narratives, but unlike *Ulysses*, the paradigmatic modernist novel, these are difficult to treat as one grand narrative. They are densely allusive, yet without an overarching explanatory myth (something that can play the role of the *Odyssey* in *Ulysses*). They do not meditate specific intertexts, but generate large numbers of intertextual references on an arbitrary basis, picking them up when necessary, leaving them aside once a more appropriate one for the specific point in the narrative is required. More than the work of any other writer, Pynchon's novels have appealed to theorists of the postmodern as parables of how postmodernity puts us in the position of receiving too many signals and dealing with too much meaning.

Chapter 4

The postmodern historical novel: Fowles, Barnes, Swift

Linda Hutcheon argues that the postmodern historical novel marks the return of 'plot and questions of reference' to postmodern fiction. Where both plot and referentiality were either disavowed in radical metafictional experimental writing – as in Barth's *Lost in the Funhouse* and Coover's *Pricksongs and Descants* – or endlessly problematized, because their authors' primary aims were to 'explode realist narrative conventions' (Hutcheon, 1988a, xii), by contrast, a work of 'historiographic metafiction' (her label for postmodern historical fiction) is still committed to telling a long and involving story, full of believable characters, which can be enjoyed by the reader in the manner of nineteenth-century realism. This explains why, of all the modes of fiction associated with postmodernism, historiographic metafiction has been 'bestselling' as well as the subject of serious academic attention. The three authors whose work we will consider in this chapter, John Fowles, Julian Barnes and Graham Swift – as well as others whom we shall consider in due course, such as Margaret Atwood and Salman Rushdie – have all enjoyed such dual acclaim. The postmodern historical novel is therefore what we might think of as 'the acceptable face of postmodernism' in literary fiction, influenced by postmodern ideas about fictionality and its relationship with reality, but also popular with a general readership on a mass scale.

As Hutcheon's term suggests, historiographic metafiction is a self-conscious work of fiction concerned with the writing of history. Metafiction, as we know, functions as a challenge to the assumptions behind literary realism and 'lays bare' its own processes of construction to remind us that reality is similarly constructed or mediated. By extension, we can say that historiographic metafiction is fiction which uses metafictional techniques to remind us that history is a construction, not something natural that equates to 'the past'. History is not 'the past', but a narrative based on documents and other material created in the past.

The accessibility of historiographic metafiction has posed problems for critics seeking to come up with an overall category of 'postmodern fiction' because it seems so different from the more avant-garde work of the great pioneers behind postmodernism, such as Beckett or Burroughs, as well as obviously 'experimental' authors such as Coover, Barth or B. S. Johnson. Brian McHale's studies of postmodern fiction, *Postmodernist Fiction* (1987) and *Constructing Postmodernism* (1992), barely mention the examples of British historiographic metafiction which are the primary concern of Hutcheon's *A Poetics of Postmodernism* (1988) and *The Politics of Postmodernism* (1988), and Alison Lee's *Realism and Power* (1990). The scope of Hutcheon's and Lee's analyses thus demonstrates that postmodernism in fiction cannot be defined as work which is non-referential or radically innovative at a formal level.

However, we noted in the previous chapter that an interest in self-reflexive historical reconstruction (somewhat contrary to received wisdom) is a strong feature of 1960s postmodern fiction, as in Vonnegut's *Slaughterhouse-Five*, for example. Staging a confrontation between metafiction and history became a dominant characteristic of the novel throughout the 1970s and the 1980s. Robert Scholes, in his 1979 study of metafiction, *Fabulation and Metafiction*, noted that the major novels of the previous decade – and he mentions work by Pynchon, Barth, Fowles and Coover – 'have tended strongly toward the apparently worn-out form of the historical novel' (Scholes, 1979, 205).

The historical novel is a long-established category of fiction, whose own history stretches back to the turn of the nineteenth century and pioneering works by Walter Scott, such as *Waverley* (1814), and includes prominent examples from later in the century such as Alexandre Dumas's *The Three Musketeers* (1844), James Fenimore Cooper's *The Last of the Mohicans* (1859), and Leo Tolstoy's *War and Peace* (1863–9). Typically it dramatizes a specific historical period a few decades at least before the time of writing and focuses on a central character (sometimes a real historical personage, sometimes a fictional one) who is affected directly in some way by real historical dramas, the outcome of which readers already know.

The classic nineteenth-century historical novel renders the conditions of the time, the way of life, and the contemporary worldview persuasively via the devices of realism. The Marxist theorist of the novel, Georg Lukács, in his classic study of the form first published in 1937, argues that its special ability was to present a 'total' picture of a society at the point of historical change, a kind of microcosmic snapshot of a real period in time, thereby enabling us effectively to use the fiction as an insight into the very historical processes which gave it its context (Lukács, 1983).

However, postmodern commentators such as Hutcheon and Hayden White note that in the nineteenth century – in stark contrast to the twentieth, for the most part – the disciplines of literature and history were regarded as quite comfortably related, not so much because history was considered fictional, but because the faith in realist art meant that the novel could be considered 'factual'. Postmodern fiction, somewhat at odds with the rest of the twentieth century (in which aesthetic practice was regarded as quite separate from historiography) once again stresses the similarity of the two modes, though tips the balance and assumes that the writing of history is dependent upon the principles of fiction.

The conviction behind this is summed up by a rhetorical question Roland Barthes asks in his essay, 'The Discourse of History':

> Does the narration of past events, which, in our culture from the time of the Greeks onwards, has generally been subject to the sanction of historical 'science', bound to the underlying standard of the 'real', and justified by the principles of 'rational' exposition – does this form of narration really differ, in some specific trait, in some indubitably distinctive feature, from imaginary narration, as we find it in the epic, the novel, and the drama?   (Barthes, 1981, 7)

Historiography has pretensions to being a kind of 'science', that is, seeing itself as a discipline which can analyse its object of study dispassionately and objectively, define its properties and measure its effects. The problem, though, as Hayden White has argued, is that the endpoint of this particular analysis remains 'a narrative mode of representation', something which amounts to a failure at both a methodological and theoretical level. 'A discipline that produces narrative accounts of its subject matter as an end in itself', he contends, 'seems methodologically unsound; one that investigates its data in the interest of telling a story about them appears theoretically deficient' (White, 1984, 1).

Historiography and fiction are both made up of narrative units (events, situations, utterances, and so on) which must be selected and ordered by a narrator, who is by definition partial, limited in the range of perspectives from which he can observe the narrative. This is as true of the historian as it is of the novelist – even allowing for the historian's responsibility to remain objective and detached. After all, the narrator of classic realist fiction often claims the same responsibility to detachment, but he or she, as a range of theorists of the novel, such as Mikhail Bakhtin, Catherine Belsey, and Colin McCabe have previously demonstrated (Bakhtin, 1973; McCabe, 1974; Belsey, 1980), inevitably favours one character over another and subtly pushes the reader to accept his or her interpretation of events.

Nor, inevitably, can *everything* be told about an episode in the past. This is obvious when we consider the sheer scale of history, which contains vast potential combinations of narrative units. To invoke a common distinction in postmodern theory, historical events are not 'found' objects, things that are effectively waiting to be picked up and represented by the historian, but 'constructed' objects. Historiography, like all narrative (indeed like all writing) involves the kind of 'frames' foregrounded by metafiction; historiographic metafiction also draws attention to these frames and their function, and often breaks them.

It would be a mistake to push this comparison too far and try to claim that history really *is* fiction, no more no less. Historiography involves narrative and formal constraints which are far more rigid than those of literature, limiting the possibilities for the kind of writing historians can actually produce. Historical writing is almost never 'creative', still less 'poetic' (though there are some examples of what we might call 'metahistory', like Simon Schama's *Dead Certainties: Unwarranted Speculations* [1998] or Peter Ackroyd's 1991 biography of Charles Dickens). Historiography must also cater for the particular expectations of its readers, who naturally assume that what they read will reflect the values of objectivity and authority.

We must also, when examining historiographic metafiction, avoid the trap of thinking of history as some naïve, old-fashioned discipline which continues to produce descriptions and analyses of historical events while remaining blissfully unaware of the problems of narrative. Like literary theory, 'historical theory' has a long-running tradition in the twentieth century (and further back, if we include philosophers like Hegel in the category), and has often debated the uses of narrative in historiography. The French *Annales* group of historians, working in the late 1960s and early 1970s, were strongly critical of narrative history. So is Hayden White, whose work (especially the two books *Metahistory: The Historical Imagination in Nineteenth-Century Europe* (1973) and *Tropics of Discourse* (1978), which examine the discipline from the perspective of narrative theory) has had a major impact in forcing historians to reconsider conventional forms of historiography.

It is also important to emphasize here that the critique mounted by works of historiographic metafiction is aimed at the writing of history, not history itself. It may be the case that history is only *accessible* to us via textual forms, as there is nothing which remains of the past except text (i.e. 'text' understood in the expanded, structuralist sense, to mean any document composed of signs which we can read, whether written, recorded orally, or visually represented). However, the actual processes of history 'itself' – that is, historical change – are not textual. As Fredric Jameson puts it in his book *The Political*

Unconscious, 'history . . . is *not* a text, for it is fundamentally non-narrative and non-representational' (Jameson, 1981, 82). Just because we cannot access them, it does not mean historical processes did not occur.

Historiographic metafiction

But of course the unbridgeable gap between the real past and representations of it is precisely what motivates the postmodern historical novel – and those critics who have written about it. Most prominent of these is Linda Hutcheon. Her definition of 'historiographic metafiction' goes much further than White's theory in insisting upon the close similarity between fiction and historiography. History and the novel, she argues, citing the theorist of history Paul Veyne, share a series of conventions: 'selection, organization, diegesis, anecdote, temporal pacing, and emplotment' (Hutcheon, 1988a, 111). Both are forms of narrative which function 'as signifying systems in our culture; both are what [the American novelist E. L.] Doctorow once called modes of "mediating the world for the purpose of introducing meaning"' – and meaning is itself constructed and imposed rather than found (Hutcheon, 1988a, 112). Most of all, she contends, the problem historiographic metafiction focuses on repeatedly is the one which also preoccupies structuralism: the recognition that language cannot refer to the real world, but only a conceptual version of it.

Hutcheon regards historiographic metafiction as practically synonymous with postmodernism in fiction (Hutcheon, 1988a, ix). Her overall understanding of postmodernism, we recall, is that it is a phenomenon characterized by *doubleness*, governed by the logic of 'both . . . and . . .' rather than 'either . . . or . . .', wholly at ease with contradiction and paradox. This doubleness is reflected in the way a work of historiographic metafiction presents a moment in history both as a vivid, believable representation *and* as a discursive, narrativized construct.

Historiographic metafiction also turns on the distinctive double relation with the reader which Hutcheon explored in her first book, *Narcissistic Narrative* (Hutcheon, 1984), as it is at once didactic, *teaching* us about history, and also – at the same time – allowing us the freedom to question, interpret, even 'co-write' its narrative (in the Barthesian sense). Rather than collapsing history and fiction into one another so that the possibility of representing 'the real' is eliminated, it problematizes the boundary, and asks the reader to explore the space in between. The reader is made aware of the fictionality of the historical material in a text while at the same time remaining conscious of its basis in real events.

The real value of the emphasis on the narrativized, textual aspects of history is not that it fatally compromises historiography, urging us to stop believing in its claims to truth, but that it 'opens up' to interpretation what would otherwise be a closed, didactic form of rhetoric. Hutcheon quotes Jameson's view (from his essay 'Periodizing the 60s') that the problems with adhering to '"old-fashioned narrative or 'realistic' historiography"' mean that the job of the historian has changed. It is not '"any longer to produce some vivid representation of history 'as it really happened', but rather to produce the *concept* of history"' (Hutcheon, 1988a, 112). Historiographic metafiction presents its readers with history *as a concept* so that the fiction comes to function as a kind of *theory*, indirectly, and often directly (as in the work of Julian Barnes or Graham Swift), asking us to consider our relation to history. 'Opening up' history to the present in this way is its special political value, for Hutcheon, for it prevents history from 'being conclusive and teleological' (Hutcheon, 1988a, 110) and asserts that 'there are only *truths* in the plural, and never one Truth' (Hutcheon, 1988a, 109).

This postmodern critique of historiography through fiction remains constructive, however. While highlighting the historian's dependence on narrative, it also asserts, conversely, the value which fiction offers historiography and the theory of history. Even though it destabilizes its own narrative, the fact is that we can learn about real historical events from a work of historiographic metafiction. Robert Coover's *The Public Burning* is one classic example, as it brought a traumatic national political event of twenty-five years before back to prominence in the United States at a critical moment. Another novel which performed a similar task on an even wider scale is Vonnegut's *Slaughterhouse-Five*, which almost single-handedly, following its publication in 1969, focused historical attention in Europe and the United States on the morality of the Allied bombing strategy designed to hasten the end of the war. Although this novel continually flaunts its fictional status, it still functions as a powerful record of what happened in Dresden in 1944.

This doubleness is what leads to the emotional power of historiographic metafiction. It is not simply a playful parody of history, making fun of our habit of believing in something which is patently fictional. Rather it affirms over and over again that history is crucial to our lives. Like the conventional realist historical novel it shows us that whether we like it or not and whether or not we have been directly affected by historical events ourselves we are the products of history and the course our lives take depends upon it. What a novel like *Slaughterhouse-Five* makes clear is that History is not some detached thing, like a great novel we read and are moved or shocked by; it is something that intervenes in our lives. The problem is how it does this and how we know what exactly happened in the past. Its accessibility may make it a more conservative form of postmodern writing, yet historiographic metafiction nevertheless engages seriously with one of the crucial dilemmas of postmodern aesthetics: the relation between the real and that which seeks to represent the real.

British historiographic metafiction

Until Hutcheon's late 1980s studies British fiction had not significantly featured in the postmodernism debate. The brief emergence of an avant-garde tradition in Britain in the late 1960s and 1970s made practically no impact on contemporary discussions about the postmodern, which featured mainly in the United States, even though writers like B. S. Johnson and Christine Brooke-Rose were producing metafictional works which could productively have been placed alongside American writing by the likes of Gass, Coover, Barth, or Barthelme.

This was not just an example of American insularity, for the fact is that the post-war British literary mainstream has always been rather conservative, especially compared with other European traditions such as the French and Italian. There may be wide-ranging historical and cultural reasons for this which are too complex to go into here (Britain's island mentality, for example, its deep-rooted suspicion of intellectualism, or even the emphasis on pragmatic and analytic philosophy over 'continental' varieties) but one important *literary* reason is the dominance of the realist tradition in fiction which has always been associated with England. As Ian Watt's landmark study *The Rise of the Novel* (1957) shows, the realist novel was rooted in England, in the work of writers like Defoe and Fielding, while nineteenth-century 'classic realism' (e.g. Dickens, George Eliot) was especially dominant in this country too.

Hutcheon's intervention in the postmodern debate opened the way for a serious consideration of some of the most important British writers to emerge in the 1980s. In a 1990 essay on 'British Historiographic Metafiction', Susan Onega lists numerous examples including John Fowles, Maureen Duffy, William Golding, Lawrence Durrell, Graham Swift, Julian Barnes, Peter Ackroyd, Rose Tremain, A. S. Byatt, Jeanette Winterson, and Jim Crace (Onega, 1995, 94). She might also have mentioned D. M. Thomas, Alasdair Gray or Salman Rushdie.

This is not to say that historiographic metafiction was an exclusively British development. I have already mentioned *The Public Burning* and *Slaughterhouse-Five*, and Hutcheon's exhaustive studies consider many other examples from North America (e.g. Doctorow's *Ragtime*), as well as texts from

South America and Europe. Nevertheless historiographic metafiction does have a particularly British relevance, given its relation to the realist literary tradition.

Alison Lee, another critic who has championed British historiographic metafiction as symptomatic of postmodern fiction, has suggested that the crucial fact is, paradoxically, the apparent conservatism of this variety of metafiction, which actually gives it an extra subversive power compared with its more obviously radical, dazzling North American counterpart. The metafiction of Gass or Barthelme, she argues, 'plays with the conventions of Realism in a more overt way' and this effectively strips these conventions of authority. By contrast, British historiographic metafiction 'firmly install[s] Realist techniques, and in some cases [such as Graham Swift's *Waterland*] seem at first to *be* Realist texts'. As a result, it means that 'postmodernist techniques challenge Realist conventions from within the very conventions they wish to subvert' (Lee, 1990, xii). This, she contends, is more powerful than a critique from outside.

In the rest of this chapter I want to consider three of the most significant examples of British postmodern historiographic metafiction: John Fowles's *The French Lieutenant's Woman* (1969), Graham Swift's *Waterland* (1983), and Julian Barnes's *Flaubert's Parrot* (1984). Each novel is written by a white, middle-class, Oxbridge-educated man, affirming that while this variety of fiction challenges the authority of an established approach to history, it is also the product of the conservative British literary establishment. Before turning to the specific examples, then, it is important to note that besides not being simply a British phenomenon, much powerful historiographic metafiction has been produced by female writers and writers from other ethnic origins than white. These bring a more precise political edge to the general question of 'opening up' a closed practice, historiography, and therefore cannot simply be reduced to a single category, as they require separate chapters to themselves. The category of historiographic metafiction will therefore be significant in the following two chapters. Nevertheless, comparatively 'mainstream' as it may be, the engaging fiction of Fowles, Swift, and Barnes provides an ideal starting-point, as it so successfully exemplifies the double-coded logic of historiographic metafiction.

John Fowles, *The French Lieutenant's Woman*

Susan Onega has written about sending a letter to the academic and novelist David Lodge in 1983 asking for other examples of 'pseudo-historical novels' like Fowles's *The French Lieutenant's Woman* only for him to reply that he couldn't think of any. By 1990, the time of her paper about British pseudo-historical novels, the situation had changed dramatically, and the list of British novelists producing this kind of work was (as we have seen) extensive. But Fowles's novel was the pioneer.

At one level *The French Lieutenant's Woman* is an extraordinarily effective pastiche of the nineteenth-century realist novel, a form Fowles clearly admires. It is as if written by a composite version of George Eliot and Thomas Hardy. *The French Lieutenant's Woman* tells an engaging love story set in the beautiful Dorset seaside town of Lyme Regis in 1867. Charles Smithson, a wealthy Victorian gentleman, heir to a title, is engaged to marry Ernestina Freeman, daughter of a representative of the emergent middle class, a haberdasher keen to see his daughter marry into a family higher up the social scale. When the novel begins, their courtship is progressing according to the codes of propriety which operated at the time. Yet Charles becomes obsessively attracted to the mysterious Sarah Woodruff – known as 'the French Lieutenant's Woman' (or 'whore') by the people of Lyme – who is a social outcast because of the stigma of having had an affair with a French sailor, who has abandoned her. Her outsider status is signified by her habit of wandering around the symbolic 'wild zone' of the Undercliff, a counter-space to the domestic interiors where proper social intercourse is conducted.

Charles begins a disastrous relationship with Sarah, breaking off his engagement to Ernestina, and following her to a hotel in Exeter where they briefly have sex. Sarah then disappears, Charles's manservant Sam betrays him, and Mr Freeman makes him sign a humiliating document acknowledging his guilt and effectively condemning him to outcast status too. When he eventually tracks Sarah down, to a house she shares with the historically real Victorian artists, the Rossettis, he discovers she has changed considerably and finds this hard to accept.

Although Fowles professed to have no particular interest in the form of the historical romance, the novel is beautifully constructed, with a faultless replication of nineteenth-century patterns of speech and period detail, and rewards the kind of in-depth reading one might perform on a Hardy novel, noting the patterns in the narrative and decoding its underlying symbolism. Fowles once commented that the novel was, like its predecessors *The Collector* and *The Magus*, 'based on more or less disguised existentialist premises' and tried 'to show an existentialist awareness before it was chronologically possible' (Fowles, 1990, 151).

Sartrean existentialism (a philosophy to which Fowles adhered) begins with the recognition that human existence is pointless, as there is no inherent purpose to life and insists that one's responsibility is therefore to determine the meaning of one's life for oneself by making committed, responsible choices.

Fowles's view is that 'the Victorian Age, especially from 1850 on, was highly existentialist in many of its personal dilemmas' (Fowles, 1990, 152). Thus his hero Charles is presented with a key moment of choice once he realizes he is attracted to Sarah. He can continue to live in 'bad faith', adhere to social convention and marry Ernestina, or he can be true to himself, break off the engagement and pursue the freedom she represents.

The pursuit of freedom is played out on a collective scale, too, as it is linked (as the novel's epigraphs suggest) to the theme of Darwinian evolution, a process governed by the ruthless logic of the 'survival of the fittest'. The novel uses historical hindsight to suggest that Charles, as a representative of 'old money', is effectively part of a dying breed, one which is being supplanted by the 'new' money associated with commerce and the middle class, embodied by the appropriately named Freeman. Charles's enthusiasm for paleontology, spending his time looking for fossils on the beach, serves partly as a metaphor for the novel's own excavation of past remnants, but also, by implication, as an analogy of Charles's status as a living fossil who will soon die out.

If this were all the novel consisted of then it would simply be a notable post-war novel, 'the nineteenth-century novel that century forgot to produce' (Conradi, 1982, 58), something like Charles Palliser's *The Quincunx* (1991). From a postmodernist perspective, it would be an example of Jameson's 'blank parody', the reflex mimicry of the past. But the novel's engagement with the past is always critical and self-conscious, and its gripping narrative is accompanied by a carefully imposed metafictional framework which enables Fowles to build in his strategies for composing the novel into the novel itself.

For the first twelve chapters of *The French Lieutenant's Woman* the reader has been able to immerse him or herself in the story, enjoying the kind of 'suspension of disbelief' required of realist novels, even though there are anachronistic reminders of the era in which the novel is composed rather than set, such as epigraphs from 1967's *Human Documents of the Victorian Golden Age*. Chapter 12 ends with the questions 'Who is Sarah? Out of what shadows does she come?'

Rather than the in-depth character-study a pastiche of the genre would lead us to expect, what follows is a remarkable act of metafictional 'frame-breaking'. Chapter 13 notoriously begins:

> I do not know. This story I am telling is all imagination. These characters I create never existed outside my own mind. If I have pretended until now to know my characters' minds and innermost thoughts, it is because I am writing in . . . a convention universally accepted at the time of my story: that the novelist stands next to God.

> He may not know all, yet he tries to pretend that he does. But I live in
> the age of Alain Robbe-Grillet and Roland Barthes; if this is a novel, it
> cannot be a novel in the modern sense.   (Fowles, 1996, 97)

The digression continues for most of the chapter, asking questions about the
degree of control an author can exercise over his fictional world. For Fowles it
is less than one might think. In the spirit of Barthes's essay 'The Death of the
Author' (written in the same year, 1967, Fowles was composing his novel) he
argues that although '[t]he novelist is still a god, since he creates . . . what has
changed is that we are no longer the gods of the Victorian image, omniscient and
decreeing; but in the new theological image, with freedom our first principle,
not authority'. For Fowles, '[t]here is only one good definition of God: the
freedom that allows other freedoms to exist' (Fowles, 1996, 99).

   After this prolonged outburst, Fowles largely retreats into the spaces outside his text as the story continues, though his intervention has permanently
changed the atmosphere, like a party following the departure of a disruptive
guest. As we read on, we do so in the light of Fowles's comments, and know that
the story we read is meant to exemplify its author's views of freedom. It also
casts the paratextual elements of the novel – the epigraphs taken mainly from
Victorian texts, such as novels, poems, and documents like medical reports,
and the occasional footnote clarifying material used in the novel – in a different light. Rather than enhancing the sense of realism, as such elements do in
George Eliot, they have the opposite effect, and remind us that this novel –
like any novel, even one by the exemplary 'classic realist' Eliot – is a piece of
rhetoric constructed by its author, a realistically drawn world but not 'the real
world'.

   For the rest of the novel we remain conscious of the fact that Fowles is
still lurking in the margins. Sure enough, as the novel gets towards the end he
reappears on two further occasions, though each time it is not simply his 'voice'
we hear, but he actually becomes a character in the text, breaking through the
conventionally sacrosanct diegetic levels of narrative. In Chapter 55 he enters a
train carriage and sits opposite the dozing Charles, wondering 'what the devil
am I going to do with you?' (Fowles, 1996, 389), and in Chapter 61 appears
outside the Rossetti house where Sarah is staying and puts back the time on
his pocket watch, effectively returning the narrative to an earlier point (441).

   Neither portrait is particularly flattering. On the first appearance Fowles
describes himself as prurient and menacing, sizing up his hero disapprovingly
in a way which 'suggest[s] something unpleasant, some kind of devious sexual
approach' (389). The second time he is a kind of 'foppish', 'Frenchified' version
of the *flâneur* (441). This is a further reminder of how implicated the realist

author is in his own text, how far he is from the detached, objective figure of convention. Intervening again, 'Fowles' explains that, normally, realist fiction 'pretends to conform to the reality: the writer puts the conflicting wants [of characters like Charles] in the ring and then describes the fight'. But this is disingenuous, for the author 'in fact fixes the fight, letting that want he himself favours win', and, as a result, subtly but firmly imposing his or her views on the reader, showing him or her 'what one thinks of the world around one – whether one is a pessimist, and optimist, what you will' (390).

True to his existentialist definition of the author as the 'freedom that allows other freedoms to exist' 'Fowles' decides he is going to 'take both sides' and show the reader two alternative versions of 'the fight' – in other words, provide us with two different endings to the novel. He claims to have no preference for either, and tosses a coin to decide which he presents last, as the second one will inevitably be seen to have been endorsed by the author as the genuine one, 'so strong is the tyranny of the last chapter' (390). The first ending conforms to the conventions of the realist form he parodies by tying up loose ends and reuniting Charles, Sarah, and Lalage, the daughter born of their brief sexual encounter. In the second Charles realizes that Sarah has manipulated him and will continue to do so and turns away before they have had a chance to speak or he has even met his daughter.

The destabilizing effect of *The French Lieutenant's Woman* comes largely from Fowles's adherence to the 'forking paths principle' which is central to postmodern narrative. Just as Coover's short stories 'The Magic Poker' and 'The Babysitter' give us contradictory versions of narrative sequences without cancelling any out, so Fowles provides us with two endings that are equally valid. In fact, before these, there has already been a possible *third* ending for the novel. In Chapter 44 Charles goes back to Ernestina, keeping his encounter with Sarah a secret, and they get married as planned and have 'what shall it be – let us say seven children' (325). There is even a possible fourth ending. As he contemplates Charles in the train 'Fowles' notes that he has 'already thought of ending Charles's career here and now; of leaving him for eternity on his way to London' (389), unsure if he will see Sarah again. This is the kind of open ending which appeals to Fowles, and resembles the ending of his earlier novel *The Magus* (1965) which finishes literally by stopping the action as if in a 'freeze-frame'.

These last two 'endings' are officially ruled out by the narrator. Yet because they have been described and remain in the book, they *exist* in the represented world of *The French Lieutenant's Woman*. Fiction, Fowles tells us, enables us to activate the various hypotheses 'about what might happen' which we 'screen in our minds' (327). This is one reason behind his assertion in Chapter 13 that all novelists write novels for one reason only: '*we wish to create worlds as real as, but other than the world that is. Or was.*' (98). His point about 'the tyranny of the last chapter' suggests that in a more rhizomatic structure, an alternative form to the page-bound novel, which is by definition linear, it might be possible for all four endings to be 'active' at the same time.

Such a space is, of course, as postmodern narrative repeatedly implies, the space in which the printed text triggers the reader's imagination. Thus *The French Lieutenant's Woman*, like potentially all texts, is a 'writerly text'. But Fowles actually polices its writerly aspect, for his insistence that we have the freedom to choose which ending we prefer is quite disingenuous. The 'third' (Charles reunited with Ernestina) and the 'fourth' (Charles remaining on the train) endings are not ones he takes seriously, the former (as he explains) because it is effectively too conventional, the second because it is not conventional enough. And in fact the first 'official' ending is apparently not one he can endorse either. Even though he takes it seriously enough to develop a long, largely irony-free chapter describing the reunion between Charles and Sarah, when they embrace at the end Charles hears 'a thousand violins cloy[ing] very rapidly without percussion' (429).

In contrast to this ironic note, the second ending, on the very last page of the novel, includes a sincere comment from the author, intervening for the last time, stating, as Charles walks away, that 'he has at last found an atom of faith in himself, a true uniqueness, on which to build' (445). Thus 'the tyranny of the last chapter' prevails and the reference to existentialism which precedes this comment indicates that it is indeed the one Fowles prefers. The problem for Sartrean existentialism often noted by commentators is that its emphasis on individual choice and freedom works against the notion of society, for one person's determination to act in good faith may impinge upon the freedom of another. This is the outcome of the 'textual existentialism' of *The French Lieutenant's Woman*: in exercising his own freedom to choose between endings, Fowles compromises the reader's capacity to choose freely.

This paradox is entirely in keeping with Linda Hutcheon's insistence about the double logic of historiographic metafiction, according to Hutcheon. *The French Lieutenant's Woman* is both didactic *and* 'writerly', simultaneously a powerful critique of realism and an attempt to revitalize it. Its replication of a Victorian novel results in a text which is simultaneously a credible portrait of a historical period *and* a self-reflexive piece of artifice, referring both outside itself to the real historical world and inside to its own workings.

Fowles's interrogation of the Victorian world from the perspective of existentialism makes *The French Lieutenant's Woman* a fascinating and valid analysis of the social and personal dilemmas faced by the Victorians: love, freedom, the emerging middle class. At the same time, its self-conscious textuality – its narratorial interventions, its epigraphs and multiple endings – reminds us that our knowledge of the nineteenth century is in fact chiefly a literary one, as it is mainly constructed, just like Fowles's own novel, from imaginative literature and historical texts. After reading it we cannot help but wonder about how accurate or inaccurate our own impression of the Victorian world, gained from other texts and media, might actually be.

Graham Swift, *Waterland*

Graham Swift's *Waterland* is similarly double with regard to 'real' history, as one of its functions is to recount the histories of the French Revolution and of the Fens region in eastern England where the novel is set. Hutcheon suggests that there are two principal modes of narration employed in historiographic metafiction: 'multiple points of view (e.g. as in [D. M.] Thomas's *The White Hotel*), or an overtly controlling narrator (as in Swift's *Waterland*)' (Hutcheon, 1988a, 117). As an example of the latter, *Waterland* presents itself in its entirety as the rambling oral narrative delivered by a disaffected history teacher to his class.

Right away this device positions the reader of the novel in a typically contradictory way: it makes it a highly didactic, rhetorical piece of text, as the reader becomes one of the listening schoolchildren with no other option than to follow his or her authoritative teacher. At the same time, the way the novel gathers together a wide range of individual narrative strands within the teacher's larger discourse places the emphasis on the reader to determine the meaning of the relationship between them.

Tom Crick has started to tell his story because he has arrived at a crisis point in his life: his wife Mary has been placed in an asylum after kidnapping a baby, his job is under threat because the school is (in a phrase with obvious symbolic resonance) 'cutting back history', and his students have become disillusioned by Crick teaching them the French Revolution, for they feel it has no relevance to the present. Worried by contemporary fears about terrorism and nuclear war, they believe – as Price, the emblematically named dissenter of the class, puts it – that what matters 'is the here and now. . . . The only important thing about history, I think, sir, is that it's got to the point where it's probably about to end' (Swift, 1992, 6–7).

Besides representing widespread fears in the 1980s about nuclear holocaust, Price's comments and the metaphorical significance of his headteacher's warning about the end of history suggest that the appropriate context for *Waterland* is the philosophical argument, often associated with postmodernism (though a counterpart is advanced in right-wing political thought of the likes of Arnold Gehlen or Francis Fukuyama), which suggests that from the late twentieth century we have entered a period of 'posthistory'. This is an argument developed by postmodern thinkers such as Fredric Jameson and Jean Baudrillard, who (in different ways) characterize postmodern culture as being increasingly devoid of historical 'depth', prone to engage continually in reflex simulations of previous historical events. This marks an alternative approach to understanding history as a 'Grand Narrative' in a Hegelian or Marxist sense, that is, as a kind of teleological progressive sequence which makes revolution possible.

Crick maintains an ambivalent attitude to history, alternatively mocking its pretensions and believing in its ability to expose the truth. It is at once a dangerously seductive fabrication and an essential mechanism for making sense of our lives. A feature of the novel is Crick's restless efforts to define history. His analogies include 'a fairy-tale' (6), 'a lucky dip of meanings' (140), and 'the Grand Narrative, the filler of vacuums, the dispeller of fears in the dark' (53). Most pertinent, though, is the dictionary definition which features as the first of the novel's two epigraphs: '*Historia, -ae,* f. **1.** inquiry, investigation, learning. **2.** a) a narrative of past events, history. b) any kind of narrative: account, tale, story'. This definition indicates that the ambiguity upon which historiographic metafiction is founded is at the heart of the very term history itself, and characterizes Crick's narrative to his listening class: a composite of official History and personal and family history ('*his* story') which draws upon a range of other kinds of fiction, such as fairytales, romance, and detective fiction (the novel's opening chapter ends with the childhood discovery of the body of one of Crick's friends floating in a lock).

One of the most important of the literary forms invoked by the novel is the retrospective first-person narrative, as suggested by the second epigraph, from Dickens's *Great Expectations*: 'Ours was the marsh country . . .'. This line indicates that the novel repeats *The French Lieutenant's Woman*'s point that our construction of the past depends frequently on *literary* material rather than any more 'authentic' documents. More precisely it also makes the comparison between the geography of the Kent marshes, where *Great Expectations* is partly set, and the East Anglian Fens. The idea of marshland, denoted by the novel's title, has metaphorical importance, too, for the continual process of 'reclaiming' the land from water which preserves the Fens and the lives of those who inhabit the region mirrors what Crick is trying to do with his own past: preserve some solidity in the face of impending collapse. 'History', he tells his class, 'if it is to keep on constructing its road into the future, must do so on solid ground' (86).

This suggests another parallel between Swift's novel and Dickens's. The protagonist of each uses his narrative to trace the origins of his present experience. In Crick's case this involves explaining his wife's breakdown by the story of her aborted pregnancy as a teenager. But it also involves uncovering a complex family story, most immediately affecting Tom, his mentally retarded brother Dick, and his father Henry (the names ironically suggesting the situation of the characters is that of every 'Tom, Dick and Harry'), which also stretches as far back into the seventeenth-century into the history of his ancestors.

But, unlike Pip, Crick's relentless storytelling and drawing of endless parallels between the stories leave him unable to establish a set of rational conclusions nor even to end the story with a proper sense of closure. He is determined 'to disentangle history from fairy-tale' (86) but finds that history and story collapse into one another: 'the more you try to dissect events, the more you lose hold of them – the more they seem to have occurred largely in people's imagination' (139–40). One reason for the adult Mary's inability to conceive is because of her crude abortion at the hands of the 'local witch' Martha Clay. But another is that Freddie Parr once dropped a live eel into Mary's knickers and, according to local legend, 'a live fish in a woman's lap will make her barren' (208).

One of *Waterland*'s most striking features is its complex structure. The vast linearity of its narrative, which stretches back over centuries and undertakes historical 'inquiry' into momentous public events such as the fall of the Bastille and the First and Second World Wars, more localized history of places, families and individuals, and curious cultural histories of things like the eel and a bottle of beer, creates a more typically postmodern *spatial* set of narrative possibilities. As Alison Lee has pointed out it is actually unlike many works of metafiction – *The French Lieutenant's Woman*, for example – in that it does not seek to 'foreground its structure'. In fact it might even be approached, she says, as a Barthesian 'readerly' text, because its story 'is so engaging and the manipulation of affect so intense that it can certainly be read (if naively) on this level' (Lee, 1990, 42).

Though it can be reassembled chronologically its narrative is not presented to the reader in a linear manner. As Lee notes, the end of the novel tells of events which occur only half way through the overall story and subsequent events are covered in the first few chapters. The narrative is effectively circular: as soon as we have finished reading we need to go back to the first chapter. Thus Crick's narrative reflects his recognition that history is not 'a well-disciplined and unflagging column marching unswervingly into the future' but something which 'goes in two directions at once. It goes backwards as it goes forwards. It loops. It takes detours' (Swift, 1992, 135).

But a more expansive metaphor than the one-dimensional 'circularity' is invited when we consider more carefully how *Waterland* works. It is made up of fifty-two chapters, each of which has a title which points to its subject-matter, most of them directly beginning with the word 'About': 'About the End of History', 'About My Grandfather', 'About Beauty and the Beast', etc. Unusually, the chapters literally run into one another. For example:

> [end of chapter 2:] let me tell you
> [title of chapter 3:] 3. ABOUT THE FENS
> [beginning of chapter 3:] which are a low-lying region in Eastern England.   (Swift, 1992, 8)

But despite the way they interlock, they are also, to an extent, interchangeable, almost as if the result of a Burroughs-style 'cut-up'. The impression is that each is self-contained and we can theoretically proceed from any one of them to any other, reading the novel the way we read a dictionary or an encyclopaedia rather than in a linear manner.

This is another novel, then, with an implicit rhizomatic structure reminiscent of the internet. It is surely no accident that one of the first hypertext projects in literary studies (now part of the well-known 'Victorianweb') was devoted to *Waterland* (Fishman, 1989). It is important not to overstate this dimension, however, for the overarching circularity of the narrative can only work with the chapters placed in the order they are; they have not simply fallen together like *The Naked Lunch*. Once again the novel is *both* readerly *and* writerly, didactically organized and open to free interpretation.

Nevertheless, aside from its *actual* structure, the novel does create a huge rhizomatic web of narratives and associations. Crick comes to seem like a machine generating story after story and suggesting pattern after pattern, and will carry on doing so eternally. Thus he embodies the two 'definitions of Man' he proffers: he is 'the story-telling animal' (Swift, 1992, 62) and 'the animal who craves meaning – but knows – [Events elude meaning]' (140). His strategy is to convince us that every story, public or personal, is somehow linked (the French Revolution somehow relates both to his wife's breakdown and to the story of his brewer grandfather's production of a special beer to mark the coronation of George V), that everything impacts on something else in a pattern of cause and effect (e.g. the watery foundations of the marsh country make the people who live there 'phlegmatic'), that everything is *equivalent* to everything else (Mary's vagina, 'a moist labyrinth of inwardly twisting, secret passages' becomes like T. S. Eliot's 'cunning corridors' of history).

Crick's determination to connect these things with one another is an example of that familiar postmodern effect: paranoid reading. He inhabits the 'significance world' of fiction, where nothing is accidental, every sign is meaningful. And of course this presents a particular challenge to the reader of *Waterland*, who is invited to inhabit a similar world. Moreover, Swift's novel, which envelops Crick's rambling narrative, adds another layer of potential significance to the narrator's web of stories and equivalences. The reader's job is to decide how far to connect these as a way of interpreting the novel. To take one example, there are numerous echoes of Christian stories in the novel, such as Tom's 'potato-head' brother Dick being named by his father Ernest Atkinson (who also happens to be his grandfather) 'The Saviour of the World', his incest perhaps (or perhaps not) causing Dick's mental retardation, while the appropriately named Mary steals a child and tells her husband she 'got it from God' (265). But this ironic reworking of the story of Christ does not 'explain' Swift's novel. It figures as just one more metanarrative which promises to keep unfathomability at bay.

Towards the end Crick tells his class: 'What do you think all these stories are for . . . . It helps to drive out fear' (241). For in the end all that is tangible in the novel is the very process of telling and listening to (or reading) stories. With appropriately circular logic, the point of the story becomes its narration.

Julian Barnes, *Flaubert's Parrot*

In its basic scenario Julian Barnes's *Flaubert's Parrot*, published two years later, in 1984, is similar to Swift's novel. Its narrator looks into history to find the truth that will also help explain his own life. His narrative is also divided into sections which could easily be arranged in a different order without disrupting any necessary coherence.

The narrator, Geoffrey Braithwaite, a recently widowed and retired English doctor, 'writes' about his obsession with the nineteenth-century French writer Gustave Flaubert and, in particular, his quest to identify the actual stuffed parrot which provided the inspiration for his 1877 story 'Un Coeur Simple'. The problem, as he explains in the novel's first chapter, is that on a visit to Normandy he has discovered two equally plausible candidates in two different Flaubert museums. He had equated the idea of finding a real historical object which had sat on Flaubert's desk as he wrote the story with 'knowing' the real man behind it. Looking at the first bird, he 'felt ardently in touch with this writer' (Barnes, 1985, 16). On discovering the second, however, he feels as if it is asking him in reply: 'The writer's voice – what makes you think it can be located that easily?' (22).

Braithwaite's dilemma is thus a metaphor for the problem at the heart of historiographic metafiction: the limits to our attempt to know the past. We cannot access it directly – all we have are textual documents (such as the letter Braithwaite has photocopied in which Flaubert mentions the stuffed parrot sitting on his desk) which divert us away from the real object or event as much as direct us towards it. Either of the parrots may be the 'real' one, but equally, as Braithwaite realizes, Flaubert may just have invented the idea of the parrot sitting on his desk. At the end of the novel, appropriately enough, the mystery of the parrot is deepened rather than solved. A Flaubert expert informs Braithwaite that the original parrot had been borrowed by Flaubert from the Museum of Natural History and then returned. When the curators of the two Flaubert museums each tried to retrieve it they were taken to a room which contained fifty stuffed parrots and then 'did the logical thing, the intelligent thing': went back to the description in 'Un Coeur Simple' and 'chose the parrot which looked most like his description' (Barnes, 1985, 187). So in this case the representation comes *before* the referent, or to recall Baudrillard's analogy about just this problem in postmodernity: the 'map precedes the territory'.

Faced with his two candidates for Flaubert's original referent, what Braithwaite embarks upon is an alternative kind of Flaubert biography, one we might legitimately describe as a work of metahistory – a piece of historiography which acknowledges its status as a subjective, incomplete, often unverifiable piece of construction. More precisely, the novel deconstructs the particular genre of historiography which is biography. We cannot 'know' Flaubert directly, but we can build up a multi-faceted portrait of him based on all the texts – fiction, letters and other documents – which he left behind or in which he 'appears', like putting together a collage made up of textual fragments in such a way that the silhouette of the person to whom they relate appears in the middle.

Braithwaite's own metaphor for this process is to compare biography to catching fish in a net, which he defines not as something for catching fish but 'a collection of holes tied together with string': 'The trawling net fills, then the biographer hauls it in, sorts, throws back, stores, fillets and sells. Yet consider what he does not catch: there is always far more of that' (38).

Braithwaite's narrative divides itself into themed chapters (not unlike Crick's strategy in *Waterland*) which enable the reader to become introduced to different facets of Flaubert. Chapter 4, for example, entitled 'The Flaubert Bestiary', is an analysis of all the different recurring animal references in Flaubert's writings and his life: bears, camels, sheep, dogs, and of course the parrot.

Chapter 9, 'The Flaubert Apocrypha', traces the references to all the books Flaubert planned to write, or imagined writing, but did not.

The result is a clever (and near academically valid) study of an important writer. It convincingly makes the point that any historical individual – just like any real-life present-day one, in fact – is not a stable, consistent unchanging character, like a portrait, but a series of different characters, all complementing and clashing with each other. This exemplifies the postmodern approach to subjectivity, of course, and it has particular consequences for history. Just as we cannot be sure what really happened in a particular historical event, or which historical object is genuine, so we cannot be sure which portrait of a person most represents the 'real' one. Subjectivity, postmodernism asserts, is always changing, always 'in process' rather than stable.

This point is made most forcefully in the second chapter of the book, 'Chronology'. It begins by presenting us with the kind of official 'Biographical Outline' which is standard practice in academic works about single authors, and moves from birth to death with all the significant events in between, such as marriages and publications. But it is followed by two other 'chronologies', each of which cover the same 'timeline' but include completely different events: the second chronology concentrates upon deaths, illnesses, and failures, while the third is made up of quotations from Flaubert about himself. These three versions represent, respectively: 'official' history, for example, public events in the writer's life; 'emotional history', or the extent to which life is affected by death and unhappiness; and Flaubert's own interpretation of his life, a first-person counterpart to the conventional detached third-person authority of the first chronology. These are three versions of a life, each designed to complement rather than rival the other.

'Chronology' also makes the point that the problem of the elusive historical referent is compounded by the fact that the historiographer is also inevitably a selective and partial narrator. This is implied in the points throughout the novel when Braithwaite unintentionally undermines his efforts to present an authoritative though multi-faceted portrait of Flaubert by spouting forth his opinions on all sorts of things, from the kinds of novel which should no longer be written, to his feelings about coincidences, to where to get the best cheese in Dieppe. In one chapter he passionately rubbishes criticisms of Flaubert and in another parodies Flaubert's *Dictionary of Received Ideas*. Moreover his examination of the author is blended with personal reminiscences, such as previous visits to France and his dealings with patients while he was a doctor.

Braithwaite is obviously an unreliable academic narrator in the tradition of Nabokov's Kinbote or Borges's unnamed narrator of 'Tlön, Uqbar, Orbis

Tertius' , whose partiality seriously compromises his narrative's sense of historical accuracy. What makes Barnes's use of the device differ from the modernist unreliable narrator is the ironic self-reflexivity of Braithwaite's discussion of the merits and problems of fiction and literary criticism. He tells us about his dislike for literary critics, meditates on what might constitute 'the perfect reader' (Barnes, 1985, 75), and discusses moments when 'a contemporary narrator hesitates, claims uncertainty, misunderstands, plays games and falls into error' (89). When Braithwaite ridicules the idea of a writer 'provid[ing] two different endings to his novel' in a pretence of 'reflecting life's variable outcomes' (89) – just like Fowles in *The French Lieutenant's Woman* – the metafictional aspect becomes a kind of ironic 'double bluff'. What we are presented with is a postmodern narrator condemning postmodern techniques.

The increasingly intrusive autobiographical element to Braithwaite's narrative and his dislike of chance and coincidence becomes explained in the appropriately numbered chapter 13 (another echo of *The French Lieutenant's Woman*) when he begins to talk directly – or as directly as he is able to – about the death of his wife and his relationship with her. He begins by stating that '[t]his is a pure story, whatever you think' (160). We realize that the trauma of her death has been increased by the fact that he made the decision not to resuscitate her as she lay in a coma, and also by the fact that she had been adulterous during their marriage and this had stopped him loving her. It becomes clear that his obsession with Flaubert stems from the parallels between his life and Flaubert's (e.g. Braithwaite's wife had a 'secret life', like Emma Bovary, Flaubert's most famous character) and becomes a way of controlling the past, or at least analysing it from a 'safe' position. Because he and his wife never spoke about her affair, it means Braithwaite has 'to invent [his] way to the truth' (165):

> Ellen. My wife: someone I feel I understand less well than a foreign writer dead for a hundred years. Is this an aberration, or is it normal? Books say: she did this because. Life says: she did this. Books are where things are explained to you; life is where things aren't. I'm not surprised some people prefer books. Books make sense of life. The only problem is that the lives they make sense of are other people's lives, never your own.
>
> (Barnes, 1985, 168)

Braithwaite's narrative is an example, to use Barnes's own description of the novel, of what psychiatrists call the 'displacement activity', as his 'inability to express his grief and his love . . . is transposed into an obsessive desire to recount to you the reader everything he knows and has found out about

Gustave Flaubert, love for whom is a more reliable constant in his life than has been love for Ellen' (Barnes, 2002, 262). Once we realize this, the preceding discussion of Flaubert comes to seem less objective still, as the very mode of analysis (e.g. the morbid second section in 'Chronology'), and the lines of enquiry he chooses to pursue (such as 'Is it ever the right time to die?' [22]) are evidence of his personal motivation.

Chapter 5

Postmodern-postcolonial fiction

Postcolonialism is concerned with the processes of colonization and its effects on different societies and cultures. Its focus is primarily on how the colonial experience has shaped not just the former colonies of Europe, but colonizing countries such as Britain, and 'settler' nations like the United States, Canada, Australia, New Zealand, and South Africa. It is important to acknowledge that the 'post' in postcolonialism does not refer simply to a historical period *after* the colonial rule of a particular country is over, such as, for example, post-August 1947 when India secured its independence from Britain. The colonial process, theorists insist, is never 'over' in the way a single event is over but is continual. India, in a variety of social, political, and cultural ways (we might consider the assassination of Benazir Bhutto in late 2007, for example) is still subject to the effects of Empire.

When it comes to literary criticism and theory, postcolonialist reading strategies concentrate on specific representations and debates in literary texts. Representation, whether through the media, art, or other cultural practices, is a crucial and powerful means of maintaining control over a people – but also a way by which the colonized can resist, subvert, or critique the colonial process. There are two main kinds of postcolonialist reading strategies: those which tease out the colonialist assumptions in European literature (e.g. classics such as Jane Austen's *Mansfield Park* or Joseph Conrad's *Heart of Darkness*), and those which examine literature produced within a once-colonized nation (e.g. Nigeria, Kenya, or India, for example) or by writers from an ethnic group within Britain and the United States.

It is within this second category of criticism that the idea of postmodernism has tended to be invoked. Postmodern strategies can be identified in fiction produced in former colonies, such as the 'magic realism' of South American writers such as Gabriel García Marquez (Colombia) and Isabel Allende (Chile). Most often, though, postmodern theory has supported postcolonialist readings of work produced within England and the United States, where there is a significant number of writers belonging to immigrant communities from previously colonized countries. This focus, after all, is what we might expect from an Anglo-American theoretical phenomenon like postmodernism, especially one which, as Linda Hutcheon has argued, is geared toward developing a critique 'from within' rather than from a detached position outside.

The very practice of writing fiction in English inevitably means positioning one's writing in relation to the 'traditional' forms, techniques and practices of the English literary tradition: conventions such as linear narrative, the development of character, and detailed empirical description. In postcolonialist texts, however, such techniques are often combined with the conscious and deliberate deployment of features of local, non-European traditions, whether oral or written. The result is a juxtaposition or cross-fertilization of genres or modes which has obvious similarities with postmodern forms of narrative. Prominent examples (returned to below) are Salman Rushdie's *Midnight's Children*, which marries the conventions of the Indian oral narrative tradition with those of the European genre of the *Bildungsroman*, and Ishmael Reed's *Mumbo Jumbo*, which articulates African identity from 'inside' the distinctively European–American genre of the detective story.

This stylistic similarity services a broadly similar philosophical position, too. Both postmodernism and postcolonialism challenge the notion of a single authoritative viewpoint which claims to be universal, which conceives of human beings as sharing an 'essential' core of subjectivity, and which is associated with European Enlightenment thought. The multicultural world we live in would seem to bear little relation to this picture, which seems designed to serve the majority and keep everyone in their place.

But we must acknowledge at this point that some postcolonial theorists have been troubled by the comparison between postmodern and postcolonial 'experience'. 'The "post" in post-colonial', as Ashcroft, Griffiths and Tiffin insist in an oft-quoted refrain, 'is not the same as the "post" in postmodernism' (Ashcroft, Griffiths and Tiffin, 1995, 118). They contend that postmodernity is just too *abstract* to be considered an experience the way postcoloniality can. Unlike postcolonialism, postmodernism 'doesn't appear to be the primary framework within which most of the world's population carries out its daily life' (118). Similarly, Simon During has argued that making a case about postmodernity being a condition which affects us all, a framework in which 'we' all live, means that the idea of *difference* is wiped out – rather ironically given the impetus of much postmodern thought (During, 1995, 125).

Yet aside from the problem of postmodernity, the fact is that the use of postmodernism in a more qualified sense of 'narrative technique' has been much less contentious in postcolonialist criticism. In this area the focus has been on how in certain texts an attitude of self-reflexivity about narrative in general, and historiography in particular – an attitude which is commonly defined as postmodern – facilitates postcolonial critique. This is what the readings of postmodern–postcolonial novels in this chapter will concentrate upon.

Narrative, in the form of metanarratives or smaller-scale rhetorical myths, is one of the principal means by which a dominant group within society can impose its values upon those it subjugates. This is made clear in the Chinese–American Maxine Hong Kingston's notable combination of fiction and memoir, *The Woman Warrior* (1975). Kingston's own identity, as the memoir shows, has been constructed through stories, primarily the cautionary tales her mother used to tell her to try to shape her into a subordinate good wife, true to Chinese custom and those cultural narratives which put pressure on her to be 'American-feminine'. But in *The Woman Warrior* Kingston effectively reclaims these narratives by rewriting them, making them her own. She demonstrates that just as narrative can be an ideological weapon, so it can also function as a response to ideology. Her memoir suggests that interrogating narrative is really about interrogating historiography.

Postmodern–postcolonial writing repeatedly suggests that the writing of history is the chief ideological means of imprisoning subjects in a subordinate social and political position. It is not surprising, then, that Linda Hutcheon's category 'historiographic metafiction' is frequently brought into the discussion in studies of contemporary postmodern–postcolonial fiction in Britain and the United States. Both postmodernism and postcolonialism, Hutcheon suggests, are engaged in a 'dialogue with history' (Hutcheon, 1995, 131). Both are reconstructing their relationship with a previous historical moment: modernism's 'ahistoricism', in the case of postmodernism, and the imposed culture of an imperial power, in the case of postcolonialism. Indeed from Hutcheon's perspective modernism can be considered the cultural counterpart of any particular colonial power because of its elitism, its impulse towards totalization, and its habit of appropriating 'local' artistic practices.

As we saw in the previous chapter, British historiographic metafiction, typically the product of white, bourgeois, Oxbridge-educated novelists, deals with history in a general, 'philosophical' sense, developing a powerful argument-in-fiction about how history works and is to be understood. A more 'postcolonial' kind of historiographic metafiction shows the more specific effects of history on a particular people. This point requires some clarification. Of course a historiographic metafiction like Swift's *Waterland* is deeply interested in the effects of history and geography on the people of the Fens region of England. However, the Crick family's experience is clearly intended to stand for Everyman's – as their names, Tom, Dick and Henry (Harry), suggest. This claim to universality is problematic from a postcolonialist perspective.

The three postmodern–postcolonial novels which are the focus of the following discussion – Salman Rushdie's *Midnight's Children*, Toni Morrison's *Beloved*, and Ishmael Reed's *Mumbo Jumbo* – could each be considered examples of historiographic metafiction. Each shows that official colonial history must be confronted by what we might call 'cultural memory', an alternative way of accessing the truth of the past through narrative which depends upon the collective memories, as flawed and partial as they are, of subjugated peoples. As a result, each of them chooses not to tell a straightforward, linear story about the past from a stable narratorial perspective but presents the reader instead with a far more challenging, multi-layered, discontinuous, even rhizomatic, narrative from a varying or unreliable narratorial point of view. Each merges together, or 'cannibalizes' (to use a provocative term from postcolonial theory) a set of conventional genres – classic realism, fantasy, Gothic ghost story, detective fiction – to challenge the notion of a single overarching metanarrative. Each, we might say, puts postmodern approaches to narrative to use in a precise political way.

Despite the understandable objections voiced by postcolonial theorists about claiming postmodernism as a general condition which can 'explain' the postcolonial, these novels suggest that the postmodern approach to narrative can usefully be regarded by those analysing some examples of postcolonial fiction as a set of general 'laws' according to which the *specific* debates addressed within the individual texts can be better understood. All narrative, postmodernism asserts, can never be universal nor objective but is always, by definition, partial, incomplete, and manipulated by its narrator for rhetorical or political purposes. The impact of this 'truth' on a specific people is what postcolonial fiction by Rushdie, Morrison and Reed powerfully portrays. Most important of all, the way postmodern narrative implicitly implores its readers to consider their role *as* readers takes on an extra urgency in postmodern–postcolonial fiction. Each of the three novels appeals to its readers to actively respond to what it tells them.

Salman Rushdie, *Midnight's Children*

Midnight's Children can be (and has been: see Lee, 1990) considered an exemplary British historiographic metafiction. It emerged at the same point in the early 1980s as other classic examples such as Swift's *Waterland*, D.M. Thomas's *The White Hotel*, and Barnes's *Flaubert's Parrot*. The parallel with *Waterland* is particularly valid, given Rushdie's novel's rambling, digressive first-person narrative, which constantly eludes its narrator's efforts to control it. Saleem

Sinai is troubled by the fact that '[t]he different parts of my somewhat compli-cated life refuse, with a wholly unreasonable obstinacy, to stay neatly in their separate compartments' (Rushdie, 1981, 187).

Like Swift in *Waterland*, Rushdie uses his novel's complex structure to demonstrate how the patterns of history impact directly on the lives of indi-viduals. Saleem refers to himself as 'handcuffed to history' because he is born precisely at the stroke of midnight on 15 August 1947 – the exact date his-tory records as marking 'India's arrival at independence' (9). This momentous accident of birth, which befalls other children too, explains Rushdie's title. The midnight children come to embody 'the new India, the dream we all shared'. It means they are 'only partially the offspring of their parents – the children of midnight were also the children *of the time*: fathered, you understand, by history' (118).

The inseparability of the individual and the historical is emphasized even more literally in *Midnight's Children* through the conceit of having Saleem's body transform throughout the novel in correspondence with the fate of the nation. His face itself comes to resemble a map of India, its blemishes repre-senting Pakistan (because, as his sadistic geography teacher Zagallo remarks, 'Pakistan ees a stain on the face of India!' [232]). Gradually his face splits and cracks, he loses a finger, then part of his scalp and hair, as the nation is scarred from conflict or its boundaries shift. At one level this might be seen as an iron-ically literal representation of the concept of the 'decentred' or 'split' subject. But the novel's literal depiction of 'human geography' (231) (as Zagallo puns) is a striking way of conveying just how powerfully the workings of history can become *imprinted* upon our sense of who we are.

Oddly, though, for all its preoccupation with writing India's history, the history in *Midnight's Children* is marred by obvious errors and embellishments. The most notorious of these is when Saleem claims Indira Gandhi had been accused by her son Sanjay for bringing about her husband Feroze's death (421). This – in an episode which confirms how dynamic the ontological confusion generated by historiographic metafiction can be – resulted in Indira Gandhi successfully prosecuting Rushdie for libel in 1984, forcing him to read out a public apology in court and his publisher to remove the passage from future editions of the novel. But more significant is Saleem's admission that he had previously made an 'error in chronology' and used the wrong date in recounting of the assassination of Mahatma Gandhi (166). This immediately leads us to question the veracity of everything else we have been told in the novel, and to question Saleem's reliability as self-appointed historian.

But here we have to understand that *Midnight's Children* does not in fact set out to provide an alternative to the 'official', colonial narrative of India.

The novel is deliberately booby-trapped as a signal that it is not to be read for its accuracy. Accuracy is not easy to determine when it comes to the history of a postcolonial nation, because reality has been swallowed up into the historiography of its colonizers. Saleem states that

> in a country where the truth is what it is instructed to be, reality quite literally ceases to exist, so that everything becomes possible except what we are told is the case; and maybe this was the difference between my Indian childhood and Pakistani adolescence – that in the first I was beset by an infinity of alternative realities, while in the second I was adrift, disorientated, amid an equally infinite number of falsenesses, unrealities and lies.   (Rushdie, 1981, 326)

Colonial rule depends upon the ideological activity of reconstructing history in the image of the present. This has the effect of erasing from the record crucial building blocks needed to construct a counter-history. In these circumstances, in the absence of reliable histories of an oppressed or colonized people, *memory* becomes crucial – however flawed it may be – because it is, as Catherine Cundy puts it in her study of Rushdie, 'the chain which connects the postcolonial subject to his or her disrupted history' (Cundy, 1996, 35). The equation between memory and identity is emphasized most directly in *Midnight's Children* when Saleem is hit on the head by a flying spittoon and goes into a state of amnesia, thus losing not only his memory but his entire sense of who he is.

As Cundy points out, 'In terms of history as it affects the individual, it does not matter *when* Gandhi was assassinated, only that he *was*, and how this impinged on the individual and collective consciousnesses of Indian citizens' (Cundy, 1996, 33). Even an alternative, personalized, and fictionalized story like Saleem's nevertheless has historical validity. He makes it clear through the text that the India he represents in his book is *his* India, one that bears a strong relation to the real nation and its history, but which is also a simulacrum in the Baudrillardian sense, a map which 'precedes the territory': 'in my India, Gandhi will continue to die at the wrong time' (Rushdie, 1981, 166). Saleem's memory may be flawed but at least it is *his* memory.

During the moment of soul-searching which results from recognizing his error, Saleem asks, 'Does one error invalidate the entire fabric?' (166). Of course the question is rhetorical: the answer can only be no. The novel implies that the fabric of narratives is the only chance we have of determining *any* meaning. While it repeats the 'message' of other historiographic metafictions, that history is purely a narrative entity, *Midnight's Children* also affirms the opposite: personal narratives, outright fictions even, are legitimate forms of history.

And this points to another significant difference between Rushdie's novel and 'white' historiographic metafiction. Rushdie's novel, for all its intertextual references to narratives in the European literary tradition, such as Laurence Sterne's *Tristram Shandy*, Günther Grass's *The Tin Drum*, and Forster's *A Passage to India*, is equally influenced by the vast, convoluted narratives in Eastern literature, such as Scheherazade's *1000 Nights* or the Indian epics *The Mahabharata* and *Ramayana*. Rushdie himself has described the novel in terms of the non-linear movements of Indian oral narrative, a form which 'goes in spirals or in loops, it every so often reiterates something that happened earlier to remind you, and then takes you off again, sometimes summarises itself, it frequently digresses off into something that the story teller appears just to have thought of, then comes back to the main thrust of the narrative' (Rushdie, 1985, 7–8). In keeping with this oral narrative context, the reader of *Midnight's Children* feels very much 'spoken to' throughout the novel, and not just because there is a built-in narratee, Padma, Saleem's lover and his 'necessary ear' (Rushdie, 1981, 149), who listens and responds to his narrative as it goes on. Saleem persistently appeals to his reader to discern the 'meaning' of his narratives. On the first page he tells us he will soon die and so 'must work fast, faster than Scheherazade, if I am to end up meaning – yes, meaning – something. I admit it: above all things I fear absurdity' (9).

Yet it would be a mistake to think that our task is to assemble the bits and pieces of the novel into one coherent biography of its narrator or an alternative history of India. Lyotard's rhetoric in *The Postmodern Condition* is not that we replace each metanarrative with a better one, but that we accept the validity of numerous localized, personalized, '*petits récits*' (Lyotard, 1984, 20). Reading *Midnight's Children* shows us that there is no one single truth about India which we must figure out, but that there are numerous competing 'truths'. History can only be encountered meaningfully by comparing, or 'swallowing', to use Saleem's own metaphor, a diet of narratives rather than subjecting oneself to one overarching narrative. 'And there are so many stories to tell, too many', he remarks at the beginning, 'such an excess of intertwined lives events miracles places rumours, so dense a commingling of the improbable and the mundane! I have been a swallower of lives; and to know me, just the one of me, you'll have to swallow the lot as well' (9).

Toni Morrison, *Beloved*

Cultural memory is even more central to Toni Morrison's *Beloved*, a novel which also uses its complex non-linear narrative structure to rewrite history.

Just as *Midnight's Children* complicates an area of existing historical knowledge, *Beloved* was conceived deliberately as a way of addressing what its author termed a 300-year-long 'national amnesia' about the subject of slavery. The need to fill in the gap means the reader of *Beloved* feels implored to respond to the narrative even more urgently than in the case of *Midnight's Children*. Its narrative structure effectively turns us into witnesses rather than just observers, urged to share the novel's judgements on history.

The novel is based on a real event which occurred in Kentucky in 1856, when an escaped slave called Margaret Garner chose to kill her own daughter rather than have her endure the suffering and degradation of being taken back into slavery. *Beloved*'s central character Sethe cuts her two-year-old daughter 'Beloved's' throat with a saw at the point of recapture for the same reason. She also tries to kill her two boys, and contemplates slaughtering her youngest daughter, Denver. It is difficult to imagine a more horrific act. Yet placing it at the heart of her novel enables Morrison powerfully to inform readers distanced by time about the horrors of the forgotten Holocaust (*Beloved*'s dedication page states simply 'Sixty Million and more') at the heart of American history. The idea of a mother killing her own baby daughter seems incomprehensible, beyond sympathy, yet the novel forces us to consider the brutal context that made such an act possible.

Beloved explodes the myth of the 'paternalist' system of slavery in the American South, which imagines black slaves as part of the extended family of a stern yet ultimately benign slavemaster. The reality was that the slaves were forced to work until breaking point in the plantations, were denied personal and family relationships that free white people took for granted, and were frequently subjected to violent abuse and humiliation. Sethe's murder of Beloved is counterbalanced by numerous acts of violence against her and her fellow slaves by their white masters on a farm ironically named 'Sweet Home' in Kentucky. A month before the murder Sethe had been whipped to the point of death before being chained up and having to endure two white boys sucking mockingly at her lactating breasts while the slavemaster looked on. Her own mother was hanged, probably for trying to flee the house where she was a slave, and one of the male slaves, Sixo, is roasted alive by the slavemaster. Even after Beloved's death Sethe is forced to have sex in order that the headstone is engraved. This is why her daughter, unnamed at the time of the murder, is known as 'Beloved', for she is still unable to afford the full inscription 'Dearly Beloved' (Morrison, 1987, 5).

With such horrific details of the everyday realities of life on the plantation, Morrison fills in the void in the established historical narrative. But she also intended *Beloved* to fill the gaps in a particular form of literary narrative.

Her interest in the topic of slavery was triggered by reading slave narratives, a genre of African-American writing which has become of particular interest to scholars of American literature in recent years. A huge number of autobiographical accounts of the experience of being a slave were produced by black African-Americans in 1840–60. They are valuable because they are personal testimonies from a community rendered voiceless by their experience, and useful to historians for the details they provide about life as a slave.

Yet they are also subject to heavy self-censorship. As Morrison has described it herself, slave narratives 'had to be authenticated by white patrons'. This means that the texts typically 'draw a veil' over the most horrific incidents in the authors' lives. They also tend to conform to a Biblical narrative trajectory, presenting their authors as sinners seeking redemption through the suffering of being a slave, a convention which points to the importance in the slave houses of indoctrinating slaves through religious education. What struck Morrison was that while the slave narrative is an autobiographical genre on the face of it, missing from its examples is a sense of who the writers really are, what they thought and how they felt: 'while I looked at the documents and felt familiar with slavery and overwhelmed by it, I wanted it to be truly felt. I wanted to translate the historical into the personal' (Schappell, 1993, 103).

Beloved, then, is a fictionalized slave narrative which, ironically, has greater truth claims than authentic slave narratives which were fictionalized for ideological reasons. Making a narrative more obviously artificial in order to present a range of 'truths' is a typically postmodern ironic strategy. And just as its fiction can suggest a more accurate 'truth', so the obvious 'constructedness' of *Beloved*'s discontinuous and fragmented narrative (considered one of the novel's most postmodern elements) conveys a truth about the workings of memory.

Reading the novel is a process of being presented with pieces of narrative from a variety of different time periods without an indication of when they took place and how they connect. This structure places special demands on the reader who, in order to understand what happens in the story has to assemble the narrative fragments into a chronological, ordered sequence. The 'present' of *Beloved* is 1873. Sethe is now living with Denver in Cincinnati as a free woman, having been spared the death sentence after the intervention of abolitionists, though she continues to be shunned by the black community for her actions. At the beginning of the novel she is reunited with one of the male slaves, Paul D. (whose name signifies his status as property rather than a member of a family), who has escaped from prison in Georgia and come to Ohio. His attempt to seek her out suggests that the black community is finally ready to forgive Sethe. Soon Paul D. moves in with her and they become lovers, and attempt to start a family. Through representing the consciousness of both characters and their conversations, the novel repeatedly revisits their pasts as slaves in the period from 1850 until 1855, the year of the death of Beloved.

The novel's refusal to detail past events in a chronological, linear sequence is quite appropriate, as both Sethe and Paul D. are determined to banish the past from their minds. We are told near the start that Sethe is trying as hard as she can 'to remember as close to nothing as was safe' (Morrison, 1987, 6). But she is quite unable to prevent vivid images of the past returning, not just horrific ones, such as young slaves hanging from the trees in the plantation, but also pictures of the sheer natural beauty of Sweet Home Farm's surroundings. In many ways the memories of beauty trouble her more, for her memory seems unwilling to distinguish between pain and happiness. It never refuses any image or event, no matter how horrific, and is always 'greedy for more': 'Why was there nothing it refused?' (70). This sense that memory has an agency all of its own takes further *Midnight's Children*'s emphasis on the elusiveness of the past.

Beloved's insistence on the dynamic power of memory has a counterpart as plot device, and this is the ghost of Beloved. From the moment she is buried, Beloved has literally been haunting Sethe's and Denver's house, 124 Bluestone, in the manner of a poltergeist. The visitations have long since caused Sethe's two sons, Buglar and Howard, to flee. Although Paul D. banishes the ghost from the house '[w]ith a table and a loud male voice' (37) soon after moving in, it is replaced by an even more disruptive presence, in the form of a mysterious young woman named – uncannily it seems – Beloved. The ghost-baby appears to have metamorphized and materialized into a young woman of exactly the age Sethe's daughter would have been had she lived. She immediately splits Sethe and Paul D. apart, causing him to leave their bed and eventually sleep outside the house in the open air. Then she seduces him. Sethe becomes obsessed with her, too, and gives up her job, her health deteriorating as if her very identity is being sucked out of her by Beloved.

Beloved is an extraordinary creation (the term 'character' does not quite seem appropriate for her). She is vulnerable, lonely, vindictive, full of rage and sexual desire, but also capable of great tenderness. She seems to be searching for all the dead infant was denied: life, love, sexual experience, vengeance. Rather than a single individual, she seems to be composed of the spirits of many other women, such as Sethe's mother-in-law Baby Suggs or even the comic little girl Topsy in *Uncle Tom's Cabin* (one of *Beloved*'s key intertexts). Her indeterminacy has prompted critics to see her as an example of postmodern characterization where character is not presented as coherent and stable but as something multifarious and endlessly 'in process' (see Duvall, 2000). Besides the uncanniness of memory itself she might also be regarded as a representative of the millions of other black people killed or silenced by slavery, or even (according to the epigraph of the novel, from Romans 9:25) one of the Israelites, cast out then forgiven by God for betraying Him: 'I will call them my people, / which were not my people; / and her beloved, / which was not beloved'.

One of Beloved's functions in the novel is to ensure that any attempt to reassemble the fragments of the narrative into a coherent order, the way one might with a non-linear modernist narrative like *The Good Soldier*, remains frustrated. Within the represented world of the story, it is impossible to decide whether the young woman Beloved is in fact a materialized ghost, the spirit of Sethe's dead daughter, or if she is simply an unhinged young woman who just happens to have the same name as a dead person. In this respect *Beloved* conforms to the tendency of postmodern narrative to keep conjectural possibilities open. We cannot dismiss the character of Beloved as being 'unreal', nor decide that she is 'real'. All we can do is say that she is both simultaneously. As such she parallels the operation of time in the novel. So vivid are Sethe's memories, and so unable is she to exert control over them, that the clear distinction between past and present is collapsed: living in the present means also living in the past.

This is a rhizomatic rather than arborescent approach to time, and as a result the novel's structure in fact resembles another rhizomatic organism, the unconscious. Sigmund Freud held that the unconscious can acknowledge no distinction between past and present, nor between right and wrong or good or bad. One of the prominent critical moves in discussing *Beloved* has been to consider it in relation to psychoanalytic theory, especially its understanding of trauma. Trauma (which comes from the Greek word for 'wound') is something too painful to be experienced directly, but which nevertheless – in keeping with the mechanism of the unconscious – makes itself felt in a displaced or disguised way. It only makes itself known through its representations, that is, by finding an outlet where it can disguise itself or displace itself onto other things, such as neurotic symptoms or dream.

Critics such as Peter Nicholls and Jill Matus have argued that structurally Morrison's novel replicates the structure of trauma (Nicholls, 1996; Matus, 1998). The narrative in *Beloved* 'enacts a circling or repetition around the traumatic event', the scene in the woodshed, which Matus calls the story's 'unspeakable heart' (Matus, 1998, 112). Although Sethe is tormented by her inability to prevent images from the past returning, there is one memory which never appears in her mind directly, and that is of the actual events in the woodshed when she murdered her daughter.

The episode is eventually rendered in terrible, haunting detail, though this is not until over half-way through the novel. It is focalized through the consciousness of 'schoolteacher', the brutal white owner of the plantation who has caught up with Sethe and her family following their escape. Doing so means that Morrison can powerfully present us with an insight into the mindset of the white slavemasters, who regard the black slaves as sub-human beings, equivalent in value to farm beasts. Schoolteacher is disturbed by Sethe's violence but only because it results in damage to some valuable stock and demonstrates that white masters must not 'mishandle' their black slaves (Morrison, 1987, 149). But confining the episode to schoolteacher's perspective also means that Sethe remains shielded from remembering the events in the woodshed herself.

Freud argues that trauma must be dealt with by a particular kind of confrontation, which psychoanalysis specializes in engineering: a full act of 'remembering' rather than merely continuing to 'repeat' neurotically (Freud, 1991). To remember trauma is effectively to 'act' upon it, rather than allow it to dictate our behaviour. This gives us a model for the patterns of repetition in the novel. The disruptive interventions of Beloved function as uncanny repetitions in the lives of Sethe and Paul D. signalling that they are both continuing to 'repeat' the past in psychoanalytic terms rather than properly 'remember' it. Indeed this is something which has been clear from the outset. In beginning with two returns from the past, Paul D.'s and Beloved's, the plot emphasizes that the past is something that must be confronted.

What is especially powerful about *Beloved* is the way its postmodernist narrative structure dovetails with this Freudian logic. The novel's complexity means that the reader is put in the position of traumatized subject. It is only on a second reading that we fully comprehend the overall framework and hence the significance of each narrative segment. The novel thus begs us to re-read it, and to do so is to 'remember' it rather than allow it to continue 'repeating' events – in other words, surprising and shocking us with its violence and Gothic elements. Because Sethe cannot 'remember' the events of the woodshed directly, it means that we need to do it for her, take on the burden.

This is a collective task, and something the novel has carefully insisted upon throughout. Although the main 'victim' of the past is perhaps Sethe, the fact that Paul D. is there with her, also burdened by his own memories (symbolized by his carrying a rusty tobacco tin round his neck containing mementoes from the past), emphasizes that this is a trauma that must be confronted together. The sense of a collective engagement with the past is strengthened by the idea of 'rememory' – an idea in which Sethe believes – which states that momentous past events leave their traces on the real world, and can also mean that one person's experience can become 'remembered' by someone else (Morrison, 1987, 35–6). Rememory thus disrupts conventional notions of time, and complicates the idea of separate, coherent identities.

Sethe's need to come to terms with the past, then, is something shared by the readers of the novel. However plausible we consider the idea of rememory in real life, there is one space where rememory does operate, and that is fiction. Reading a novel causes us to take on the memories of its characters as our own. *Beloved* represents Morrison's challenge to her readership – especially an American one – to overcome the 'national amnesia' about slavery and 'remember' it fully. It is therefore a novel with an insistent message, though its triumph is that this message is delivered without didacticism but by the text remaining a puzzle that cannot completely be solved. *Beloved* never lapses into theoretical polemic but remains a beautiful, shocking work of art.

Ishmael Reed, *Mumbo Jumbo*

Given its sheer stylistic exuberance Ishmael Reed's *Mumbo Jumbo* (1972) is even more obviously 'postmodern' than *Beloved* or *Midnight's Children*. In it, passages of original narrative are punctuated continuously by reproductions of historical documents such as paintings, period advertisements, photographs, song lyrics, and a facsimile of a handwritten letter, as well as different textual forms like dramatic dialogue, epigraphs, quotations, and footnotes, and visual effects such as drawings, cartoons, shaded areas and extensive capitalized or italicized passages. The first chapter comes before the epigraphs and title page, and the novel ends with a 'Partial Bibliography' of 104 items.

Its juxtaposition of numerous different kinds of texts – often by other authors than Reed – is once again reminiscent of Burroughs's 'cut-up' method, though instead of 'punk' as a musical analogy for *Mumbo Jumbo*'s style, a more appropriate one would be jazz. As one of Reed's major influences, the writer Ralph Ellison, once told him in an interview: 'anywhere I find a critic who has an idea or a concept that seems useful, I grab it. Eclecticism is the word. Like a jazz musician who creates his own style from the styles around him, I play by ear' (Ellison, 1978, 132).

As such the novel is as parodic and textually inventive as anything by Coover or Barth, and can be seen as emerging from the same melting-pot of metafictional experimentation and left-wing social awareness which produced the US metafictionists. However, Reed is dedicated to developing 'the true Afro-American aesthetic' in his writing (Martin, 1984, n.p.), and this suggests that *Mumbo Jumbo*'s intertextuality is less about deconstructing previous traditions such as realism and modernism and more about productively mapping out African–American culture, from the slave narratives to modernists such as Ellison. This is born out by the vast number of intertextual allusions in *Mumbo*

Jumbo (mapped out by Henry Louis Gates Jr's exhaustive reading of the novel in his book *Figures of Black*) to texts not just in the Black American tradition but to key influences on this tradition, such as Egyptian mythology.

Reed's emphasis on the 'Afro-American aesthetic' suggests, too, that the novel, as literary form, may be conceived differently by black writers to the white American metafictionists of the 1960s. Because the African–American experience has tended to be more extensively explored in other media, primarily music (and music is one of *Mumbo Jumbo*'s subjects), it means the novel retains a freshness and sense of potential for black American writing which has disappeared from its 'exhausted' white counterpart.

Comparing Reed with the white American metafictionists might even lead us to consider more dynamically the relation between postmodernism and postcolonialism in a specifically American context. While American literary theory and practice undoubtedly share a critical heritage with its European counterparts, drawing on the same European theorists such as Foucault, Derrida, Lyotard, etc., the fact is also that US culture is *itself* thoroughly 'postcolonial' as a result of the nation's multicultural history. Reed has pointed to a prevalent misunderstanding about the United States, that it is 'an extension of European civilization' (Martin, 1984). As *Mumbo Jumbo* demonstrates, the nation is just as much influenced by Africa. Rather than regarding postmodernism as something which suddenly erupts in American writing in the 1960s as a 'decentring force', one which undermines 'the categories of a universal authority', it can be regarded instead as a confirmation of 'the essentially subversive nature of much American literature throughout its development: subversive, that is, of the authority of the European centre and its forms and expectations' (Ashcroft, Griffiths and Tiffin, 1988, 163).

If we follow this logic, we might be led to conclude that American literature is always already postmodern. More plausibly, though, we might argue that American literature can be regarded as profoundly shaped by postcolonial experience from the outset; it is writing which has always, at some level, set out to subvert Eurocentric metanarratives. The subversive, parodic elements we associate with postmodernism can be regarded, as Reed suggests in *Mumbo Jumbo*, as rooted in African art and culture.

Mumbo Jumbo gears its self-reflexive pyrotechnics towards examining the cultural expression of blackness and what this signifies in modern white (American) civilization. It focuses on a real historical period: what is commonly regarded as the beginning of the 'Jazz Age' in the 1920s in the US, a time when Black American music – jazz, ragtime and blues – and their associated lifestyle and values suddenly exploded into popular culture. One of the key triggers for this 'Negro vogue' was the 'Harlem Renaissance', the impact of a community of black artists associated with the Harlem neighbourhood of New York City in the 1920s and early 1930s (including writers such as Langston Hughes and Zora Neale Hurston).

The novel's term for this moment, however, is 'Jes Grew'. This curious label can be explained by a statement in *The Book of American Negro Poetry* by the black writer James Weldon Johnson, included as an epigraph in *Mumbo Jumbo*, which affirms that 'The earliest Ragtime songs, like Topsy, "jes' grew"'. Topsy, the little girl in Stowe's *Uncle Tom's Cabin* (1852), has never known her parents, and when asked (in stage versions of the novel popular in the early 1850s) if she knew who made her, she replies, 'I jes' grew!'

The fact that *Uncle Tom's Cabin* trades on numerous racist stereotypes of black people, even though it was written by an abolitionist, signals immediately that the name Jes Grew is treated ironically by the novel. The idea of its sudden eruption sums up the unease of the white authorities in the face of a dangerous carnivalesque force. Carnival, as the literary philosopher Bakhtin argues, is an oppositional energy – exhibited at its purest in actual street carnivals which permits the subjugated to have a momentary outlet for their frustrations in the form of fun and laughter – which works to undo the strict hierarchies and codes of behaviour by which modern, Western, Enlightenment society is organized.

From the outset the novel plays on the idea of the music as 'infectious', as something one cannot help dancing or tapping one's foot to, and as a phenomenon whose popularity spreads rapidly, by describing it as a plague. The first chapter makes it clear that this is in fact an 'anti-plague', for where plagues are normally 'accompanied by bad air [. . .] Jes Grew victims said that the air was as clear as they had ever seen it and that there was the aroma of roses and perfumes which had never before enticed their nostrils' (Reed, 1972, 6). However, the (white) authorities in New Orleans and across the American South treat it as if it were a real outbreak, and marshall all their resources to stamp it out.

It becomes clear early on in the novel that what Jes Grew really stands for is the energy and vibrancy associated with *blackness*. Blackness is presented by the book as a force signifying freedom of language, body and also thought which exists in powerful opposition to the repressive, ordered value-systems of 'whiteness'. Music is indeed the most palpable signifier of blackness. Black music, which realistically can be considered the roots of all the dominant contemporary musical styles (rock n' roll, soul, rap, hip hop and R&B), has had an enormous influence on post-war US – and consequently British and

European – 'white' popular culture throughout the twentieth and twenty-first centuries, shaping social phenomena such as lifestyle, language, and fashion. This is a very powerful kind of cultural 'colonization', and there seems to be a special irony that such a subjugated part of the American population (especially so during the time of *Mumbo Jumbo*'s composition in the early 1970s) could wield so much cultural influence.

But the other reason why the name Jes Grew is to be taken ironically is that African–American music did not simply explode out of nowhere in the 1920s. Rather the moment was itself prepared for by previous cultural conditions and practices. The poet Franklin Rosemont has argued that twentieth-century black American music 'originated in the culture of the slaves who were systematically deprived of the more "refined" instruments of human expression' (Salaam, 1995, 351). They were prevented from reading or writing, and even from using drums or other instruments in case these were used as a call to arms to other groups of slaves nearby. This meant that other modes of creative expression, such as writing or art, were denied to them and they had no option but to direct their creative energies towards the spoken word, chanting, or rhythmical movement, the kind of activities permissible on the plantation.

Music, then, is a clear example of how one can read an entire cultural history into a cultural practice. Black music was shaped by the experience of slavery and its very nature can be interpreted as a response to this experience and its social consequences. It is not enough, Kalamu ya Salaam argues, to claim that black music is influential because it is 'so good'. The fact is that it is good because in America 'where our people were uniformly denied the opportunities of concrete expression and mass assembly, all our soul was poured into the ephemerality of music' (Salaam, 1995, 353). Far from being a creation that 'jes grew', music is to black Americans,

> our mother tongue. Our music is a language used not only to express ourselves, but also to assert ourselves in world affairs. Additionally [it] serves as a unifying force in our external conflict with our colonizers and as a unifying force in encouraging us to struggle against the internalization of oppressive concepts as well as struggle against our own weaknesses. (Salaam, 1995, 375)

These arguments serve as a useful summary of what are perhaps the two driving forces behind Reed's novel: its interest in what constitutes 'blackness', and its very structuralist assumption that every cultural phenomenon 'means' something only *in relation to* other things. Cultural forms and specific texts do not 'just grow' out of nothing.

While it is 'about' music on its surface, *Mumbo Jumbo* is really more deeply concerned with literature. This is clear from its paratextual form, and also from the way it deals with its comic-thriller plot. *Mumbo Jumbo* spins out a yarn that shows the spread of Jes Grew is no accident, but is because the 'plague' is deliberately travelling from the American South to New York in order to 'cohabit' with its 'text'. 'Jes Grew is seeking its words. Its text', we are informed early on. 'For what good is liturgy without a text?' (Reed, 1972, 6). Realizing this, the authorities enlist the help of a detective, PaPa LaBas, to discover its source and to get to the text before Jes Grew can.

The idea of a search for a key text is a dominant motif in a particular sub-genre of postmodern writing (which we shall consider fully in Chapter 7), the 'metaphysical' or 'anti-' detective story. LaBas's quest means that *Mumbo Jumbo* is on one level a parody of detective fiction in both its classic English 'clue-puzzle' and American 'private-eye' forms, which becomes positively Borgesian in its expansion from a basic thriller plot into a vast conspiracy ranging across history and involving hidden texts. This expansion is what makes it a postmodern detective novel, as it frustrates the reader's desire to arrive at the satisfying closure provided in classic detective fiction. LaBas calls himself 'a jack-legged detective of the metaphysical who was on the case' (211–12), and the novel's fragmented form invites its reader to become 'literary detective', moving from one extract or parody to another in an effort to decode what it all means, only to find there is no satisfactory solution. Even though LaBas finds out who the murderer is, the mysterious Jes Grew text is never found.

Thus *Mumbo Jumbo* provides a postcolonial spin to the critique of the Enlightenment which drives postmodern detective fiction. The implication – as Richard Swope has argued – is that the framework of classic detective fiction is representative of the puritanical Western/Eurocentric tradition of rationalist thought which Reed seeks to challenge (Swope, 2002).

LaBas does manage to trace the recent explosion of Jes Grew back to an ancient Egyptian dance craze which had taken New Orleans by storm in the 1890s and to discover that Jes Grew is a combination of three African traditions: African dance, the Egyptian myth of Osiris, and Haitian voodoo. Its genealogy suggests that, of course, the Jes Grew 'text' (which is actually called the 'Book of Thoth', named after another Egyptian God) symbolizes more than simply the spirit of the Jazz Age but nothing less than what Gates terms 'the text of blackness' itself. In other words Jes Grew is a manifestation of the very essence of African–American culture, the vitality of which makes it so influential and subversive to white American culture (representatives of which in the novel are called 'the Atonists', an Egyptian mythological term denoting the dehumanizing ethic associated with the god Set, in contrast to impulses towards natural expression associated with the god Osiris).

Mumbo Jumbo's openness about the 'constructed' nature of texts is why Gates considers the novel an exemplary postmodern one. *Mumbo Jumbo* flaunts its intertextuality rather than conceals it 'under the illusion of unity', as a modernist text does. The 'Partial Bibliography' is the most obvious example of this deliberate exposure, as its references demonstrate that all texts 'are intertexts, full of intratexts. Our notions of originality, [Reed's] critique suggests, are more related to convention and material relationships than to some supposedly transcendent truth' (Gates, 1989, 256).

This suggests, in fact, that the idea of 'Jes Grew' or 'blackness' being reducible to an authoritative Word, or set of clear commandments, is untenable and runs counter to the very spirit of Jes Grew. It is not surprising that the Jes Grew text cannot be found. If Jes Grew signifies blackness, then blackness is not an essence, but a vast network of linked influences and traditions. It is not, in Gates's words, a 'transcendent signified', but rather something which 'must be produced in a dynamic process and manifested in discrete forms, as in black music and black speech acts' (Gates, 1989, 272).

Gates here offers a response to the critique of postmodernism advanced by another prominent African-American cultural critic, bell hooks, who had contended that the postmodern rhetoric against unified subjectivity was problematic at a point in history when black people, through popular cultural forms like rap music, were beginning successfully to articulate a positive and specifically 'black' identity. Even more controversially, Gates might be suggesting that just as we can regard American literature as always already postmodern so we might even see the spirit of blackness and postmodernism as equivalent.

The paradox implicit in his reading of the novel, however, is that while the novel may be read as affirming the impossibility of condensing blackness into a single text, it does point to a version of this text which actually exists – and that is itself. After all it is within Reed's complex, endlessly inventive and multi-layered narrative, and nowhere else, that the history of Jes Grew is comprehensively set out (even though it does this via postmodern self-reflexivity rather than modernist illusory unity). *Mumbo Jumbo* both 'jes grew' and didn't 'jes grew'. On one hand, like all fiction, it developed piece by piece out of an idea which Reed developed through historical research, textual appropriation and creative imagination. But, on the other hand, its paratextual, intertextual status means that it is the product of its author's immersion in popular and literary culture – not just black American but also (as the use of the detective genre shows) white as well.

We are by now familiar with the idea that one of the definitive aspects of post-modernism is its contradictory nature. *Mumbo Jumbo*, like other postmodern-postcolonial texts, shows that the use of postmodern literary form to explore the experience of a particular group of people has the effect of making this experience both specific and universal.

Chapter 6

Postmodern fiction by women: Carter, Atwood, Acker

Gender is an especially problematic issue when it comes to postmodern theory. A cursory glance at the roster of prominent names in the postmodern debate might lead to an obvious question: where have all the women gone? Indeed a version of this question informs part of the argument of two important contributions to the debate at its highpoint in the 1980s, Craig Owens's 'The Discourse of Others: Feminists and Postmodernism' (Owens, 1983) and Andreas Huyssen's 1984 essay, 'Mapping the Postmodern' (Huyssen, 2002). Their assumption is that feminism ought to find something of value in postmodernism, for it is about challenging authority and asserting difference.

These discussions by male theorists did serve to provoke many feminist theorists into the debate. Sandra Harding, for example, protested that feminism can only go so far in throwing out Enlightenment *ideals* (Enlightenment assumptions and prejudices are another matter), for, like Marxism, it is by definition committed to some of these, such as emancipation (Harding, 1990, 99). Sabina Lovibond took this argument further by identifying in the championing of postmodernist theoretical principles by male theorists 'a collective *fantasy* of masculinist agency or identity', one exposed by Owens's and Huyssen's assumption that it is humiliating to be 'caught out' – as they imply feminists are – 'longing for a world of human subjects sufficiently "centred" to speak to and understand one another' (Lovibond, 1989, 19).

Most powerfully, perhaps, the cultural critic Meaghan Morris pointed out that the very question implicitly posed by Owens and Huyssen was actually the problem. Wondering where all the women have gone is 'perhaps the latest version of the "why have there been no great women artists (mathematicians, scientists . . .)?" conundrum' (Morris, 2002, 393). Of course, as students on University English courses know as well as anyone, there *are* great women writers wherever we care to look in literary history. The problem is that for us to recognize them as 'great' they have to be isolated by literary critics from a masculinist frame of reference that limits them; they have to be judged on grounds other than those set out by masculinist views of art. Likewise, in the postmodern debate, argued Morris, important women theorists – and she cites many, including Hélène Cixous, Luce Irigaray, Gayatri Chakravorty Spivak, Jacqueline Rose, Donna Haraway, Teresa de Lauretis, Angela McRobbie, Judith Williamson – *have* shaped the postmodern debate but have then been excluded from the critical canon because they do not *explicitly* address the question of postmodernism or write within the theoretical parameters set by male theorists which mark the discussion.

For similar reasons, no doubt, the postmodern 'canon' has included relatively few women writers. It would be possible to make the case for others (e.g. Jeanette Winterson, Sarah Waters, Siri Hustvedt), though as an introduction to the novelists most consistently associated with the postmodern, this is not the job for this book. However, another feminist critic to address the question of postmodernism and feminism, Bonnie Zimmerman, argued in response to Owens and Huyssen that one of the problems of connecting the two when it comes to literature is that most women writers, no matter their feminist credentials, remain committed 'to realism, to creating an authentic female voice, and to portraying authentic female experience' (Zimmerman, 1986, 186). What is striking about the writers featured in this chapter is that this is not the case.

Angela Carter, Margaret Atwood, and Kathy Acker are the three female novelists who have been most consistently considered in the light of postmodern ideas (a fourth would be Toni Morrison, whose work we considered in the previous chapter.) Treating them in a chapter of their own runs the risk of suggesting that they somehow, as women, figure *outside* the postmodern mainstream, when in terms of the subject matter of their work (e.g. sexuality, subjectivity, history etc.) and its formal techniques (e.g. intertextuality, metafiction, 'cut-ups') their work is quite representative of postmodern aesthetics. Each draws freely and critically from the mass of literary and cultural myths which shape contemporary culture. But, at the same time, their work directs its postmodern techniques towards uncompromisingly feminist ends, continually insisting on what is different about female experience of the contemporary world and why this needs to be taken into account.

While they have certainly been appreciated by women readers and critics for having created an authentic voice and portraying female experience, the forms they write in are firmly anti-realist. There can be no doubt that – unlike many 'experimental' authors – this formal innovation has helped Atwood and Carter, in particular, become appreciated on a mass scale. Both are now central to the contemporary fiction canon, their work having generated a whole secondary industry of academic books, study notes and scholarly essays. The case is rather different for the 'aesthetic terrorist', Kathy Acker, but we'll come to this in due course.

Like postcolonial theorists, feminists have found it problematic to appropriate postmodern theory in their arguments. Postmodern *aesthetic* strategies, however, have proved useful to feminist novelists. More precisely, metafiction, a naturally critical strategy, a form of 'theory-in-practice', is employed by Carter and Atwood not to question just literary history but the kind of 'masculinist' discourse which has dominated history, science, and academic argument on a wider scale. More precisely, what each of these writers do is to use postmodern strategies in order to critique and subvert the Enlightenment metanarrative, but also caution against chipping away at it until there is *nothing* left.

Here their 'position' parallels the one adopted by the theorist Patricia Waugh, who has argued that postmodernism is valuable for its critical potential, as a kind of reading strategy which can question and subvert Enlightenment texts (literary realism or philosophy) but ought not to be imagined as contributing more directly to feminist politics, as pointing the way to a feminist way of life (Waugh, 1992). In particular, each of the three writers might be seen to be addressing what Lyotard identified as the demise of the metanarrative. Social and cultural perceptions of gender are sustained by a particular metanarrative which implies the universality of male experience, and that women are only objects in a male drama. Besides their various formal techniques, the work of these writers is postmodern in their continued challenging of this metanarrative.

Angela Carter

In her 1983 essay 'Notes from the Front Line', Angela Carter states that the 'investigation of the social fictions that regulate our lives . . . is what I've concerned myself with consciously' ever since the beginning of her career in the 1960s (Carter, 1997, 38). Exposing 'social fictions' is what we might consider an eminently 'postmodern' aim, one quite in tune with the kind of postmodern theory we discussed in the Introduction. At one level some of her novels can be read as *allegories* of the effects of postmodernity and postmodern ideas. Indeed Carter was quite at home with theory, and in her interviews happily discussed Barthes, Nietzsche and Foucault alongside medieval and nineteenth-century literature.

For all her learned quality, what is notable, though, is the sense of sheer *excess* that we get from reading Carter. Her prose is rich, heavy, intoxicating and sensual, packed with feelings, images, sounds, smells, elaborate metaphors and ideas. Her style is comic, gothic, grotesque, sexually explicit, and (as H. G. Wells famously said of Joyce) gratuitously 'cloacal' (Wells, 1917, 710).

Her plots, too, are nothing short of outrageous, featuring such things as a man being turned into a woman and a city under attack by a powerful 'desire machine'. Her characters are outlandish, monstrous figures, she-wolves and bird women. Her fiction is obviously non-realist, and generically 'promiscuous', ranging across, as Lorna Sage put it, 'romance, spies, porn, crime, gothic, science fiction' (Day, 1998, 9).

The most important 'social fiction' Carter wanted to explore was about gender. Her writing was a way of 'answering back' after years of 'being told what I ought to think, and how I ought to behave, and how I ought to write, even, because I was a woman and men thought they had a right to tell me how to feel' (Carter, 1993, 5). Deconstructing the gender metanarrative is clearly the function of one of her most celebrated collections of short stories, *The Bloody Chamber* (1979). Each story is a reworking of a different fairytale or myth – cultural narratives which perpetuate the overall masculinist metanarrative – as Andrea Dworkin's ironic description of the traditional fairytale reveals:

> The lessons are simple, and we learn them well. Men and women are different, absolute opposites. The heroic prince can never be confused with Cinderella, or Snow-White or Sleeping Beauty. She could never do what he does at all, let alone better. . . . Where he is erect, she is supine. Where he is awake, she is asleep. Where he is active, she is passive. Where she is erect, or awake, or active, she is evil and must be destroyed.
>
> (Dworkin, 1974, 79–80)

The title tale, for example, is a version of 'Bluebeard's Castle', one that is remarkably faithful to the conventional tale except that the heroine is saved by a mixture of her own ingenuity and her mother, rather than a band of brothers.

Carter's writing displays an exuberant delight in storytelling, apparently for its own sake – though she insisted that narrative was valuable as a way of fulfilling the fundamental human impulse to make sense of our own lives through narrative. She defined narrative as 'an argument stated in fictional terms' (Carter 1993, 2) and this is a useful way of describing her work's combination of narrative excess and philosophical debate. In what follows I will consider two novels which critics have tended to discuss in terms of postmodern philosophy, and which both demonstrate Carter's ability to create fables for our modern times, outlandish, fantasy-fictions, but which make pertinent points about the real world.

The first of these is *The Infernal Desire Machines of Doctor Hoffman*, published in 1972. It is set in an unnamed South American country whose capital, once characterized by its 'smug, impenetrable, bourgeois affluence' (Carter,

1994, 16) has been placed under siege by the sinister figure of Doctor Hoffman. The assault involves the machines of the novel's title – which cause the most secret desires and fantasies of the city's inhabitants to become objectively real, trapping them 'in some downward-drooping convoluted spiral of unreality from which [they] could never escape' (20). The plot concerns the attempts of the city to defend itself against the threat. Its narrator – Desiderio, whose name itself, critics have pointed out, evokes the Italian term for 'desire' (Day, 1998, 65) – is enlisted by the city's Minister of Determination, who remains immune to Hoffman's attack, to track down and assassinate him. The problem Desiderio faces is that, as a result of Hoffman's revolution, everything he sees and feels during his quest is generated by his own desire. The places he goes to, the people he interacts with, the time-frames he thinks he is within, are imaginary constructs.

As critics have noted (Suleiman, 1994; Day, 1998; Robinson, 2000) the story reads on one level as an analogy of the postmodern critique of Enlightenment philosophy. Before Hoffman's attack, the city figures as a model of empiricism and order. The (appropriately named, of course) Minister of Determination:

> believed that the city – which he took as a microcosm of the universe – contained a finite set of objects and a finite set of their combinations and therefore a list could be made of all possible distinct forms which were logically viable. These could be counted, organized into a conceptual framework and so form a kind of checklist for the verification of all phenomena.   (Carter, 1994, 24)

Desiderio is despatched from this world like a descendant of Swift's Gulliver, encountering people and places on his route which destabilize his faith in rationality and empiricism.

The psychoanalytic conception of reality, we recall from the Introduction, is to regard it as something we all tacitly agree to share – because not to do so would mean that we could not function as social beings – but which varies from person to person depending upon their specific perspective. Dr Hoffman rewrites the Cartesian *cogito* from 'I think therefore I am' into 'I DESIRE, THEREFORE I EXIST' (Carter, 1994, 211). As a result he ushers into this Enlightenment world what might be described as a 'crisis of representation'. His machine makes reality relative to the inhabitants of the city. What this means is that he doesn't simply change the city, he changes the city *for each of* its inhabitants, whose imaginations are responsible for transforming it according to their desires. No one there can now agree on what is real or not: everything is subject to change according to the different value systems and beliefs and desires, fantasies and anxieties of who is doing the perceiving. There can now be no single stable figure of authority presiding over this world, just as no author can dictate the meanings generated by a novel.

What results is in fact not a single world but a series of worlds. Carter's novel, in this way, might be regarded as also a portrayal in fiction of Brian McHale's theory about postmodernism's 'ontological dominant'. Her novel does not break down the boundary between the fictional and the real world in the way metafiction does, nor leave the reader unsure about what is to be taken as real or not in its world, as in Coover's 'The Babysitter' or Nabokov's *Pale Fire*. Yet it informs us about how reality is understood in postmodernity, as a network of worlds rather than one unified world.

Although the world created by Dr Hoffman can be read allegorically as a post-Lyotardian one where metanarratives no longer function, one metanarrative remains tellingly in place, and this is the narrative about men subjugating women. The kinds of fantasies and desires made real by Dr Hoffman's machine often involve acts of sexual violence against women. This is a feature of the people Desiderio encounters in his quest to find Dr Hoffman: the blind peep-show proprietor whose images are often of abused women, the dehumanized women of the 'River People', the sinister Count who believes that 'since there is no God, well, there is no damnation either' (Carter, 1994, 124) and inhabits a brothel where women have been replaced by literal embodiments of his desire unleashed by Dr Hoffman: 'sinister, inverted mutations, part clockwork, part vegetable and part brute' (132).

This might be seen as Carter's own response to the assumption by male critics like Owens and Huyssen that the postmodern discourse of liberation is valuable from a feminist perspective. The cumulative examples of male abuse of women in Carter's novel cautions that postmodern relativism is not necessarily beneficial to all. If we are to assume that everyone's perspective is valid and every '*petit récit*' contains its own truth, does this not legitimate some of the unsavoury and dangerous aspects of society which the patriarchal order of Enlightenment society managed to keep broadly under control, such as racism and sexual violence?

This is why, although he has become seduced by the liberation Hoffman's machines can offer during his quest, it is still necessary for Desiderio to kill Doctor Hoffman by the end of the novel. While masquerading as the agent of liberation, ultimately his machine licenses a destructive form of selfishness, where everyone attempts to impose their desires on those of the other. This is why, too, though it might seem to be another male act of violence against a woman, Desiderio must get rid of Hoffman's daughter Albertina, for she turns out to be nothing more than the Doctor's puppet, a representative of this dangerous relativism. In the end we realize that Desiderio has been faced with a false choice, for it is really between two forms of totalitarianism.

The second novel we shall consider here, *The Passion of New Eve* (1977), also underlines the difficulties of freeing ourselves from the trap of the gender metanarrative. Carter suggested that this novel set out deliberately 'to say some quite specific things about the production of femininity' (Haffenden, 1985, 86). One of these things is a thesis which was to become a mainstay of postmodern theory, the idea that gender is, as the theorist Judith Butler termed it, 'performative', rather than anything fixed or essential (Butler, 1990a, 271). One's *sex* is fixed, in that one is stuck with being *biologically* a man or a woman depending upon how one happens to turn out at birth (though of course this can be altered, as *The Passion of New Eve* in fact explores) but one's *sexuality* (one's sexual preferences and how they are expressed or repressed) and one's *gender* (how one presents oneself to the outside world as either a man or a woman) is something acquired and conditioned. Our sexual identities are constructed through the kind of 'social fictions' which Carter's fiction unmasks.

The Passion of New Eve is at once rigorously theoretical (using seventies terms like 'phallocentric') and completely over-the-top: filmed as faithfully as possible it would resemble a cross between a *Carry On!* film and a Hammer Horror. It is a testament to the invention and pace of Carter's writing that we take it seriously at all. It is narrated in the first person by an Englishman called Evelyn – note the appropriately androgynous name – who is fascinated by the Hollywood actress, Tristessa de St Ange, billed as '[t]he most beautiful woman in the world' and every man's desire. Like Greta Garbo, Tristessa has suddenly removed herself from the Hollywood glitter in her forties, and become a recluse. Like *Dr Hoffman* it is essentially a quest-narrative, as Evelyn sets out to find her.

His picaresque adventures begin in London, move to a seedy New York and then the deserts of Colorado, where he is captured and imprisoned by a mysterious all-female sect and taken to Beulah. The commune worship 'Mother', a 'sacred monster', a grotesque caricature of femininity, who dons a large black mask, a false curly beard, and has gigantic limbs and two rows of breasts ('so that, in theory, she could suckle four babies at one time' [Carter, 1992, 59]). The commune is working towards a utopia where woman is simply 'the antithesis in the dialectic of creation' and their kidnapping of Evelyn is the first step in their plan to begin 'the feminisation of Father Time' (67) by kidnapping men who wander into the desert, castrating them and turning them into women.

This is when Evelyn, after much elaborate surgery, hormone replacement, and instructional lectures from Sophia, the apologist of the regime, becomes the 'new Eve' of the title, 'the perfect specimen of womanhood' (68). Mother's plan is that he will then be impregnated from the reserves of his own semen, collected after he is ceremonially raped by Mother, so that s/he will become perfectly self-sufficient, the first woman able to both 'seed' and 'fruit' herself (76). When cast out into the desert by Mother's commune, 'Eve/lyn' is immediately captured by another group, only this time one ruled by a man, a one-eyed and one-legged poet called Zero. Evelyn is especially vulnerable as a woman and her capture makes us even more aware of the impact her bodily differences from men have on a woman's capacity for agency. Having been raped 'unceremoniously' by Zero (86), Evelyn is immersed in his polygamous harem of women, all of whom are expected to indulge their master's sadistic sexual whims and end up loving him all the more for it.

Zero is also obsessed by Tristessa and eventually he and his harem, with Eve/lyn in tow, manage to find her, holed up in a glass mansion, like a Gothic version of Elvis Presley's Graceland, full of cheap piped music and waxwork figures of dead Hollywood celebrities. They tear off Tristessa's clothes to reveal, to their disgust, his penis. Eve realizes, '*[t]hat* was why he had been the perfect man's woman! He had made himself the shrine of his own desires, had made of himself the only woman he could have loved!' (128–9). Inevitably, once they escape Zero, Tristessa and Eve have sex, both of them in different ways examples of the 'female man'.

The Passion of New Eve thereby demonstrates how gender performance involves a complex relation between substance and image (Butler, 1990b, 22–32). Each of the 'sacred monsters' – Tristessa, Zero, Mother, Eve/lyn herself eventually – seem to represent different gender stereotypes: for example, Zero as Alpha Male, Mother as Phallic Mother. These emphasize the idea of gender as performance which is central to the tales of both Evelyn and Tristessa. Tristessa illustrates how in postmodernity the signifier 'man' or 'woman' has little to do with the referent. What is important is the *signified* which has been attached to it by culture. The novel's main setting, the United States – regarded by Baudrillard as a literal embodiment of hyperreality, a universe of signs detached from any referent – is the appropriate location to put forward this argument.

One of the 'specific things' *The Passion of New Eve* wants to say about women, then, is the way that femininity becomes a commodity, in particular how 'Hollywood produc[es] illusions as tangible commodities' (Haffenden, 1985, 86). The second, related point *The Passion of New Eve* makes about gender is similar to the conclusion of *Dr Hoffman*. Although there is no substance other than the surface, this does not, in fact, lead to a completely free play of signification but merely another form of imprisonment. What happens is that this 'perfect specimen of womanhood' still ends up as a man's conception of the perfectly desirable woman. Gazing at herself in the mirror for the first time, Eve/lyn realizes that 'They had turned me into the *Playboy* centre fold. I was the object of all the unfocused desires that had even existed in my own head. I had become my own masturbatory fantasy. And – how can I put it – the cock in my head, still, twitched at the sight of myself' (Carter, 1992, 75). Similarly the novel shows that 'a woman is indeed beautiful only in so far as she incarnates most completely the secret aspirations of man' (Carter, 1992, 129). This is what enables Tristessa to become the most beautiful woman in the world. The lesson she has learned about this inequality is perhaps why, when Eve/lyn is offered her genitals back at the end (implying that she could somehow go through the whole experiment backwards) she refuses.

Ultimately, for all the explicit theoretically informed context and subject matter of both *Dr Hoffman* and *New Eve*, it is the *style* that makes Carter's fiction postmodern. Her work trades on myths, but her writing is resolutely anti-mythic (she once stated that she was 'in the demythologising business' [Carter, 1997, 38]) – and this makes her *post*-modern, in that she rejects the mythic explanations which typically underpin the works of high modernism. Like *Gravity's Rainbow* and *Waterland*, Carter's work plays with myth, teasing the reader into making connections.

Eve/lyn repeatedly describes her story as a 'maze' further into which she must continually go to find its truth – or the way out. But it is also, of course, a labyrinth for the *reader* to become lost in. This is one function of Carter's use of myth in the novel. Its narrative self-consciously evokes the stories of Oedipus, Lilith, Lot's wife, Samson and Delilah, etc. as well as more contemporary pop-cultural parallels like *The Lost Island of Dr Moreau*. But none offer a foundational structure for reading the novel – they are used in the style of the *bricoleuse*, objects 'found' by chance as the author's imagination takes the narrative along certain paths only to be discarded when another, more appropriate one, comes to mind. *New Eve*, typical of postmodern fiction, seduces us into interpretation, only to frustrate our efforts. Carter's is a strategy whereby reference to myth is used not to add layers of explanatory meaning in the manner of modernist fiction, but ultimately to *demystify* – that is, to use myth to illustrate, ironically, how dangerously dependent we (i.e. the subjects of patriarchal culture) are on myths as a way of experiencing the world and making sense of it.

Margaret Atwood

The Canadian writer Margaret Atwood resembles Carter in the generic variation of her fiction, though rather than invoking a host of different genres all at the same time, like Carter, Atwood seems systematically to choose a different genre in each successive novel. Nevertheless the recurrent concern in all her fiction is with the constructed nature of history and the way cultural myths operate as kinds of scripts that dictate our behaviour. A more conventional kind of 'feminist rewriting' takes place in Atwood's work, compared to Carter's. Novels such as *The Handmaid's Tale* and *Alias Grace* effectively write history from an explicitly feminine perspective, one which contests the authoritative 'masculinist' narrative that constitutes much official history. It is a common concern of those writers (mainly, but also postmodern historians) that the narrative of history inevitably leaves the powerless unvoiced. This includes ethnic minorities, the colonized, the marginalized, and, especially in earlier times than our own, women.

In this respect Atwood's work exemplifies Linda Hutcheon's category of historiographic metafiction (Hutcheon, 1988a, 21). She produces historiographic metafictions from a feminist viewpoint, a strategy that has been labelled 'herstory'. Consequently, as realism is the natural form for the traditional, linear view of history, it follows that each of her novels might justifiably be read as a critique of the conventions of realism, exposing the ideological foundations of the mode and challenging its pretence that it is a 'natural' form of storytelling – albeit in a more subtle and double-coded way (since it preserves some realist elements, like all historiographic metafiction) than an earlier tradition of North American metafictionists.

The interrogation of both traditional historiography and realism are central to the achievements of *The Handmaid's Tale*. The novel is, to borrow Angela Carter's description of her own work, a 'speculative fiction'. It is a dystopia in the tradition of Yevgenie Zamyatin's *We* (1921), Huxley's *Brave New World* (1932), and Orwell's *1984* (1948), set in the not-too-distant future. Typically the dystopian genre, a science fiction sub-genre, depicts a fearful, paranoid world in the near future in which individual liberty has been severely compromised by a brutal totalitarian regime which regards people as units of data or orders them to conform to repressive social norms rather than treat them as individuals. It is a critical commonplace to say that a work of science fiction is actually a diagnosis of the present rather than a prediction of the future.

The Handmaid's Tale expresses Atwood's concern about the rise of reactionary politics and culture in 1980s America (represented by the Reagan administration). Perhaps unsurprisingly, as it was published in the middle of that decade, *The Handmaid's Tale* quickly became famous and notorious, a fixture on school syllabi but also the subject of frequent complaints about its perceived anti-religious sentiment.

The novel is set in Cambridge, Massachusetts, where, following a revolution, the US constitution – traditionally considered a sacred foundation of American life – has been abolished and the country is now the Republic of Gilead, a

Christian theocracy, run along the lines of Biblical fundamentalism. Freedom for citizens is severely limited, with social roles rigidly maintained by ideological means and by force. Literacy, for example, is being deliberately eroded, with pictures replacing words on labels in shops and women being forbidden to read, while non-conformists are deported to the 'colonies', and dissidents and homosexuals are put to death publically at 'The Wall', outside what was formerly Harvard University.

Women are the most subjugated group in Gileadean society. Black and Jewish women are removed from society completely, while the rest are segregated into seven categories: Wives, Daughters, Widows, Aunts, Marthas, Handmaids, and Econowives. Only upper-class couples are permitted to have children, though Gilead is beset by desperately low fertility rates following previous environmental catastrophes, pollution, and chemical leaks, which have seen the colonies made dangerously toxic by pollution and much of Gilead uninhabitable. As a result the privileged turn to 'handmaids' as surrogate mothers for their children. Handmaids are treated like slaves. They have no names of their own, but are given names which denote who they belong to.

The novel's narrator and central character is one of these handmaids, Offred (whose Commander is Fred). She is permitted to leave the house only to go shopping in the company of another handmaid, is unable to close the door to her room, must visit the doctor frequently to check for disease, and is subject to constant scrutiny by 'the Eyes', Gilead's secret police force. At the appropriate point in her menstrual cycle Offred must have sex with the Commander – in silence and exhibiting no sign of pleasure or independence – while the Commander's wife, Serena Joy, sits behind her, holding her hands. Handmaids are allowed up to three placements with different couples to see if they are able to have children, and, if not, they are deported to the colonies as Unwomen. Fred and Serena are Offred's third placement, without success so far, and if there is no conception, she faces deportation.

The conventions of the regime might be regarded as literalized versions of aspects of the experience of being a Western woman in the 1980s, even in a free society: under constant scrutiny by the male gaze (the Eyes), and valued chiefly as sexual objects whose appearance and behaviour is prescribed by the way that male desire is encoded in the marketing and advertising apparatus. The novel thus makes use of the specific power of dystopian fiction: it is not simply a 'wouldn't it be awful if . . . ?' kind of cautionary tale, but an intensification and formalization of attitudes in our own world. Atwood is careful to show that Gilead is not the result of a sudden, unprecedented lurch to the right. In fact it represents simply the worst of two evils for women. During flashbacks into Offred's past we learn that Gilead came into being in a climate of increasing social disorder, the symptoms of which were severe abuse of women, such as easily available pornography, prostitution, and violent attacks. The novel also shows that although Gilead eventually collapses, it reverts only to a similar state of affairs to those which led to its gestation, with little change for women.

The novel takes the form of an oral narrative, recorded onto tape, in which Offred tells of Gilead, but also – in the form of dreams and memories – the story of her previous existence. Offred, the daughter of a feminist activist (and single mother), had an affair with a man called Luke, who divorced his wife and had a child with Offred. During the military coup which saw the rise of Gilead, they attempted to flee across the border to Canada, but were caught and separated. Offred has never seen husband or daughter since. Serena Joy arranges for Offred to have sex with her Commander's gardener and chauffeur, Nick, in the hope that Offred will become pregnant and the baby can be presented as the Commander's. As an incentive, Serena promises to give Offred a picture of her lost daughter, thus revealing that she has always known her whereabouts. What Serena doesn't realize is that Offred and Nick have begun an affair. Offred then learns of the existence of a covert resistance group entitled Mayday.

The ending of *The Handmaid's Tale* is famously ambiguous. Having found out about a trip to Jezebel's, a secret club for commanders, Serena sends Offred to her room to await punishment. As she sees the black van of the Eyes coming to get her Nick enters her room and tells her not to worry because in fact the men in the van work for Mayday. Offred assumes they will take her to what is known amongst the subjugated women of Gilead as 'The Underground Femaleroad'. The novel ends as she is taken away – but whether this is by the Eyes or by the resistance movement is unclear, just as it is unclear whether Nick is part of Mayday or an Eye, working for Gilead.

Besides telling this story Offred's narrative contains occasional digressions about the problems of constructing accurate historical narrative. At one point she comments

> This is a reconstruction. All of it is a reconstruction. It's a reconstruction now, in my head, as I lie flat on my single bed rehearsing what I should or shouldn't have said, what I should or shouldn't have done, how I should have played it. . . . When I get out of here, if I'm ever able to set this down, in any form, even in the form of one voice to another, it will be a reconstruction then too, at yet another remove. It's impossible to say a thing exactly the way it was, because what you say can never be exact, you always have to leave something out, there are too many parts,

> sides, crosscurrents, nuances, too many gestures, which could mean this
> or that, too many shapes which can never be fully described, too many
> flavours, in the air or in the tongue, half-colours, too many.
>
> (Atwood, 1996a, 144)

We recognize here the familiar postmodern concern about the unnarrated
events which figure in the gaps and margins of any narrative. In the novel's
epilogue, 'Historical Notes', we realize that Offred has indeed managed to
'set it all down'. This section takes the form of a transcript of a talk given
by a Cambridge University Professor, one Professor Pieixoto, to the Twelfth
Symposium on Gileadean Studies in Nunavit in Arctic Canada in 2195. His
lecture focuses on what has become a significant document in 'Gileadean
studies', the tapes of Offred's story – given the Chaucerian title *The Handmaid's
Tale* by a Professor – which, he says, were discovered in Bangor in Maine, 'a
prominent way-station in what our author refers to as "The Underground
Femaleroad"' (313) where it was, he surmises, recorded in a Mayday safe-
house. His research has led him to identify the Commander as a 'real' historical
figure (probably one Frederick Waterford or B. Frederick Judd).

'Historical Notes' is the most debated section of *The Handmaid's Tale* by
critics. It is the kind of fictional paratext which commonly appends postmodern
novels – for example, *Pale Fire*, Iris Murdoch's *The Black Prince*, Ian McEwan's
Enduring Love – which at once recalls the eighteenth-century tradition of
ensuring verisimilitude through editorials and postscripts, and invites its reader
to focus on its processes of construction and indeed those of all narratives. The
most obvious effect is that it is a self-reflexive commentary on the novel we've
almost finished, its own first piece of criticism. As in *Pale Fire* we have an
academic commenting on a work of literature given the same title as the novel
we have read.

In his discussion of the status of the story Pieixoto comments on the nature
of its narrative and thus continues Offred's story, up to a point. It becomes
clear that he has been the translator of what we have read. But this revelation
also means that her voice has come to us mediated through his; the woman's
monologue has been filtered through a man's narrative, moreover one who
cautions his readers against the cultural bias of judging Gilead too harshly,
for he considers the Republic an attempt to ensure the survival of humanity
in the face of falling birthrates and environmental disaster. He claims to have
transcribed her oral narrative, and we reasonably may wonder if he has edited
this too.

This means that 'Historical Notes' is at once the source of hope and depress-
ing familiarity. It solves the mystery of Nick's fidelity, making it clear from the

very existence of the tape that Nick *was* in fact a member of Mayday, who helped his lover to escape (even though there is no indication of what happened to Offred: if she had escaped, the Professor assumes, she would surely have turned up in England or Canada and published a proper account). Thus it brings a small counterbalance to the novel's negative depiction of men, showing that some can be trusted. However, even though the date of the Historical Notes is also the source of hope, as it shows that the Gilead regime eventually died out and has been replaced by a more liberal one, the very nature of the Professor's lecture confirms that the historical position of women is really no better. His lecture concentrates on the early commanders and their role in developing Gilead, and accuses Offred of missing key events. His discourse thus positions women as insignificant footnotes to a predominantly male history. As Coral Ann Howells has put it, 'His reconstruction effects a radical shift from "herstory" to "history"... the historical facts that Pieixoto selects as significant effectively erase Offred from the Gileadean narrative' (Howells, 2005, 107). And this is something that Offred herself has foreseen, noting in her narrative that 'from the point of view of future history... we'll be invisible' (Atwood, 1996a, 240).

Offred describes her narrative as the reconstruction of a reconstruction. Pieixoto's translation ensures that it is reconstructed at one further remove. Effectively his role means that her narrative is treated in a similar way to her body: appropriated by a patriarchal male for the benefit of an overall metanarrative. Pieixoto thus gives us one reading of *The Handmaid's Tale* – one which works on a metafictional level, of course, as it is partly a commentary on Atwood's novel. However the layerings of narrative point to another twist in how we respond to the story's message. The epilogue reveals that Gilead has become a research area, a historical period subject to academic analysis. The more we study a regime, the more we might learn its lessons. Subsequent readings of *The Handmaid's Tale* after Pieixoto's – as well as readings of Atwood's novel, subtly prompted by this metafictional logic, might therefore reach alternative and more feminist conclusions to his.

Atwood's novel *Alias Grace* (1996) examines deeply ingrained cultural attitudes to women in a different way. The 'Historical Notes' section in *The Handmaid's Tale* is about imagined research on an unearthed narrative, which turns out to be inadequate. In *Alias Grace* Atwood attempts something similar herself, only this time combining real research on a real text, but interwoven with fiction. Her novel tells the story of Grace Marks, a sixteen-year-old immigrant servant girl who, in 1843, along with fellow-servant James McDermott, was convicted of killing their employer Thomas Kinnear and his housekeeper Nancy Montgomery in Upper Canada. McDermott was hanged and Marks spent thirty years in prison until she was pardoned. She moved to New York State whereupon she vanished from all official records. Marks's involvement in the murder and her motivations have always been unclear. The most common version of the story is that Kinnear and Montgomery were having an affair, and Marks was jealous at the status this provided Montgomery in the household. Marks herself, however, always claimed that she could not remember the events surrounding the murder, and gave conflicting explanations, once claiming to have been possessed by the spirit of a dead friend.

Alias Grace bears out Atwood's conviction that while history might set out 'to provide us with grand patterns and overall schemes' it would fall apart 'without its brick-by-brick, life-by-life, day-by-day foundation'. She continues: 'Whoever tells you that history is not about individuals, only about large trends and movements, is lying' (Atwood, 1997, 6–7). Grace Marks's story is one such small unit in history. But it is also a problematic one, because of the impenetrable kernel of mystery at its heart caused by the fact that the case has been built up by the testimony of so many witnesses, and the testimony of the only survivor of the four people involved, Grace Marks, is so contradictory.

In *Alias Grace* Atwood uses fiction to do something other than try to solve a historical mystery, however. While it deals with its period as seriously as a historian might (the number of texts in the Acknowledgements section at the end suggest this) the novel is also the product of Atwood's decision to invent material, '[w]here mere hints and outright gaps exist in the records' (Atwood, 1996b, 467). The obvious result of her exercising this aesthetic licence is the invention of a character, a practitioner of the new medical science of 'mental pathology', Dr Simon Jordan, who interviews Grace in an effort to help her relive the experience of the murders and remove the traumatic blockage. Atwood's aestheticization of history has the effect of shifting the focus onto masculinist historiographical processes rather than on the case in question.

Running through the novel is the metaphor of the patchwork quilt. Grace is an expert quilter and during her discussions with Jordan sews together her fabric blocks. It is clear (Grace alludes to it herself) that there is a parallel between constructing narrative and stitching together a quilt, traditionally a matter of making something new from old fragments of fabric. Indeed – as the image of a quilt block pattern prefacing each of its fifteen sections suggests – this is how Atwood has put her own narrative together, combining a huge range of different texts: epigraphs taken from contemporary sources (e.g. newspaper reports of the case, Marks's Confession, pen portraits of Marks and McDermott from a contemporary account of the trial), more tangential period texts, such as Coventry Patmore's *The Angel in the House* (1854) and Robert Browning's 'Childe Roland' (1855), as well as the texts Atwood invents:

Grace's oral narrative; her interior monologue; a third-person, present-tense, description of meetings and dialogue between Jordan and Grace; and numerous letters written by each. The impression from reading Atwood's huge novel is consequently of a bewildering mass of voices and texts which have been 'quilted' together by the author. The mass of documentation does nothing to clarify past events but reminds the reader that history itself is a patchwork quilt of texts, and in order for it to mean anything, it must be stitched together by a narrator.

Atwood's own historical quilting process was a matter of trying to untangle the web of stories about Grace Marks. Debate about her case continued throughout the nineteenth century, and saw her become the object of a number of competing narratives – those which advanced prejudices against the Irish and the Jews, or the poor, or articulated nineteenth-century fears about the 'mad woman' and the threats of female desire to masculinist authority. In particular, as Atwood says in the 'Author's Afterword', the accounts of the case 'reflected contemporary ambiguity about the nature of women: was Grace a female fiend and temptress, the instigator of the crime and the real murderer of Nancy Montgomery, or was she an unwilling victim, forced to keep silent by McDermott's threats and by fear for her own life?' (Atwood, 1996b, 464).

Rather than try to determine what exactly Marks was, Atwood is interested in how authority attempts to categorize and explain different 'types' of people. Her narrative reveals Marks as a victim of what the philosopher Michel Foucault called 'disciplinary regimes' (Foucault, 1995, 193). These operate via the 'dividing practice', the grouping of kinds of people into various subdivisions of the 'normal' and the 'abnormal' (e.g. in the courts, the criminal is marked off from the non-criminal; in psychiatric clinics, the sane from the mad; in hospitals, the healthy from the sick). Thereby a disciplinary regime is able to build up a picture of the *normal* person, which then enables deviations from this constructed norm to be easily identified and isolated. Grace Marks is classified as abnormal by the discourses of two disciplinary mechanisms in particular: firstly the legal apparatus (through her trial, sentencing, and pardon) and then the medical apparatus, through the efforts of Simon Jordan to understand her. While sympathetic up to a point, trying to establish whether or not she is innocent in her own interests, Jordan is also attempting to *explain* Grace along the lines of the dividing practice. Significantly, though, he fails, and abandons the case, feeling so unsettled by the experience that he is close to 'nervous exhaustion'. '*Not to know*', he reflects, ' – to snatch at hints and portents, at intimations, at tantalizing whispers – it is as bad as being haunted. Sometimes at night her face floats before me in the darkness, like some lovely and enigmatic mirage' (Atwood, 1996b, 424).

Atwood, like Angela Carter, has a fondness for the Gothic, and uses it in her fiction to disrupt the (frequently masculinist) processes of rational investigation and analysis. In her 1993 novel *The Robber Bride*, for example, the demonic woman of the title, Zenia, returns from the dead to complicate the serious historiographical analysis of the character Tony, who writes the opening and closing sections. In literary history, the Gothic represents a parallel force to those of philosophical rationalism and realism which were emerging at the same time (the eighteenth century) and trades in elements which exceed definitions and labels and cannot be contained by conventional theorizing. In *Alias Grace* the Gothic elements of the central character – her prison nightmares, apparent split personality, the thin disembodied voice she uses when under hypnosis – represent a powerful counter-force to Jordan's theorizing, and ultimately win out.

Kathy Acker

Carter's and Atwood's writing is highly intertextual. References to other texts – myths, fairytales, works of pop culture and literature – abound. It is clear from considering novels like *Alias Grace* or *The Passion of New Eve* that this kind of intertextuality is not the aimless reflex of pastiche, which Fredric Jameson thinks typifies the postmodern, but a much more considered version, closer to Hutcheon's understanding of postmodern parody, which enables it to make pertinent points about postmodernity.

The Handmaid's Tale, for example, as well as being a feminist version of the kind of dystopia produced by Orwell, Huxley and, especially, Zamyatin, is, as Hutcheon has noted, a 'serious parodic echoing and inverting of the canonical *Scarlet Letter*' (Hutcheon, 1988a, 139). Nathaniel Hawthorne's novel, one of the foundational texts of American fiction, is set in Puritan New England in the seventeenth century, itself a formative time for America. Like *The Handmaid's Tale* it is a framed narrative, prefaced by a statement by its narrator insisting that what follows is based on an original document. It concerns Hester Prynne, a married Englishwoman who, waiting for her husband to join her in America, becomes pregnant by another man, refuses to name him, and is punished when she and her daughter are ostracized and pilloried by the community, and she is forced to wear the red letter 'A' (for 'Adulteress') on her bosom. The story is about religious hypocrisy, as it turns out that the father of Hester's child is a minister, Arthur Dimmesdale, who lacks the moral courage to share her punishment.

The work of Kathy Acker takes this strategic use of intertexts to outrageous levels, while remaining deadly serious and committed to a broadly feminist agenda. Take *her* intertextual incorporation of *The Scarlet Letter*, in *Blood and Guts in High School* (1978). It is the story of a ten-year-old girl, Janey Smith, who is having a sexual relationship with her own father. Having fallen in love with another woman, he sends her to school in New York, and the text details her escapades in the city, which involve numerous sexual partners, joining a gang named the Scorpions, surviving a fatal car crash, being kidnapped by a white slave ring and sold into prostitution, having an affair with President Carter, developing cancer, having a relationship with the French writer Jean Genet, meeting capitalist rulers in Egypt called Mr Fuckface, Mr Blowjob, and Mr Knockwurst, and then dying at the age of fourteen. While imprisoned by a Mr Linker, a Persian slave trader, Janey writes a lengthy 'book report' on *The Scarlet Letter*, in which she seems to have metamorphosed into a version of Hester Prynne, and enters into an abusive relationship with a Reverend Dimwit.

Acker said that when writing the novel 'it was in my mind to do a traditional narrative' (Friedman, 1989, 20), but even this brief summary makes it clear that Acker's fiction is about as far from a 'traditional narrative' as one could imagine. The story opens with a conventional piece of third-person narration but is immediately interrupted by dramatic dialogue, poems, and pornographic drawings of genitals and sex acts apparently there to illustrate specific lines in the narrative, and soon becomes even more fragmented as it features Janey's diary, her letters, and extracts from a range of literary texts – Hawthorne, Mallarmé, and Genet. Susan E. Hawkins has called this progressive incorporation of more and more different kinds of texts, 'textual breakdown', a formal parallel to the 'bodily' and 'characterological' breakdown detailed in the novel (Hawkins, 2004, 644). The 'punk porn' (Phillips, 1994, 173) use of *The Scarlet Letter* is therefore one of a number of ways Acker's text conveys the inappropriateness or even the impossibility of expressing oneself through 'traditional narrative'.

Acker is often said to have injected literature with the values of 'punk' rock, the kind of music which upset the order of things in the late 1970s by challenging the rock-music orthodoxy – and other social establishments – with its aggressive, nihilist style and lyrics. What makes Acker's fiction most obviously 'punk' is its obscenity. Just as the Sex Pistols easily demonized themselves by saying the F-word on national television in 1976, so Acker's novels are full of gratuitous explicit sex scenes. *Blood and Guts in High School* was banned in South Africa and in Germany (with the transcript of the court ruling incorporated in Acker's 1991 collection *Hannibal Lecter, My Father*), and her work was seized by Canadian authorities following the Butler ruling on pornography in Canada in 1992.

Another 'punk' element of her writing is her incorporation of the world of pop culture into her fiction, and more precisely the way it is crudely set alongside high literary and philosophical sources. Acker's work is an excellent illustration of the typically postmodern impulse identified by Leslie Fiedler to 'cross the border, close the gap' between high and low culture. In her 1986 novel *Don Quixote*, for example, the protagonist (only this time Don Quixote is a woman) tells a story which is actually the plotline of the 1973 Japanese monster movie *Godzilla vs. Megalon*. In the film both monsters have been produced as a result of the testing of weapons, something which is explained as a 'rational behaviour'. The plot ends, true to the genre, with the two beasts fighting to decide the fate of the world. However, in the version recounted by Acker's Quixote they suddenly pause and start to discuss human reason, one monster saying to the other:

> In the modern period, exchange value has come to dominate society; all qualities have been and are reduced to quantitative equivalences. This process inheres in the concept of reason. For reason, on the one hand, signifies the idea of a free, human, social life. On the other hand, reason is the court of judgement, of calculation, the instrument of domination, and the means for the greatest exploitation of nature. As in de Sade's novels... (Acker, 1986, 72)

It is a parody of serious philosophical discourse, the epitome of Enlightenment thinking. Yet by placing it incongruously in the middle of a mass-market low-budget movie, its pretentions are exposed and punctured.

But what accounts, most of all, for Acker's 'punk aesthetic', besides obscenity and the closing of the cultural gap, is its relationship to other texts. As Larry McCaffrey has said, the central method of 'punk aesthetics' is 'crossing images over unexpectedly': 'profaning, mocking, and otherwise decontextualizing sacred texts... into blasphemous metatexts' (McCaffrey, 1989, 221). The use of *The Scarlet Letter* in *Blood and Guts in High School* marked the point at which Acker began seriously to employ plagiarism as an aesthetic strategy in her work. The list of writers from whose work she steals in her fiction is lengthy and includes classic and canonical writers such as Shakespeare, Dickens, the Brontës, Joyce, Mary Shelley, Cervantes, Keats, Faulkner, theorists such as Deleuze and Guattari, contemporary writers such as Harold Robbins and William Gibson, as well as works of pornography, and extracts from the journals and letters of real people.

This kind of aggressive appropriation has been regarded by some as a defining characteristic of postmodernism. It also reinforces the idea that postmodernism prevents us from ignoring the cultural, constructed nature of existence.

The most obvious precursor to Acker here is William Burroughs, and Acker is one of the few authors to have used his 'cut-up' method extensively rather than just expressing admiration for it. Acker's method also has parallels in postmodern visual art: from Marcel Duchamp's 'readymades', his provocative re-presentation of 'found' objects, such as drawing a moustache and goatee on a reproduction of Da Vinci's *Mona Lisa* and re-titling it *LHOOQ* (an acronym which read quickly in French translates as 'she has a hot ass' – 1919), through to her contemporary, Sherrie Levine, who exhibited as her own work photocopies of the work of great modern artists like the photography of Walker Evans or the paintings of Vincent Van Gogh.

Acker always spoke about the strategy of appropriation rather ambivalently, as simultaneously a deliberate, legitimate aesthetic practice, 'a literary theory' and 'a literary method' (Friedman, 1989, 120), a way of 'inhabiting [other texts] in some way so that I can do something with them' and, more impulsively, as something that she could not help but do: 'I have always used appropriation in my works because I simply can't write any other way' (Acker, 1997, 27). She spoke of the genesis of her writing as being when she was six years old finding her mother's porn books and hiding them inside her Agatha Christie novels: 'That's why I originally became a writer – to write Agatha Christie-type books, but my mind is fucked up' (Friedman, 1989, 20).

Where an author like D.M. Thomas, who has incorporated the work of others in his fiction in a more seamless way, has spent much of his career defending himself against accusations of plagiarism, Acker always acknowledged her lifting of the words of others defiantly, claiming it was a legitimate aesthetic strategy. This is not to say that it was always free of controversy. In 1975 she was forced to issue a public apology to the publishers of Harold Robbins for using 1500 words of a sex scene from his novel *Pirate* in her *The Adult Life of Toulouse-Lautrec* (under the heading 'the true story of a rich woman: I Want to Be Raped Every Night!') after they threatened to sue.

Acker's plagiarism is blatant. But this is what makes it hard to see in terms of the definition of plagiarism, as a devious attempt to pass off the work of others as one's own. This is because her insertion of other texts seems random, free-associative, almost deliberately clumsy and slapdash, as if to make what she is doing as obvious as possible. Typically her practice is to take an extract from a text and stick it roughly into her own fiction, with an additional sub-heading added, and occasionally names or pronouns changed. The opening of her *Great Expectations*, for example, begins with a chapter entitled 'Plagiarism', the first lines of which are: 'My father's name being Pirrip, and my Christian name Philip, my infant tongue could make of both names nothing longer or more explicit than Peter. So I called myself Peter, and came to be called

Peter.' These two sentences are identical to the two which begin Dickens's *Great Expectations*, except for the change of the name 'Pip' to 'Peter'. Such 'cutting and pasting' is a different way of using an intertext than the carefully interwoven, systematic interrogation of a particular source we find in *The Handmaid's Tale*. It is the apparent solution of the *bricoleuse* who needed a *Bildungsroman* and picked the first one to hand, hurriedly changing only what is necessary to appropriate it.

Brian McHale, considering Acker's insertion of passages from William Gibson's cyberpunk novel *Neuromancer* (1984) into her *Empire of the Senseless* (1988), argues that the act of appropriation is entirely 'pointless', with 'no discernible purpose apart from that of producing the "sampling" effect itself' (McHale, 1992, 235). He sees it therefore as an example of Jameson's 'blank parody' (Jameson, 1991, 17). But, at the risk of sounding glib, the pointlessness is actually the point. It causes us to revise Jameson's dismissal of pastiche as an uncritical strategy, for Acker demonstrates that pastiche has a powerful critical edge when it becomes *too* faithful, as it were, moving from homage into outright theft. Her strategy of incorporation makes valid points about origins, sources, and reading.

In its sheer brazenness, Acker's plagiarism makes the reader an active one. The simple act of giving her novels the same titles as *Don Quixote* or *Great Expectations* instantly makes the reader question their knowledge of literary history. Wasn't it Cervantes and Dickens who wrote these texts? How can someone else be claiming to write them? She is actually doing what Borges only imagined his fictional author Pierre Menard doing, 'writing' a classic text word for word and making it strangely 'almost infinitely richer' (Borges, 1989b, 69). To call one's novel *Great Expectations* is a provocative act and one which instantly positions the reader in terms of their expectations. Imagine writing a novel and calling it *Hamlet* or *Middlemarch*. The practice immediately provides a frame for our reading, setting up interpretive parameters involving themes from the original novel, such as origins, love, or the nature of capital, as well as preparing for a reinterpretation of Dickens's text. It has been suggested, for example, that the sadistic sexual acts in which the hero/heroine is forced to indulge in Acker's *Great Expectations* serves to comment on the 'exhibitionist masochism' of Dickens's hero, who suffers 'exquisitely' at the hands of Estella (Mukherjee, 2005, 114).

If there is a story in Acker's *Great Expectations*, it revolves around the narrator's attempt to deal with the effects of her mother's suicide. But really, rather than a single narrative, what we are confronted by is a continual evocation of specific *kinds* of narrative – confessional, the epistolary novel, the realist novel.

This has the effect of playing on the 'great expectations' (as in 'considerable') built up in the reader by Acker's borrowed title and its first lines. The experience of reading Acker leads us to question received wisdom about the unity and originality of realist fiction. All fiction, it suggests, is a patchwork of the words of others and pre-existing generic and discursive conventions – despite the efforts of the realist author to pass it all off as a coherent, organic whole. Dickens's *Great Expectations* is about the achievement of its protagonist to 'control' his life through narrative, after being controlled by others throughout the story – effectively being inserted into their narratives.

Acker's aggressive intertextuality also functions as a critique of one of the founding myths of our culture, the Romantic ideal of original authorship. Where the Romantics conceived of an author as a bard singularly possessed by inspiration, although this was itself a disguise for the ideology of capitalist ownership, which becomes important at the same time (Nesbit, 1995), the postmodern conception emphasizes that whatever role 'genius' or extreme skill might play in literary composition, it is really a matter of a writer selecting from a number of available conventions and discourses (Barthes, 1977b), or reinterpreting or 'misreading' influential works which already exist (Bloom, 1973).

Acker's work is a commentary not just on authorship but on the condition of being a *female* author. She explained her choice of specific texts as if more or less at random, because they were what she happened to be reading. Her *Don Quixote*, for example, was a text she couldn't help thinking of when she was about to go through her own abortion and this is why the narrator's abortion is presented as the ironic equivalent of the male knight's quest for Love, her 'puke green' paper hospital suit her 'armour', her wheelchair her steed. Yet her selections also tend to be some of the most canonical, foundational texts in particular traditions – and this means written by men: *Don Quixote*, commonly acknowledged to be the first novel 'proper', *Great Expectations*, one of the key Victorian *Bildungsroman*, Twain's *Huckleberry Finn*, the archetypal American quest for identity, Gibson's *Neuromancer*, the paradigmatic 'cyberpunk' text. Typically her strategy is to make the protagonist a woman. Acker's appropriation of these texts makes us reflect on this fact and wonder why women are not usually the pioneers of new modes of fiction and how the great works of literature would differ if they had been written by women.

Blood and Guts in High School, for example, shows how Acker's strategy causes us to reflect on the typical male *Bildungsroman*. The *Bildungsroman* is also known by its French name '*education sentimentale*' and tends to be a matter of its protagonist overcoming problems on the journey to maturity. In

Blood and Guts in High School, by contrast, education comes from the constant repetition of the same brutal pattern. Jenny is 'fucked' violently (there's no other word for what passes for sex in this novel) and then rejected by a series of men – continuing the pattern set by her father. Sentimental education here is not a question of progressively gaining greater awareness about the world and how one responds to it, but a matter of the same brutal point being hammered-home repeatedly (and literally). The structure (divided into three parts, 'Inside high school', 'Outside high school' and 'A Journey to the end of the night') explains the title in that it suggests that all of life is crystallized in the High School, presented by the novel as a place, with its brutal violence and indiscriminate fucking, which functions as a microcosm of America itself (Hawkins, 2004).

Though Acker tends to use rites-of-passage texts, the accompanying ideology about consistent, autonomous subjectivity is most certainly not there. The implication in texts like *Great Expectations* and *Jane Eyre* is that the protagonist remains essentially the same person despite the trials and tribulations documented in the story – perhaps because of them, since they bring out his or her essential nature. These characters *change*, but only in the sense that they mature. In Acker's versions, the juxtaposing of different texts, voices, and discourses means that there is no consistency of sexual identity or subjectivity in the characters. Her 'Pip' metamorphoses into something between a version of Dickens's Pip, a woman who is perhaps the author herself, as well as other characters such as the French poet Rimbaud, and the film director Pasolini. This fluidity is underlined by the different kinds of narration, ranging from the measured tones of the borrowed passages from Dickens's original to dark, obscene Burrovian streams-of-consciousness: 'I want: every part changes (the meaning of) every other part so there's no absolute/heroic/dictatorial/S&M meaning/part the soldier's onyx-dusted fingers touch her face orgasm makes him shoot saliva over the baby's buttery skull' (Acker, 2002, 152).

Nevertheless a more consistent identity *does* recur in Acker's fiction and that is her own, as the example of the abortion motif in her *Don Quixote* shows. Although their work challenges realist assumptions about autonomous identity, Carter's and Atwood's fiction preserve the traditional boundary between the author's real life and her fictional world. Acker breaks down the boundary between these worlds by incorporating her own story into her fiction, in a way typical of a more exhibitionist style of postmodern authorship – as visible in the work of celebrity-artists such as Tracey Emin.

But the work of all three novelists suggests in different ways that postmodernism is less about writing than *reading* (though of course particular reading strategies are made possible by the way a text is written). This reminds us of Patricia Waugh's point that one of the values of postmodernism for women is as a particular *reading strategy*, a way of interpreting contemporary reality. As Nicola Pitchford puts it, postmodernism enables feminist readers 'to manipulate texts to make meanings that further their ability to affect the political and social conditions of postmodernity' (Pitchford, 2002, 21).

Chapter 7

Two postmodern genres: cyberpunk and 'metaphysical' detective fiction

Despite its near-definitive tendency to problematize or collapse generic boundaries (demonstrated in many of the readings in this book) postmodern fiction, like any current within literary history, has inevitably favoured some genres over others, though not of course using them 'straight', but adapting and subverting them. This chapter assesses the way that postmodern literary fiction co-opts two popular narrative genres – science fiction and detective fiction – and the implications of this for understanding how postmodern fiction works.

Sci-fi and cyberpunk

Science fiction, and its potential to offer an alternative to realism – and a critique of it – has proved central to postmodernism. We have noted this already with regard to writers such as Burroughs, Vonnegut, Atwood, and Acker, each of whom draws on sci-fi in their work.

The reason for this is explained by Brian McHale, the theorist who has made the most valuable contribution to the study of the relationship between postmodernism and science fiction, and its subgenre cyberpunk. We recall that science fiction plays a key role in his poetics of postmodernism, as 'it is the ontological genre *par excellence* (as the detective story is the epistemological genre *par excellence*), and so serves as a source of materials and models for postmodernist writers' (McHale, 1987, 16). This is because both postmodernism and sci-fi make use of 'the universal fictional resource of presentation of virtual space'. Of course, as we considered in Chapter 1, 'projecting virtual space' is a definitive characteristic of *all* fiction. But McHale's point is that few modes of writing 'foreground and exploit the spatial dimension to the degree that SF and postmodernist texts do' (McHale, 1992, 247).

Both, he thinks, share origins in medieval romance, fiction which uses 'enclosed spaces *within* the romance world: castles, enchanted forests, walled gardens and bowers' which function as 'scale-models or miniature analogues of worlds' and thus allow us to explore what is normally directly unrepresentable in fiction and has to remain implicit, what McHale describes as 'the very "world-ness" of world' (McHale, 1992, 247). In science fiction the castles or enchanted forests are replaced by 'domed space colonies, orbiting space-stations, subter-ranean cities' (McHale, 1992, 247).

McHale argues that the late twentieth century witnessed a gradual 'science-fictionalization of postmodernism'. More than just the deployment of motifs and *topoi* from science fiction in non-generic texts (e.g. *Slaughterhouse-Five, The Passion of New Eve,* or *The Handmaid's Tale*) McHale is referring to the way postmodern texts confront one world with another at a *structural* level – that is, when the structure of a text is built around the juxtaposition of or inter-relationship between two worlds. Sci-fi 'proper' tends to do this literally, telling stories about interplanetary travel or beings from one planet visiting another. But without dealing with 'outer space', postmodern fiction also sets world against world. An example would be Alasdair Gray's novel *Lanark* (1982). Without drawing on the sci-fi genre, it features a double narrative involving two parallel worlds, the real-life Glasgow being set against the fictional Unthank, both of which reflect on each other. (The outcome is that the represented Glasgow is revealed, inevitably, as a fictional construction in important ways.)

But just as postmodernism has been 'science-fictionalized' the converse is true, according to McHale, and sci-fi has become increasingly 'postmodern-ized', that is, by reinforcing its interest in confronting worlds with a self-reflexive concern with *literary* worlds. This is central to the most postmodern incarna-tion of science fiction, its late-twentieth-century subgenre, cyberpunk.

Cyberpunk is best understood as a wave of radical science fiction which emerged in the 1980s and 1990s and which built upon the 'new wave' science fiction by the likes of Ballard, Aldiss, and Moorcock. This movement was more concerned with what Ballard termed 'inner space' ('an imaginary realm in which on the one hand the outer world of reality, and on the other the inner world of the mind meet and merge', as in surrealist art by the likes of Magritte or Dali [Ballard, 1968, 106]) than 'outer' space and displayed a specific pre-occupation with the decline of the contemporary world. Cyberpunk's lifespan as a pioneering literary 'movement' was comparatively brief (Bukatman, 1993, 137), beginning in 1984 with the publication of William Gibson's *Neuromancer,* and continuing for a decade or so with works by other authors such as Bruce Sterling, John Shirley, Rudy Rucker, Lewis Shiner, and Pat Cadigan (though a number of 'postcyberpunk' genres, such as 'biopunk' and 'steampunk', have been identified by some critics).

The term 'cyberpunk' was first used as the title of a short story written by Bruce Bethke in 1983, but became widely used in 1984 to describe Gibson's *Neuromancer.* In particular, it is concerned with the way that new technology enables us to enter into a kind of 'virtual reality' (this term was coined by Gibson). The term cyberpunk itself is a neologism. Its first part, 'cyber', is a short form of the word 'cybernetics', a term used by the mathematician Norbert Wiener in 1948 to refer to a new science which, broadly speaking, explored the relationship between human beings and machines, and, more precisely, linked communications theory (how information is transmitted, for example through the media) and control theory (which analyzes the behaviour of 'dynamical' systems).

But the 'cyber' in cyberpunk also relates to two other relevant uses of the prefix. The first is 'cyborg', a hybrid of human and machine in whom the machine elements are integrated into the human body in order to enhance its natural capabilities (Featherstone and Burrows, 1995, 2). The cyborg is most obviously exemplified in the 1987 film *Robocop*, and has been the subject of an important contribution to the postmodern debate, Donna Haraway's feminist essay, 'The Cyborg Manifesto' (1985). There she explains the mythic value of the figure of the cyborg in breaking down the boundaries which have structured Western existence since the Enlightenment: private and public, nature and culture, human and machine, physical and non-physical. The second related term is 'cyberspace' – another one coined by Gibson – to describe a space generated in the mind of a person operating or being controlled by a computer system, which also takes over his or her entire nervous system.

The 'punk' in the title refers mainly to the kind of *attitude* this fiction was seen to embody: anti-authoritarian, rebellious, and fascinated by the seedy world of drugs and machismo which punk rock symbolized. Cyberpunk is also associated – either through depiction within its pages, or by association on the cultural scene – with other youth subcultures in music and style. Punk rock, which in England emerged in the late 1970s, famously had a 'do-it-yourself' aesthetic whereby anyone could pick up a guitar or a microphone and be in a band regardless of talent or training.

Gibson's comments about writing his novel *Neuromancer* at times present himself as an uncertain amateur, putting together bits and pieces from fiction he knew to produce something original (McCaffrey, 1991a, 267). But this reminds us too that 'punk aesthetics' (McCaffrey, 1991a, 221) refers to the method of *bricolage*, the kind of cannibalizing of pre-existing genres and texts by cyberpunk authors we have considered in relation to Kathy Acker, a mixing of high and low cultural forms and a countering of the myth of the author as originary genius.

Cyberpunk recycles the clichéd conventions of classic science fiction – 'the robots and the braineaters and the starships', as Rudy Rucker once put it (Rucker, 1999, 462), as well as some of those associated with other literary forms and authors. Mark Bould points out that *Neuromancer* exhibits 'traces' of Dashiell Hammett, Raymond Chandler, Nelson Algren, J. G. Ballard, William Burroughs, Robert Stone, Howard Hawks, and John Carpenter, and 'cobbles together' the character Molly 'out of Wolverine and Cyclops from Marvel Comics's *X-Men*'. Gibson confessed that the interior descriptions in his *The Difference Engine* were all lifted more or less straight from Victorian novels (Bould, 2005, 219).

Where 'classic' twentieth-century science fiction (e.g. by the likes of Frank Herbert or Arthur C. Clarke) is set in a world far in the future, cyberpunk takes as its setting earth in the near future. The assumption behind it is that as a result of technological change and the revolution of what sociologists call the 'second media age' (namely the advent of computer-based and digital methods of communication), we are on the point of entering a new era, one characterized by the way that technology can remake the human body and the world. The settings of cyberpunk conform to McHale's notion of 'microworlds', those elements descended from the romance which enable readers to explore how worlds are *made*. McHale suggests that the cyberpunk version of these microworlds is typically more of an 'orbiting slum', a 'shabby, neglected, unsuccessful, technologically-outdated' world, than a shiny, technologically advanced world, like the Death Star in *Star Wars*. Such a world is depicted – so vividly that the novel is often regarded as initiating the entire genre – in William Gibson's *Neuromancer*, by far the most important and celebrated text in the cyberpunk canon.

William Gibson, *Neuromancer*

It is actually unfair to claim that *Neuromancer* kicks off cyberpunk all by itself, for Gibson was part of a 'school' of similar writers emerging at the same time, such as Sterling, Shirley, and Shiner. Nevertheless *Neuromancer* did strike reviewers as something quite different from existing science fiction, a new fictional genre, one moreover that was wholly in tune with the 'postmodern condition'. The cities which provide its setting are teeming with different types of people, and the practice of corporate branding present in our world has been taken to extremes. Name-checked throughout the novel are Braun coffee-makers, Sony computer monitors, Citröen cars, the 'Mitsubishi bank of America', while employees have their company's logos tattooed on the backs of their hands.

Two elements of *Neuromancer* (and this is in fact true of the whole genre of cyberpunk) are particularly distinctive. First, there is Gibson's ability to create a powerfully-realized, detailed world – one close enough to our own to be instantly recognizable, and far enough in the future to be disturbingly plausible. We might describe this as the 'cyber' element of the novel, its virtual world realized in the virtual world of narrative fiction. Secondly, there is Gibson's liberal deployment not just of elements of previous texts but of the conventions of other kinds of fiction (the 'punk' element).

Neuromancer is set in an unspecified near-future period on earth. There are references which suggest a recent Third World War. The two main locations for the novel are Japan, a country which fascinates Gibson as it seems a kind of hyperreal future-world which already exists, and the United States. The USA is known as 'the Sprawl', an image which suggests a vast urban conglomeration stretching the length of its Eastern Seaboard. Almost paradoxically, one of the reasons this world is so convincing is that there are no 'history lessons' inserted in the plot for the benefit of the reader (as they are in dystopias such as *1984* and *The Handmaid's Tale*), no direct guidance offered by the narrator to the reader. The history of this world and the present way of life are simply implied, we pick up on them as we go along, and this makes us feel as if we have suddenly entered into a fully functioning world. It thus bears out McHale's point about science fiction, that it inserts a network of 'innovations' into our familiar understanding of our own world, causing a kind of ontological disruption: is this our world just a few years hence, or a completely different one?

The locations in *Neuromancer* are all urban, 'downtown', places, thronging with crowds and populated by a cast of lowlifes, criminals, and businessmen out for what they can get. Technology does not appear to have improved the quality of life for the inhabitants of Earth. Cash is now illegal (things are paid for via cards or bio-implants), most food is reconstituted, there is a constant intake of mood-enhancing, mind-altering drugs. The most significant difference from our world (or at least that of the early 1980s when the novel was written) is the ability for the inhabitants of the cities to inhabit virtual reality. They do this mainly for entertainment, as when they enter the 'simstim' (or 'simulated stimulus'), a system which triggers not only the visual and aural senses, like TV, but also touch, taste, and smell. Gibson's general idea of people living in a structured 'virtual' realm has been widely credited with predicting the internet.

But cyberspace also 'exists' as a more concrete space for certain inhabitants of the world to visit. Cyberspace, also known in *Neuromancer* as 'the Matrix' (and the famous film of that name might, incidentally, be seen as late cyberpunk) is defined by the novel (via a voice-over in an imaginary educational documentary) as:

A consensual hallucination experienced daily by billions of legitimate operators, in every nation, by children being taught mathematical concepts . . . A graphic representation of data abstracted from the banks of every computer in the human system. Unthinkable complexity. Lines of light ranged in the nonspace of the mind, clusters and constellations of data. Like city lights, receding . . .   (Gibson, 1995, 67)

The Matrix enables a person to enter another part of the world from wherever he or she is, and experience things by proxy, through the body of another, and even continue to exist after he or she has died. The plot of *Neuromancer* revolves around the existence of its hero, Case, in cyberspace. In fact, cyberspace is his very *raison d'être*: he refers contemptuously to bodily activities, such as travel, as 'meat things' (Gibson, 1995, 97). Case is a 'console cowboy' (39), a middle-man thief who specializes in stealing hacker software for more powerful thieves. Having made the 'classic mistake' (12) of stealing from these, his own bosses, he is punished by having his nervous system damaged by mycotoxin. Consequently he is prevented from accessing cyberspace, the place where his work was previously conducted and, more painfully, is also deprived of the addictive high of cruising through this world.

The novel begins as, his career over and increasingly enmired in drug abuse, he tries in vain to obtain a cybernetic implant from the black market dealers in Chiba City in Japan, only to be suddenly 'rescued' by a mysterious ex-Special Forces gang leader named Armitage. In exchange for repairing his neurological damage and curing his drug addiction by modifying his pancreas (thus making him into a cyborg), Case must work for Armitage, using his skills as a hacker to secure vital information for him. He is paired up with another cyborg, Molly Millions, a professional criminal who has had mirrored glasses inset surgically into her eye sockets and razorblades protruding from her fingernails, and together they embark on a labyrinthine series of adventures as they assemble a crack team to do the work, coming up against a series of hostile organizations and individuals such as the secret Tessier-Ashpool clan and their cyber-ninja Hideo, and the two halves of a huge independent Artificial Intelligence construction, 'Wintermute' and 'Neuromancer'.

More detailed summary of the plot would sound even more ridiculous and incomprehensible. This is partly due to the effect of the typical sci-fi fondness for complex names and organizations, but also because the plot owes a great deal to the conventions of the romance, a genre which specializes in the marvellous and the fantastic, and typically features questing heroes. A common element of the romance is a convoluted, labyrinthine plot full of twists and turns and peopled by characters who are not who they seem.

This is, in fact, where we need to consider the second distinctive feature of *Neuromancer*, its use of previous genres. It invokes the genre of the romance, but more precisely, in keeping with its logic of recycling, echoes the conventions of two other quintessentially modern American descendants of the romance, the 'hard-boiled' detective story, as pioneered by Dashiell Hammett and especially (in this instance) Raymond Chandler, and the Western. Case is an incarnation of both the questing private investigator and the gun-toting outlaw who is nevertheless working against a greater evil. An even closer relative is the video game, which is also typically a version of the romance, as the novel reads as if Case is progressing through the levels of an action-adventure game.

Reading *Neuromancer* is like being in a dream where it seems as if all the generic motifs – private-eye quest, the sexy S&M female sidekick, the assemblage of a team of talented crooks and misfits – have been encountered somewhere before. 'Neuromancer' refers to one half of a vast AI construction which can generate cyberspace, in ways that recall another descendant of the romance, the Gothic novel (the activity of the computer hacker, guessing passwords to access secret worlds, is compared to the practice of summoning up dark spirits). Yet of course the term also signals that the novel constructs a 'new romance' out of the bits and pieces of the old.

What is especially interesting about Gibson's novel is the way that its two most characteristic elements – its imaginary world and its *bricolage* – actually come together to reinforce one another, so that its form mirrors the 'constructed' nature of the world it projects. *Neuromancer*'s locations are remorselessly urban, a world where no distinction is possible any longer between the natural and the constructed, as suggested by the famous first line of the novel which compares the sky to 'the color of television, tuned to a dead channel' (Gibson, 1995, 9). Similarly, the 'punk aesthetic' of the novel emphasizes the fact that the narrative is not 'natural', but has been assembled from bits and pieces of existing texts and genres.

This is not the only way in which the story of *Neuromancer* implicitly comments on literary production and consumption. A parallel which is not made explicit at any point in the text (*Neuromancer* is not metafictional in the way many postmodern novels are) but which is bound to strike any student of literature, is how the thrills and benefits of entering cyberspace, as Gibson envisages it in this novel, resembles the act of reading fiction – especially, in fact, the kind of thrilling plots favoured by modern descendants of the romance genre which the novel draws upon, such as the private-eye novel, sci-fi, and the Western. Cyberspace means that Case can appear in alternative locations no matter where he is stationed. It also means he can experience the world from the perspective of another person (as he frequently does through Molly).

Though Case's travels in cyberspace have their 'real' dangers (he nearly ends up trapped in cyberspace forever by 'Neuromancer') there is still a valid parallel between them and the experience of reading the novel. Reading *Neuromancer* involves entering a version of 'cyberspace' – safer but no less vivid. This is common in the box-like structures of the romance, where the reader experiences all the twists and turns of the plot just at the same time as the hero, and is faced with the same uncertainty about characters and situations which confront him or her.

This aspect illustrates McHale's thesis that the microworlds of science fiction and cyberpunk enable the *idea* of world itself – how it actually operates, how we relate to it – to be represented. It also reminds us, once again, that fiction creates multiple worlds, and worlds which are larger than their textual depiction. A concept associated with science fiction is that of the *multiverse*, a term used first by the philosopher William James to describe a universe lacking order or governing principles, but which tends to be used in science fiction to refer to multiple, co-existent worlds. While the multiverse may be imagined as something which exists in the diegesis of a work of science fiction, it also refers to the kind of proto-sci-fi experiments with narrative space we find in the like of Borges's 'The Garden of Forking Paths', Pynchon's *The Crying of Lot 49* and Coover's 'The Magic Poker'. However, to equate cyberspace to fiction, as the logic of *Neuromancer* suggests, also leads us to a paradoxical conclusion. Cyberspace may be a radical prediction of a very different future, but another way of looking at it might be as simply a more powerful version of what realist fiction has always been able to do. Realism enables us to enter different worlds and experience things through the minds of people who are not us.

Detective fiction

Critics are in broad agreement that the detective story 'proper' begins in 1841, with the publication of Edgar Allan Poe's 'The Murders in the Rue Morgue'. By 'proper' I mean that elements of the genre which were to become instantly recognizable as detective fiction are more or less in place in this tale. It has a distinctive 'tripartite' structure, by which the narrative focuses first on the discovery of a crime, then on the casting of suspicion on the members of a community, and finally (the longest part) on the mechanism of investigation and solution. Most importantly, in the character of Chevalier Auguste Dupin, Poe's enigmatic detective, the cornerstone of the tradition was put in place. The conventions initiated by Poe in 'Murders in the Rue Morgue' and two further stories featuring Dupin, 'The Mystery of Marie Rôget' (1842) and

'The Purloined Letter' (1845), were subsequently 'formalized' over forty years later with the advent of the Sherlock Holmes stories by Sir Arthur Conan Doyle (1887–1913) and then the Agatha Christie-led 'Golden Age' of 'clue-puzzle' detective fiction in the 1920s and 1930s. Consequently the detective story is often associated with modernity. It is the genre above all in which the modernist/Enlightenment fantasy of order and control finds expression. Each classic detective story ends with a restoration of social order and a resolution of the mystery with which it began – suggesting that social cohesion and hierarchy is preserved and that the human mind, the rational faculties (supported by scientific techniques) reign supreme.

It is a commonplace of the study of the detective genre that its representation of detective-work figures as the complement to the practice of reading texts. The detective is a figure whose job is to decode signs and impose narrative order upon an apparently chaotic mass of detail. The reader consequently becomes a 'literary' detective engaged in a similar process of interpretation to the detective, doubling him in his quest to decode a series of signs and arrive at a final meaning. Jorge Luis Borges, who was fascinated by the detective story, once stated that Edgar Allan Poe, in inventing the detective story, really invented the *reader* of the detective story. That is to say, 'a reader who reads with incredulity, with suspicion, with a special kind of suspicion' (Borges 1985, 16). This form of reading, 'paranoid reading', became, as we noted in Chapter 1, institutionalized by the time of modernism and 'practical criticism' (the 1920s and 1930s) – the same moment detective fiction reached its highpoint with the 'Golden Age'.

Paranoid reading is central to the subgenre of detective fiction known variously as the 'metaphysical' detective story, the 'anti-detective' story or the 'postmodern' detective story, which is defined by Patricia Merivale and Susan Elizabeth Sweeney in their collection *Detecting Texts* as 'a text that parodies or subverts traditional detective-story conventions – such as narrative closure and the detective's role as surrogate reader – with the intention, or at least the effect, of asking questions about mysteries of being and knowing which transcend the mere machinations of the mystery plot' (Merivale and Sweeney, 1999, 2). It is acknowledged by the editors and many of the contributors to the collection, that this form of fiction is a particularly postmodern phenomenon. It deploys the techniques of metafiction and intertextuality, frequently referencing classic detective stories by Poe and Doyle. In particular, postmodern detective fiction draws the reader into the activity of 'paranoid reading' only to frustrate his or her efforts at interpretation. This is at work in each of the three of the most celebrated examples which I shall go on to discuss here – Borges's 'Death and the Compass' (1941), Umberto Eco's *The Name of the Rose* (1980) and Paul Auster's *City of Glass* (1985).

Jorge Luis Borges, 'Death and the Compass'

Exemplifying the ingenious response to the 'exhaustion' of fictional forms which so impressed John Barth, Jorge Luis Borges wrote a sequence of three short intellectual thrillers which systematically revisited Poe's three great originary detective stories: where 'The Murders in the Rue Morgue' was published in 1841, Borges's 'Death and the Compass' appeared 100 years later; 'The Garden of Forking Paths' was published 100 years after Poe's 'The Mystery of Marie Rôget' in 1942. 'Ibn-Hakam al-Bokhari, Murdered in His Labyrinth' (1950) lapsed a little behind the centenary of 'The Purloined Letter' (he intended this to follow the pattern and appear in 1945, but found this the hardest to complete).

Rather than exact parodies or variations, Borges's tales parody more generally the epistemological dominant of the classic 'clue-puzzle' detective story by disrupting the realist singular world of classic detective fiction. The most powerful of these is Borges's short story 'Death and the Compass' ('La Muerte y La Brújula'). The story tells of how the great detective Erik Lönnrot is called in to investigate the mysterious murder of one Marcel Yarmolinsky who had been the occupant of a room next door to a famous set of precious jewels. The echoes of Poe's detective fiction are overt, from the outset. Yarmolinsky has been killed in a locked room, as in 'The Murders in the Rue Morgue' (a convention which was to become a staple of the genre), while Lönnrot is a version of the flamboyant eccentric detective *à la* Dupin or Holmes – one who indeed 'believed himself a pure reasoner, an Auguste Dupin' (Borges, 1989, 106).

At the crime scene the dull plodding sidekick figure, Treviranus, another integral feature of the detective genre, exemplified in Doyle's Watson, whose function is to intensify the awe and mystery surrounding the detective, immediately guesses that because the jewels were 'the finest sapphires in the world' owned by the Tetrarch of Galilee, the murder represents a botched robbery: breaking into the wrong room, the thief was confronted by Yarmolinsky, and was forced to kill him. Playing to type, confident almost to the point of smugness, Lönnrot replies:

> Possible, but not interesting. . . . You'll reply that reality hasn't the least obligation to be interesting. And I'll answer you that reality may avoid that obligation but that hypotheses may not. In the hypothesis that you propose, chance intervenes copiously. Here we have a dead rabbi; I would prefer a purely rabbinical explanation, not the imaginary mischances of an imaginary robber.   (Borges, 1989, 107)

In the classic Sherlock Holmes tale, Lönnrot would be proved right, and the solution much more complex than it seems. His suspicions seem to have foundation, too, given that in Yarmolinsky's typewriter is a sheet of paper stating, '*The first letter of the Name has been uttered*'. Sure enough, this murder is swiftly followed by two other deaths. Yarmolinsky was murdered in the north of the city on 3 December, and on the night of 3 January, a second body, that of Daniel Azevedo (incidentally, Borges's family surname on his mother's side), is found in the west of the city. Chalked over the 'conventional diamond-shaped' patterns on the walls of the shop where he is found is the sentence, '*The second letter of the Name has been uttered*'.

The third murder, of one Gryphius-Ginzberg, appears to have taken place (though no body is found) on the night of 3 February in the east of the town, after the words '*The last letter of the Name has been uttered*' are found scrawled on the wall where the victim has made a desperate phone call to Treviranus. It seems the killings are over, and to underline this Treviranus receives a letter accompanied by a map of the city which informs him that there will be no more murders as the three deaths in the north, west, and east form 'the perfect vertices of a mystic equilateral triangle' (Borges, 1989, 112).

Lönnrot is not convinced, however. The first victim, Yarmolinsky, was a noted Talmudic scholar amongst whose possessions had been found a study of the Tetragrammaton – a word with four letters, which refers to the Hebrew secret name for God. It seems obvious to him that there will be a further murder in the south of the city, completing a diamond equivalent to the four points on the compass and the four letters of the Tetragrammaton. Furthermore, given that in Jewish culture each day begins at sundown rather than midnight, it means that each murder has actually been committed on the fourth of the month. This means that the fourth and final murder will be on 3/4 March. Using a compass on the map of the city Lönnrot pinpoints the location of the final murder, a deserted villa named Triste-le-Roy. He goes there intending to catch the criminal in the act and discovers an eerie, disorientatingly labyrinthine building. This is when the twist in the tale is clear. Lying in wait for *him* is a master criminal named Red Scharlach.

Scharlach informs him that the first murder was indeed, just as Treviranus had suspected, a bungled robbery. The man who turned out to be the second victim, Daniel Azevedo, attempting to double-cross the other members of Scharlach's gang and steal the jewels, entered the rabbi's room by mistake and had to kill him. Reading about Lönnrot's investigation in the newspaper, Scharlach hatched a plan to catch him, and thereby gain revenge on an old adversary: 'I swore by the god who looks with two faces and by all the gods of fever and of mirrors that I would weave a labyrinth around the man who had imprisoned my brother' (Borges, 1989, 115). Knowing Lönnrot's fondness for a 'rabbinical explanation' Scharlach plants clues that will seem to the detective to confirm his theory about the murders being aligned to the Tetragrammaton. He kills the double-crosser Azevedo and himself pretends to be Gryphius-Ginzberg in locations which will prompt in Lönnrot's mind associations with the figure of a diamond, which in arcane theology signifies the mirror-relationship between God (the upper triangle of the diamond) and the universe (the lower triangle). Despite Lönnrot's attempts to have the last word by telling Scharlach that in his labyrinth 'there are three lines too many', Scharlach shoots him dead.

The story is thus a powerful and comic parody of many of the established conventions of clue-puzzle detective fiction. The dumb sidekick figure has got it right from the start, whereas the detective's brillant deductive capacity is revealed as flawed – or entirely unsuited to the world in which he tries to exercise it. The criminal is victorious, ensuring that although there is a decisive closure to this detective story, it is not the one we expect from the classics of the genre, where order, restored by the detective, again reigns supreme. Moreover, it is the criminal who delivers the classic dénouement speech. It is appropriate his name is a twisted pronunciation of 'Sherlock'. The title underlines what Borges's story does to the rationalist tradition of conventional detective fiction. The compass is a symbol of the values of the Enlightenment, a human invention designed to help us master our environment. Yet all it does in this story is lead to the death – literal and also symbolic perhaps – of the ultra-rationalist detective.

Umberto Eco, *The Name of the Rose*

In many ways Umberto Eco is the true inheritor of Borges's legacy. His world – in other words, the frame of reference in his critical writings, the bookish world of obscure references and texts – is similar to that of Borges's. *The Name of the Rose* might be considered a novel-length attempt to continue in the Borgesian tradition of the 'metaphysical detective'. It is a text about texts, full of references to other, obscure, texts. It features labyrinths both literal (central to the setting is a vast open-air library) and metaphorical (the attempts of the detective-figure and the reader to make sense of the bewildering number of clues). Moreover, it is very aware of the Borgesian influence. Eco's title itself recalls the repeated refrain of 'Death and the Compass', 'the first letter of the Name has been uttered', while it is an obvious academic in-joke that the master-criminal here, a blind scholar who inhabits the heart of the library-labyrinth, is one Jorge of Burgos, who ends the novel by tearing out the pages of a priceless lost volume and cramming them into his mouth.

Its introduction, ostensibly written by Eco himself to explain how he came by the manuscript and how it has, over the centuries, been subject to numerous retranslations, rewritings, and the addition of supplements, signals clearly to the reader the problem of determining truth if it is embedded inside a text. This is exacerbated by the fact Eco presents his story as a translation of a text which has already been translated: 'On sober reflection, I find few reasons for publishing my Italian version of an obscure, neo-Gothic French version of a seventeenth-century Latin edition of a work written in Latin by a German monk towards the end of the fourteenth century' (Eco, 1984, 15). In other words, as Eco put it later, Adso's narrative exists 'on a fourth level of encasement, inside three other narratives: I am saying what Vallet said that Mabillon said that Adso said . . . ' (Eco, 1985, 20).

Just as Adso's own text has ostensibly been continually lost and found again, so the plot itself revolves around a lost text, namely the second volume of Aristotle's *Poetics* (on comedy) about which academic speculation has been intense, for its existence would perhaps have had profound consequences for Western aesthetics. The novel is set in an Italian monastery in 1327, where two familiar generic archetypes – transported back in time 500 years before the advent of detective fiction proper – are summoned following the murder of one of the monks. The Sherlock Holmes figure is a Franciscan monk named Sir William of Baskerville (again, note the in-joke), capable of brilliant deductive 'introductory exercises' like his ancestor/descendant, while his apprentice Adso of Melk, like Watson, accompanies the detective and narrates the story. As in 'Death and the Compass' a series of apparently linked murders follow the initial one, though there are five this time, and the mystery deepens. While the monks in the Abbey are convinced that the murders are evidence of demonic possession in the face of the Second Coming of Christ, Sir William chooses to seek a solution through the familiar methods of classic detective fiction, empirical reasoning, and deduction.

Yet one of the ironies of *The Name of the Rose* is that while Sir William's methods solve numerous mysteries (e.g. discovering the identity of the lost Aristotle text, cracking the code of a secret message written by Venantius, and figuring out the complex structure of the labyrinthine library), when it comes to the sequence of murders, he is defeated. Like Lönnrot, he assumes that there is a pattern to the murders based upon the biblical narrative of the Apocalypse, but turns out to be quite mistaken. Nevertheless, his mistakes *do* lead him to the master-criminal Jorge, and his vast labyrinthine library. This is the supreme irony: it is only as a result of his *misreading* of the case that he is able to arrive at the heart of the labyrinth. Sir William delivers a dénouement which (in an ironic reversal of the detective tradition) explains his own errors:

I arrived at Jorge seeking one criminal for all the crimes and we discovered that each crime was committed by a different person, or by no one. I arrived at Jorge pursuing the plan of a perverse and rational mind, and there was no plan, or, rather, Jorge himself was overcome by his own initial design and there began a sequence of causes, and concauses, and of causes contradicting one another, which proceeded on their own, creating relations that did not stem from any plan. Where is all my wisdom, then? I behaved stubbornly, pursuing a semblance of order, when I should have known well that there is no order in the universe.

(Eco, 1984, 492)

In Eco's *Reflections on The Name of the Rose*, which I have often referred to in this book, he notes that the experience of writing *The Name of the Rose* led him to rediscover 'what writers have always known (and have told us again and again): books always speak of other books, and every story tells a story that has already been told' (Eco, 1985, 20). His switch from writing criticism to writing fiction actually strengthens his literary-critical conviction that a novel 'is a machine for generating interpretations' (Eco, 1985, 8). Maintaining this principle – in fact trying to ensure that the reader is disoriented by the mass of signifiers within his text – was central to his aim in writing the novel.

It is this logic which determined his choice of title. Aware that a book's title plays a significant role in shaping the reader's interpretations of the text, he initially planned to short-circuit the process by titling the novel *Adso of Melk*, after its narrator – an ambition which, not surprisingly, dismayed his publisher. But he liked *The Name of the Rose*, 'because the rose is a symbolic figure so rich in meanings that by now it has hardly any meaning left: Dante's mystic rose, and go lovely rose, the Wars of the Roses, rose thou art sick, too many rings around Rosie, a rose by any other name, a rose is a rose is a rose, the Rosicrucians' (Eco, 1985, 3). This overload of signification means the title is less about the actual case narrated in the novel, and more about semiotics: the name of the rose is its signifier, but its signifieds are multiple, so much so that they indicate how words refer simply to other words and little else. In demonstrating the polysemy of language generally and fiction specifically, *The Name of the Rose* makes its reader duplicate the activity engaged in by its detective. Arriving at a 'final' interpretation of the novel by imposing upon its patterns of meaning a decisive set of signifieds, is impossible. The network of allusions is so densely wrought that there are potentially hundreds of lines of enquiry which the reader may choose to follow – a veritable labyrinth of potential meaning.

Eco argues that the popularity of detective fiction is precisely because the genre as a whole – not just later parodies of the classic works – raises the kind of questions regarded as definitive of the 'metaphysical' tradition. It is not because detective fiction enables readers to confront death in a displaced manner nor derive consolation from the 'modernist' closure of the text. Rather it is because, like medical diagnosis, scientific research, and philosophy, 'the crime novel represents a kind of conjecture, pure and simple' – and its revelation gratifies us because '[e]very story of investigation and conjecture tells us something that we have always been close to knowing' (Eco, 1985, 54).

This is where we can return to the comparison of different kinds of maze Eco develops in *Reflections on The Name of the Rose*, and which we considered in Chapter 1. For Eco, seeking satisfaction – perhaps even truth – via conjecture works like entering a labyrinth and trying to find the exit. Where sometimes this process is completely straightforward, as in Theseus's labyrinth, and in other labyrinths, like the 'mannerist maze'(Eco, 1985, 57), more complex but still possible through trial and error, the most baffling and powerful kind of labyrinth is the 'rhizomatic' one, with 'no center, no periphery, no exit, because it is potentially infinite' and 'so constructed that every path can be connected with every other one' (Eco, 1985, 57).

Whether or not we subscribe to the implication here that the patterns of conjecture involved in detective fiction makes the genre 'rhizomatic' by definition, it certainly explains the effect of *postmodern* detective fiction – and, by extension (as we have explored in Chapter 1), postmodern narrative as a whole. Eco describes his own novel by claiming that its library is 'still a mannerist labyrinth' (Eco, 1985, 57) (after all, Sir William can work it out) but that 'the world in which William realizes he is living already has a rhizome structure: that is, it can be structured but is never structured definitively' (Eco, 1985, 58). This is indeed the effect of *The Name of the Rose*, which sends the reader on a constant chase for clues, parodying the entire experience of reading detective fiction, all while it lets him or her indulge in it.

Paul Auster, *City of Glass*

The idea that the *experience* of reading detective fiction makes a cognitive point 'emotionally', or via the senses rather than the mind, is a significant one when it comes to postmodern fiction. This was the central point made in one of the first essays to examine the 'anti-detective' story in the context of postmodernism, William Spanos's 1972 essay 'The Detective and the Boundary: Some Notes on the Postmodern Literary Imagination', an interesting complement to Susan Sontag's call for an 'erotics' rather than a hermeneutics of literature (which we considered in Chapter 1).

Spanos argues that postmodern detective fiction makes the same point as anti-rationalist philosophy, but does so through its form rather than through argument, refusing the satisfactory closure of the conventional detective novel and thereby rejecting the Enlightenment faith in teleology (Spanos, 2002).

Spanos's view that we *feel* the anti-rationalism in fiction where we process it cognitively in philosophy applies to another paradigmatic example of the postmodern detective story – Paul Auster's slim novel, *City of Glass,* first published thirteen years after Spanos's theory, in 1985. The novel is the first in a sequence of 'metaphysical' detective stories known as *The New York Trilogy,* and is followed by *Ghosts* and *The Locked Room* (both 1986), each of which draw inventively on detective conventions – not just the classic British analytic model, but also the 'hard-boiled' US tradition. In fact, *City of Glass* is perhaps the most 'canonical' postmodern detective fiction, and one reason for this is that it interrogates the connection between reading and detective fiction persistently, suggestively, and (in a surprising way) movingly. It does so through the simple premise of telling the story of a man fascinated by detective fiction who takes on a case as a real detective. Its hero is a fusion of the amateur, 'armchair' detective who tries to solve a puzzle, familiar from Conan Doyle and Agatha Christie texts, with the professional American private investigator who pounds the mean streets in search of a missing person.

Daniel Quinn is a writer of detective stories and also an avid reader of the genre, someone who loves detective stories because of,

> their sense of plenitude and economy. In the good mystery there is nothing wasted, no sentence, no word that is not significant. . . . The detective is the one who looks, who listens, who moves through this morass of objects and events in search of the thought, the idea that will pull all these things together and make sense of them. In effect, the writer and the detective are interchangeable. The reader sees the world through the detective's eye, experiencing the proliferation of its details as if for the first time.   (Auster, 1987, 8)

At a low point in his life following the failure of his marriage, and looking to escape the literary world, Quinn starts to receive misdirected telephone calls asking urgently to be put in touch with a private detective, one 'Paul Auster. Of the Auster Detective Agency' (Auster, 1987, 7). After dismissing them initially, he impulsively pretends he is a real detective and takes on the case, drawing on the knowledge of detective conventions he has gained from writing and reading detective fiction.

The metafictional effect of the novel is immediately clear: what we have is a writer of detective fiction, masquerading as Paul Auster – someone, moreover, who writes under the *nom-de-plume* William Wilson, the name of a character in an Edgar Allan Poe story who is the narrator's uncanny double. This, we recall, is a clear example of metafiction's capacity to destabilize ontological boundaries, for reading Auster's name in the story makes us question whether Auster is really the novelist or whether the story is not fiction but true. At one point, Quinn meets 'Auster', complete with the author's real-life wife and son, and discusses with him the question of authorship in *Don Quixote* (as Quinn later reflects, he shares his initials with Cervantes's character). The considerable network of intertextual references in *City of Glass*, including, for example, references to Melville and Hammett, extends the metafictional dimension of Auster's story, emphasizing that this is a novel about novels rather than anything in the 'real' world.

Initially Quinn's task is to protect a certain Peter Stillman from his deranged father, also called Peter Stillman, who has gone missing. But the quest to find him is doomed practically from the outset. Lying in wait for him at Grand Central Station in New York Quinn encounters two apparently identical suspects and realizes, to his horror, that '[t]here was nothing he could do now that would not be a mistake. Whatever choice he made – and he had to make a choice – would be arbitrary, a submission to chance'. Nevertheless, he chooses one (the second), a 'shuffling . . . shabby creature, . . . broken down and disconnected from his surroundings' (Auster, 1987, 56) and then tails him over the course of several weeks, waiting outside his apartment each day for him to emerge, and obsessively recording his movements in a red notebook he has bought, until eventually, having given up everything – home, health, sanity – in the pursuit, and convinced that 'the only thing he felt now was the man's impenetrability' (67), Quinn becomes a shabby tramp-like figure himself.

The novel ends enigmatically with a description of Quinn's last days lying on the floor in the Stillman's empty apartment, sleeping, hallucinating that he is being provided with delicious meals, and continuing to write down his thoughts. Finally the narrator – hitherto remaining in the background, now becoming more visible – reports on Quinn's disappearance, and his and 'Auster's' efforts to find out what happened to him. They visit the apartment themselves and find only the red notebook, the last sentence of which reads, 'What will happen when there are no more pages in the red notebook?' (131). This, of course, is a neat self-reflexive ending, as we have a fictional character who disappears once the words run out, that is, once the author has stopped writing him into existence. But Auster's work contains a poignancy that is more powerful than the kind of playful self-reflexive literary games associated with an earlier generation of American metafictional writers, such as Coover and Barth.

Like other postmodern detective stories, *City of Glass* works as a critique of rationalist – or 'paranoid' – reading strategies. But what is especially interesting about Auster's novel in the context of detective fiction, as Jeffrey Nealon has argued, is what it says about *writing* and the process of detection. In his influential essay on the genre, 'The Typology of Detective Fiction', Tzvetan Todorov (drawing on a 1926 article by the detective writer S. S. Van Dine) posits a homology that aligns the author with the criminal rather than the detective: 'author : reader = criminal : detective' (Todorov, 1977, 49). However, Nealon contends that Auster's trilogy shows that although the author is the one who establishes the labyrinthine plot into which the reader must enter, s/he is *also* 'the one who searches – perhaps more desperately than the reader – for its end, for [to quote *City of Glass*] "the idea that will pull all these things together and make sense of them"' (Nealon, 1999, 118). 'For the reader', Nealon writes, 'the mystery always ends, regardless of whether it is solved. . . . No such luxury is available to the writer or the detective. Once they enter the space of the mystery, there is no guarantee of an ordered conclusion – no guarantee even of the closure afforded the reader by the final period placed after the final sentence' (Nealon, 1999, 118). The detective is the person who is faced with apparently random and unconnected phenomena: a death, for example, and a range of clues. His job is ultimately to show that these apparently chance elements link together into a meaningful narrative which can uncover the means, motive, and opportunity to commit the crime, and the identity of the criminal.

More than an interrogation of reading, Quinn's engagement with the Stillman case is actually a dramatization of the act of *writing*, of trying to make some kind of narrative sense out of the chaos of the world. As with other examples of metafiction, Auster's strategy here is to make the metaphorical literal – more precisely, in the case of *City of Glass*, the analogy between writing and detective-work. For Quinn, in fact, these activities become more than analogous but progressively indistinguishable from one another. Once he has purchased his red notebook Quinn becomes obsessed with recording everything Stillman does, to the point at which he takes to writing while actually following him, making notes while walking. While this is obviously a source of pathos, it is also ironic that the very job Quinn took on to escape a purely textual world has ultimately entailed returning to it more directly and desperately than ever.

Auster's novel is influenced by the work of the literary philosopher Maurice Blanchot (whose work Auster translated in the 1970s). Though not a postmodernist theorist, Blanchot's thinking bears an interesting relationship to the postmodern. It begins with the assumption that we are living in a 'time of transition' between an earlier world where the 'human condition' could be understood by reference to God, and our own 'absurdist', post-religious – we might say, postmodern – culture. Against this background, Blanchot considers what we might call the *mystery* of literature. Why do we write? Why does what is written have such a strange power over us? Writing is strange, he insists, because it does not *refer* to the world (though it is naturally assumed that it does) yet exists as part of it. This means that literature exists independently of the writer's own existence: though it is produced *by* the writer, what is written also takes its place as a separate entity in the world (Blanchot, 1989).

A positive effect of this independence is that writing can ensure a certain kind of immortality for the writer, as he or she 'lives on' posthumously through his or her achievements. More disturbingly, though, it means that writing makes the writer's existence *irrelevant*, for his or her work can be read without any reference to himself or herself.

The act of writing, then, for Blanchot, is tantamount to confronting one's own non-existence. This accounts for the impulse to write and the curious consequences for our own sense of identity when we do so – what Blanchot refers to as the 'demand of writing'. This notion leads him to distinguish between the 'book' and the 'work', concepts which might usefully be seen as the counterpart of Roland Barthes's opposition between 'work' and 'text', except that it uses how something is written rather than read as the basis for the distinction. For Blanchot, the book is the object that we buy in the shop, and is what we read and write about: it bears the author's name and is bound up with the network of cultural meaning and economic exchange that characterizes the everyday modern world. The 'work', on the other hand, is what is produced by responding to the 'demand of writing'; it is the space into which the writer 'disappears'. From a Blanchotian perspective, it is the work rather than the book to which Kafka and, to a lesser extent, Beckett are concerned with.

Blanchot's distinction between work and book can be felt behind *City of Glass*, which on one level is nothing other than a dramatization of Blanchot's idea of the mystery of 'the work'. It is significant that Quinn's detective – from whom he is trying to escape – is named 'Max Work'. While Quinn's failure in detective-work amounts to a clear failure of reading (that is, an inability to decode the ambiguous signifiers his case presents him with) it is more fully the result of entering into a kind of *writing*. This aspect distinguishes Auster's *The New York Trilogy* from other 'canonical' works of metaphysical detective fiction, such as 'Death and the Compass' or *The Name of the Rose*, in that his detectives are to be envisaged as surrogate *writers* rather than simply readers. As he becomes lost in the labyrinthine plot of his case Quinn resembles the writer surrendering to the force of the Blanchotian 'work'. He is never sure of where his writing will take him.

City of Glass thus underlines the fact that postmodern detective fiction is not simply geared towards mounting a critique of classic detective fiction, but is about our engagement with literature itself. Detective fiction is typically condemned as an inferior generic form of writing. But its postmodern incarnation makes us think of it as precisely the opposite; as a genre which is naturally metafictional and which causes us – like all postmodern fiction does, in some way – to meditate on the practices of writing and reading fiction.

Chapter 8

Fiction of the 'postmodern condition': Ballard, DeLillo, Ellis

Conclusion: 'ficto-criticism'

The final chapter in this book turns to three important post-war writers whose fiction explores the psychological effects of postmodernity on the individuals who live in it: J. G. Ballard, Don DeLillo, and Bret Easton Ellis. Their work can therefore be (and has been) considered in relation to the theories of postmodernism and postmodernity with which we began this book, especially those by the 'Holy Trinity' of postmodern theorists, Jameson, Lyotard, and Baudrillard. Indeed Ballard and DeLillo in particular have been regarded as theorists-by-proxy themselves, producing the kind of work Noel King has termed 'ficto-criticism', writing which uses fiction explicitly to analyse cultural and social patterns as an alternative to 'pure' theory (King, 1991).

The discussion will focus on key novels by each writer: Ballard's *Crash*, DeLillo's *White Noise* and *Libra*, and Ellis's *American Psycho*. Each of these novels depict, in different ways, a world which is increasingly divorced from the real as a result of the pervasive power of technology and systems of representation which dominate our culture: television, the media, advertising, and marketing. The consequence for the individual is that the self is experienced as being emptied of substance, lacking coherence and consistency. In each case the implication is that the logic of the 'Möbius strip' (a geometrical twisted figure-of-eight structure where the outside edge becomes the inside and vice versa) operates with regard to what were once stable boundaries between society and the individual, private and public, inside and outside. 'External' social patterns, such as the logic of the surface and the image, are replicated on the 'inside' of the self, while, conversely, private individual desires, fantasies and anxieties seem to shape wider social and cultural dynamics.

A particular feature of the psychology of the characters depicted in the work of the three writers in question here is what J. G. Ballard once called 'the death of affect'. 'Affect' is a term used by psychiatrists and psychoanalysts to refer to emotion, as in 'being affected by' something. It is assumed that this is a fundamental part of existing as a normal social being, because it is how we make sense of our own experiences, and – crucially – how we empathize with the experiences of those around us. Ballard's conviction is that our ability to feel genuine emotion has been disappearing since the late twentieth century. Support for this idea comes in Jameson's reading of the pathologies of postmodernity in *Postmodernism, or the Cultural Logic of Late Capitalism*, central to which is a 'waning of affect'. Jameson, we recall, argues that postmodernity has ushered in a change in the structure of expressing and feeling emotions. Where once we had anxiety, neurosis, and *anomie*, expressions of 'the centred subject', now, 'since there is no longer a self present to do the feeling' we are more subject to the more 'free-floating and impersonal' emotions which Lyotard terms 'intensities' (Jameson, 1991, 16).

Another thing that unites the fiction considered in this chapter is that its postmodernism operates chiefly at the level of content rather than form. Throughout this book I have been suggesting that if there is anything that defines the many different kinds of fiction to have been labelled 'postmodern' over the past four decades or so it is to be identified at the level of form. In other words, it is not what postmodern fiction tells us that makes it postmodern, it is what it *does*. Specifically, postmodern fiction reminds readers of the nature of fictionality and causes them to reflect upon the process of deriving meaning from narrative. The work of Ballard, DeLillo, and Ellis for the most part provides something of an exception to this rule in that it eschews the kind of radical formal experimentation favoured by earlier postmodernists (there are exceptions in some of the early work of the first two writers, while there are subtly metafictional elements to Ellis's *American Psycho*, as I shall show). Because these writers have been linked so consistently to postmodernism it would be impossible to ignore them in a book such as this. Yet for the reasons mentioned above, their work does also emphasize the *constructed* nature of postmodern existence, its dependence upon narrative and representation, in a way that provides a fascinating complement to the more overtly self-reflexive writing of authors considered previously in this book.

In fact, reading the work of these novelists suggests that so completely has our experience of reality become shaped by postmodern systems of representation that a neat separation of 'reality' and 'fiction', of 'world' and 'book', upon which the category of metafiction depends, is actually no longer tenable and even rather quaint. As such, the novels considered here underline the point which other postmodern fictions dealt with in this book have made repeatedly, that real life is mediated through narrative and aesthetic technique, just as much as fiction. They remind us, too, that fiction – whether or not it has been labelled 'postmodern' – is always, to some degree, self-reflexive.

J. G. Ballard, *Crash*

In an introduction written to accompany the 1975 French edition of his novel, *Crash* (1973), J. G. Ballard explains the psychopathologies which drive contemporary society:

> the marriage of reason and nightmare which has dominated the 20th century has given birth to an ever more ambiguous world.... Over our lives preside the great twin leitmotifs of the 20th century – sex and paranoia.... Voyeurism, self-disgust, the infantile basis of our dreams and longings – these diseases of the psyche have now culminated in the most terrifying casualty of the century: the death of affect.
>
> (Ballard, 1995a, 4)

Where twentieth-century existence was underscored by an increasing faith in rationality, embodied in the application of scientific and logical principles to social communication and systems of social life, such as communications and the media, technology, cars and aeroplanes, and the cinema, Ballard also thinks that this resulted in a perverse counter-effect whereby such developments tap into and massage, perhaps even produce, the *irrational* desires within us all. The advances of technology, he thinks, effect a return to a kind of infantile state, 'where any demand, any possibility, whether for life-styles, travel, sexual roles and identities, can be satisfied instantly' (4).

More precisely, Ballard argues that the intensities of the twentieth century have resulted in a reversal of the *roles* played in everyday existence by the world of fiction and the world of reality: 'In the past we have always assumed that the external world around us has represented reality, however confusing or uncertain, and that the inner world of our minds, its dreams, hopes, ambitions, represented the realm of fantasy and the imagination' (Ballard, 1995a, 4). This stable opposition has now been eroded. Ballard's view is that where once we would retreat from everyday social reality into the world of our imagination – serviced by art forms such as the novel and cinema – now the outside world is so 'fictional' as a result of the systems of 'mass-merchandizing, advertising, politics conducted as a branch of advertising', that '[t]he most prudent and effective method of dealing with the world around us is to assume that it is a complete fiction – conversely, the one small node of reality left to us is inside our own heads' (4).

The experience is like living 'inside an enormous novel', and this reversal presents the writer of fiction with a special challenge. The author's task is no longer to 'preside over his characters like an examiner, knowing all the questions in advance', inventing 'a self-sufficient and self-enclosed world' and disregarding questions about his own 'motives, prejudices and psychopathology'. Rather he ought to be more like the 'scientist, whether on safari or in his laboratory, faced with an unknown terrain or subject'. This author has a duty to reject the stance of 'moral authority' favoured by the writers of realist novels and instead offer the reader 'the contents of his own head, a set of options and imaginative alternatives' (5–6).

Although brief, Ballard's Introduction to *Crash* amounts to an extraordinarily vital and enduringly relevant manifesto for postmodern fiction, at once in tune with the critiques of realism being advanced by novelists like B. S. Johnson and John Barth and cultural critics like Susan Sontag in the late 1960s and early 1970s, but also prefiguring more sustained critiques of postmodern culture mounted in the 1980s by the likes of Jameson (who uses a number of similar terms to Ballard) and Jean Baudrillard. It perhaps goes without saying that the Introduction also sketches out the landscape of Ballard's own fiction.

Yet what is curious about Ballard is that most of his fiction is, on the surface, much less radical than one might expect from one who rejects the English 'bourgeois novel' so strongly and argues for writers to be 'scientists on safari' who empty the contents of their heads on to the page. While the form of some of Ballard's 1970s short stories and his extraordinary collection *The Atrocity Exhibition* (1970) – which parallels the techniques of 1950s and 1960s 'Pop Artists' by assembling a series of 'condensed novels' to create a spatial effect, as if each scene or motif is a 3-D object which we can walk around and view from different perspectives – is 'experimental', the rest of Ballard's fiction appears rather conventional, favouring linear plots narrated in a consistent third-person 'omniscient' voice.

However, critics have suggested that it is in fact Ballard's superficial 'normality' that makes his work so unsettling. Roger Luckhurst has argued that Ballard's distinctive strategy in his fiction is to unsettle the distinction between generic boundaries and thus disturb our expectations (Luckhurst, 1997). Andrzej Gasiorek has argued that the use of a traditional linear structure to accommodate shocking subject-matter refuses to allow readers any 'distance' or 'estrangement' from the content, inviting them into the novel in a familiar realist way but then making them feel uncomfortable (Gasiorek, 2007, 17).

This is certainly what happens in Ballard's *Crash*, which the author describes as 'an extreme metaphor for an extreme situation, a kit of desperate measures only for use in an extreme crisis' (Ballard, 1995a, 6). The novel clearly also puts into practice the strategy of refusing the 'moral authority' of the realist writer, instead 'offer[ing] the reader the contents of [the writer's] head' (5–6). Given its subject-matter, though, it is natural for readers to wonder about Ballard's sanity (as did the writer of a publisher's report on the novel in

1971, who famously wrote 'This author is beyond psychiatric help. Do Not Publish').

Crash is a particularly graphic exploration of the erotics of the car crash, its underlying thesis spelled out by a comment by William Burroughs, one of Ballard's key influences, that 'an auto crash can be more sexually stimulating than a pornographic picture' (Burroughs, 2001, 7). Narrated by 'Ballard', it tells the story of Vaughan, a former 'TV scientist' whose existence is governed by sexual fantasies about women and car crashes. 'Ballard' becomes Vaughan's 'assistant' and accompanies him on visits to the crash-tests at the Road Research Laboratory in West London and on tours of the motorways seeking out 'nightmare collisions', stopping to watch the rescue attempts, even filming a fatally-injured woman driver when first to arrive on the scene. He watches uncomfortably as Vaughan takes women to have sex in crashed cars in scrapwrecking yards.

As well as these real crashes he and Vaughan endlessly imagine more and more exotic collisions, car-crash victims and wounds, especially those involving celebrities: Jayne Mansfield, Albert Camus, and John F. Kennedy. Vaughan becomes the leader of an underground community of alienated people, all of whom have been victims of car crashes and who gather together to re-enact famous car crashes. Eventually he begins to stalk Elizabeth Taylor, taking pictures of her as she leaves her hotel room, which he combines with images of wounds from a textbook on plastic surgery to form a collage. Vaughan's ultimate fantasy is to die with the actress in a car crash and inevitably gets killed when he tries to smash 'Ballard's' car into the limousine in which Taylor is a passenger.

The novel is a kind of perverse postmodern reworking of the classic modernist mode, the retrospective narrative. 'Ballard' is fascinated by Vaughan much in the way that Nick Carraway is by Jay Gatsby in *The Great Gatsby*. After Vaughan's death – and this is what gives his narrative much of its impetus – 'Ballard' subscribes increasingly to his friend's perverse psychology and philosophy, telling his story in order to support Vaughan's conviction that he had discovered 'the keys to a new sexuality born from a perverse technology' (Ballard, 1995b, 13). The surrogate novelist 'Ballard' thus plays the role of a 'scientist on safari', exploring unknown psycho-sexual territory.

The idea of a 'new sexuality born from a perverse technology' can be illuminated by what the theorist Mark Seltzer calls 'wound culture'. A wound is where a body is literally torn apart, so someone looking at it is able to see what's inside, and what happens to the body when the surface is broken apart. 'Wound culture', Seltzer argues, is a powerful way of conceiving of modern and postmodern society. We are attracted to what Ballard calls the 'atrocity exhibition' on a mass scale, fascinated by 'the shock of contact between bodies and technologies: a shock of contact that encodes, in turn, a breakdown in the distinction between the individual and the mass and between private and public registers' (Seltzer, 1998, 253).

This is why, Seltzer argues, we are fascinated by depictions of violence in contemporary culture – especially artistic and media representations of serial killing, Seltzer's main subject – but, more generally, why we are preoccupied by events and artwork which show us 'the opening of private and bodily and psychic interiors' (Seltzer, 1998, 253). The work of Ballard, whom Seltzer describes as 'one of the compulsive cartographers of wound culture' (Seltzer, 1998, 264), is preoccupied by the collapsing of internal and external space, and the private and the public sphere. As Vaughan photographs the young accident-victim Gabrielle, 'Ballard' records that 'her canny eyes were clearly aware of his real interest in her' (Ballard, 1995b, 100) – and this not just the literal opening of her body suggested by her scars, nor even her sex (an outdated term for which is 'wound'), but the desire to see into the interior of her body and psyche.

In his 'photographic workshop' (Ballard, 1995b, 96), where there are hundreds of photographs of crashes and victims, Vaughan hands 'Ballard' Gabrielle's 'dossier', which documents first the crash scene in which she is surrounded by police, medics, and spectators, then her severe injuries in the crash, then the wreckage of her car, then her recuperation in hospital. With huge scars on her legs, leg clamps and back braces, she comes to seem a more permanent embodiment of the marriage between technology and sex which is momentarily enacted with every car crash. The car crash has transformed her radically, from 'a conventional young woman whose symmetrical face and unstretched skin spelled out the whole economy of a cosy and passive life, of minor flirtations in the backs of cheap cars enjoyed without any sense of the real possibilities of her body' to a woman 'reborn' as a deeply sexualized cyborg, a hybrid combination of human sexuality and the erotics of technology. The motorized chromium wheelchair she occupies – a miniature car to which the body is welded – has the effect of making her openly sexualized, emphasizing her knees and pubis to the men who look on, her male physiotherapist, Vaughan, and 'Ballard': 'The crushed body of the sports car had turned her into a creature of free and perverse sexuality, releasing within its twisted bulkheads and leaking engine coolant all the deviant possibilities of her sex' (Ballard, 1995b, 99). The continual references to fluids, both manufactured and bodily (semen and blood from the human, and engine coolant and petrol from the car) symbolizes the merging of inside and outside, human being and machine. Gabrielle is only in fact the most obvious example of a character who exhibits change *outwardly* as a way of advertising the change in psychology inside. Vaughan himself, who seems to be permanently attached to his camera, embodies this combination, as if he is not just the possessor of a new psychology, but an example of a new species formed by the blending together of sex and technology.

This summary ought to be enough to suggest why *Crash* is one of the most notorious novels of the twentieth century and was the subject of much moral outrage. Yet as extreme and perverse as its story is, it develops, on a number of levels, a serious critique of contemporary culture, more extensive than Ballard's Introduction.

To begin with, the novel's strategy is really just to make literal what is an enduring metaphor in contemporary culture: the status of the automobile as an eroticized object, most commonly suggested by a car being described as an 'extension of a man's penis'. Its story depicts a culture in which the imaginary has come to stand in for the real – in Baudrillardian terms, a hyperreal world which can no longer distinguish original from copy. The characters in *Crash* engage with all the suggestive, sensual images of the car which are circulated through the marketing and advertising apparatus rather than its reality: a dangerous piece of technology which we should be wary of.

At one level the novel represents Ballard's amazement at how a rational, advanced society such as ours can tolerate the kind of 'perverse technology' involved in the production of high-speed motor cars – especially those high-lighted by Ralph Nader in his famous 1956 exposé, *Unsafe at Any Speed,* which revealed that US car companies were reluctant to spend money on safety features, and, worse, included 'designed-in dangers' in their cars (e.g. the Chevrolet Corvair), such as an excessively heavy rear engine or a steering column that could impale the driver. For Ballard this is clear evidence of 'some deviant logic unfolding . . . , more powerful than that provided by reason' (Ballard, 1995b, 6). *Crash* explores the way in which human nature has changed as a result of the impact of modern technology, and how this is bound up with an unhealthy attitude towards mediatized celebrity and the image. *Crash*'s characters can only experience sexual arousal while engaging with technology (cars obviously, but also architecture). At the heart of Vaughan's perverse activities are the devices of visual technology, such as the camera, film, and the photocopier (which Ballard uses to blow up the collage-pictures of Elizabeth Taylor).

This behaviour is evidence of the 'death of affect'. One of the most distinctive features of all of Ballard's fiction – from the novels which immediately followed *Crash*, *Concrete Island* (1973) and *High-Rise* (1975) (the three making up what critics have called the 'urban disaster trilogy') to the more recent novels *Cocaine Nights* (1996), *Super-Cannes* (2000), and *Millenium People* (2003) – is the depiction of affectless characters. But rather than portraying a world of robotic people, playing out routine existence in emotional isolation from others, Ballard's dramatization of the 'death of affect' is a matter either of presenting characters who go through the motions of having 'feelings', in fact taking them to excess, as a kind of reflex action, a learned behaviour of how to act *as if* one were human, or depicting people who become aroused or stimulated by things which normally would not trigger desire in this way.

Don DeLillo, *White Noise* and *Libra*

As with Ballard, critics respond to DeLillo's work not simply for its aesthetic merits, but because of its status as 'ficto-criticism'. As his comments in interviews attest, the author himself is quite comfortable with this view of him as public intellectual rather than just private author, as he is deeply interested in ideas. The downside is that DeLillo's fiction, which often chooses ambitiously to deal with the crucial events in contemporary history head on (such as the assassination of John F. Kennedy in *Libra*, or 9/11 in *Falling Man*), has often been compared by critics to journalism, a form of writing predicated on fact and accurate insight, and found wanting. But DeLillo's fiction delivers an alternative kind of insight into contemporary culture and society not least because the dominant feature of the contemporary world is the way it is shaped by images and narratives, and fiction trades in precisely these things.

DeLillo's early novels, *Americana* (1971), *End Zone* (1972), and *Ratner's Star* (1976), bear affinities with the experimental tradition of US writing which privileged metafiction. However, his 'breakthrough' novel was the satirical *White Noise*, published in 1984, which has been the source of most critical interest in his work. It is set in the kind of hyperreal US suburban town which we all recognize from American sitcoms and Peter Weir's 1997 film *The Truman Show*, and features as protagonist Jack Gladney, a university professor in 'Hitler Studies' (a subject that enables him to salve his own fears of death as the monstrous mass murder of the Nazis makes them pale in comparison). Following a toxic spillage, the citizens start to become ill and the story tells of the evacuation of Jack and his family and his uncovering of a mystery about the drugs designed to alleviate the symptoms caused by the accident.

There is therefore an absorbing plot to *White Noise*. Yet the most interesting feature of the novel is the apparently incidental detail. Much of it is taken up with Jack (who is the narrator) recounting his perceptions of postmodern existence after observing his students and his family, reporting his discussions with his friend, fellow professor (of Popular Culture) Murray Siskind, and meditating on death. It is in this dimension of *White Noise* that the novel's preoccupation with one of the key aspects of the postmodern condition is revealed: the fact that contemporary culture is characterized by an overload of communication, information and representations, transmitted through the media, advertising and marketing systems, and the effect this has upon post-modern subjects.

'White noise' is the term for the cacophonic merging of sounds which we hear when TV reception is interrupted or during audio feedback, but has a more general sense – one that certainly figures in this novel – as referring to the babble of different messages transmitted constantly in our media-driven culture. The 'airborne toxic event' which constitutes the main dramatic catalyst to the novel's plot is paralleled by the effects of a more metaphorical 'white noise' of information systems. This is suggested in the novel by television, Siskind urging his students to 'Look at the wealth of data concealed in the grid, in the bright packaging, the jingles, the slice-of-life commercials, the products hurtling out of darkness, the coded messages and endless repetitions, like chants, like mantras. "*Coke is it, Coke is it, Coke is it.*"' (DeLillo, 1984, 50–1). Where the airborne toxins cause those who come into contact with them to become unwell, so the cacophony of messages and signals propelled through the air by the various communications and informations systems of postmodernity cause the 'health' of the postmodern subject to deteriorate.

Two comic episodes in the novel are often cited by critics who see in them a parallel with Jean Baudrillard's diagnosis of postmodernity as a hyperreal cul-ture, one in which the real is continually inaccessible and simulated through representations. The first is where Siskind and Gladney drive to see a tourist attraction known as 'the most photographed barn in America' and pass five signs advertising this fact before arriving – along with forty cars, a tour bus and tourists with cameras – at the site. Siskind, a kind of apologist for post-modernism, comments approvingly on the effect of the hype: 'No one sees the barn. . . . Once you've seen the signs about the barn, it becomes impossible to see the barn' (DeLillo, 1984, 12). What he means is that the signs condition the viewers' response to the barn so that looking at it is a matter of witnessing the spectacle surrounding it rather than noticing anything significant about the barn itself. The image tourists are seeking is not the barn but the 'aura' about the barn's celebrity. It gives them a new spiritual sense of identity, which Siskind likens to a 'religious experience' (12).

The second episode is when Jack and his family are being evacuated to protect them from the effects of the toxic spillage. The evacuation is being co-ordinated by an organization called SIMUVAC, which one of its employees informs Jack stands for 'simulated evacuation', an important new state programme. When Jack points out that 'this evacuation isn't simulated. It's real', the technician replies: 'We know that. But we thought we could use it as a model'. A real event, in other words, provides the opportunity to prepare for a more accurate simulation. Jack asks him how this is going, and is informed that:

> The insertion curve isn't as smooth as we would like. There's a probability excess. Plus which we don't have our victims laid out where we'd want them if this was an actual simulation. In other words we're forced to take our victims as we find them. . . . You have to make allowances for the fact that everything we see tonight is real. There's a lot of polishing we still have to do.   (DeLillo, 1984, 139)

Both these events are illustrations of Baudrillard's conviction about how 'the code', or the systems which make the world meaningful, produces copies that stand in for the real. In fact they make it especially clear that Baudrillard's argument isn't simply about lamenting the loss of something present and stable (the real), but about how our experience of reality is actually *produced* by simulation. The most photographed barn itself is effectively produced by the aura surrounding it, because it is impossible to see it as anything else, while the simulated evacuation modelled by SIMUVAC is intended to condition real evacuations in future.

Everywhere in the world of *White Noise* is the sense that the constructions of the spheres of media, marketing, and advertising shape real events and behaviour rather than respond to them or represent them. Jack notices, for example, that the symptoms his daughters, Steffie and Denise, experience following the toxic spillage are precisely those which have been described in the news bulletin which precedes the one they are watching (according to an apparent logic which Elaine Showalter has noted in real epidemics such as 'Gulf War Syndrome' and 'Toxic Shock Syndrome' where the media seems to transmit symptoms via suggestions [Showalter, 1998]).

Similarly many of the incidental details in the novel suggest that the capacity of representations or words to reflect reality is severely weakened. The novel is full of references to food, but it is always the processed, packaged variety, purchased in the sterile world of the supermarket: peanuts, popcorn, pretzels, pizza, etc. Siskind (of course) celebrates the 'flavorless packaging' of the generic brands in his basket as 'the last avant-garde. Bold new forms. The power to shock' (DeLillo, 1984, 18) but Gladney is disturbed that even the apparently authentic, natural products such as fruit have taken on the appearance of packaged foods: 'The fruit was gleaming and wet, hard-edged. There was a self-conscious quality about it. It looked carefully observed, like four-color fruit in a guide to photography' (DeLillo, 1984, 170).

At a more pervasive level *White Noise* suggests that language itself can no longer refer to reality. Throughout the novel there are references to the products, brand names, and companies which are omnipresent in the everyday experience of postmodernity, some real, some made up: Panasonic, The Airport Marriott, Dacron, Red Devil. DeLillo's strategy – comic but often strangely poignant – is to insert these names suddenly and randomly into passages of prose. When musing on his wife Babette's fear of death, for example, the paragraph ends with the words 'Mastercard, Visa, American Express'. The strategy has the effect of demonstrating directly how the words bear no relation to reality, but at the same time also suggest that they take on a deeper, more mysterious, meaning in the lives of postmodern subjects. While asleep, Steffie utters two words which the listening Gladney assumes 'have a ritual meaning, part of a verbal spell or exotic chant' – *Toyota Celica*: 'A long moment passed before I realized this was the name of an automobile. The truth only amazed me more. The utterance was beautiful and mysterious, gold-shot with looming wonder. It was like the name of an ancient power in the sky, tablet-carved in cuneiform' (DeLillo, 1984, 155).

White Noise diagnoses contemporary culture as one saturated by the logic of the representation. DeLillo approaches this question from a different angle in his next novel, *Libra* (1988), which was a huge bestseller in the United States. It tells the story of the real historical figure, Lee Harvey Oswald, the man who was arrested on suspicion of having shot President Kennedy in 1963 and who was then gunned down himself two days later by the mysterious Jack Ruby. More precisely *Libra* develops two narratives which gradually merge into one: besides Oswald's biography, it tells the story of a conspiracy begun by the CIA official Win Everett who decides, on the second anniversary of the Bay of Pigs (17th April 1963) that Kennedy's increasingly conciliatory attitude to Cuba must cease, and looks to create an 'electrifying event' to marshall popular and government opinion against the Cubans.

Both narratives are rooted in established historical fact, though like all the events surrounding the assassination of JFK they are both also full of gaps which DeLillo fills in through fictionalization. The conspiracy story, while plausible, is impossible to verify, and for this reason DeLillo was regarded by some commentators as having joined the ranks of the many conspiracy theorists who treat events in US political history with the greatest suspicion, and also the new leader of the US tradition of 'paranoid novelists', such as Burroughs, Mailer, and Pynchon.

But, as Frank Lentricchia has pointed out, DeLillo's novel does not actually advance a water-tight conspiracy theory. He leaves out many of the necessary elements required to make the conspiracy narrative surrounding the assassination most plausible, such as the conspirators somehow ensuring that Oswald was given the job at the Texas School Book Depository or that the motorcade would pass directly beneath his window in that building. The novel's real interest in the assassination and Oswald's role in it is because the event confirmed the degree to which American reality and history are dependent upon representations rather than the real. These representations generate a myriad narratives which are all plausible but, equally, are also virtual or fictional. Conspiracy theory is a classic example of this, as are other interpretations of Oswald's motives (but which remain speculative as so little is really known about him) such as his possible Oedipal desire to be the fatherless slayer of America's great father figure.

This points to one way of understanding the title. Oswald is a 'negative libran', and consequently considers his character as 'somewhat steady and impulsive. Easily, easily, easily influenced. Poised to make the dangerous leap' (DeLillo, 2006a, 315). Astrology is a system which shapes reality by explaining our actions according to a particular narrative or even determining how we act in a given situation. The fact that the title does not specifically identify Oswald as the Libran suggests that Libra is intended to signify more generally. Oswald is an extreme version of the way postmodernity makes us all into creatures of the image too. Libra figures perhaps as an alternative name for postmodern America: a country of subjects swallowed up by the logic of representation, easily influenced, impulsive and ready to make a 'dangerous leap'.

The particular proliferation of narratives and representations, all of which separate us further from the real rather than take us closer to it, is why, according to N. H. Reeve, *Libra* is a postmodern historical novel very unlike Hutcheon's 'historiographic metafiction' which challenges and subverts established 'official' versions of history. The problem is that the story of John F. Kennedy's assassination has never had an 'authorized' version – or, at least, the closest thing that came to it, the official Warren Report, developed a narrative which was challenged right from the outset by conspiracy theories. Moreoever, Reeve suggests, the assassination-story, which comes to us through a range of contestable and fragmented narrative forms (the Zapruder film, contemporary news reporting, etc.) 'has itself already done more than any postmodern novel to undermine the supposed authority of historical accounts and objective overviews' (Reeve, 1999, 138).

The numerous conspiracies surrounding the assassination flourish because there is so much that remains mysterious – despite so much of the event having been recorded on film and audio tape and its aftermath being subject to such intense scrutiny. In a new Introduction to the novel published in 2006 DeLillo notes wryly how the advances in technology in recent years promise to determine whether there were three, four, or even five shots fired (the latter two numbers would make it a conspiracy because the time permitted would only have allowed Oswald to fire three times) (DeLillo, 2006a, viii–ix) but implies that will not cease speculation.

The novel suggests that the mystery reigns not despite the technology of the image but because of it. The very nature of television is that the image seduces the viewer away from any reality it refers to. Partly this is due to the distinctive TV logic Fredric Jameson notes, of replaying and reconstructing events – something which becomes even more pronounced during the news media's response to a crisis (Jameson, 1991, 355). But it is also because of a more fundamental fact, that the image sucks the meaning out of an event and causes us to focus on the image itself.

DeLillo's interest in the figure of Oswald is not just because he is at the heart of what the CIA historian Nicholas Branch thinks of as the 'seven seconds that broke the back of the American century' (DeLillo, 2006a, 181) but that he is also a pure creature of the media. Even his name is conferred upon him by the media, as the novel notes. Where he was known simply as Lee Oswald throughout his life, the media insisted upon calling him by his full name, Lee Harvey Oswald, as if to emphasize that he was the double of John Fitzgerald Kennedy.

In an interview DeLillo noted that '[s]omeone who knew Oswald referred to him as an actor in real life, and I do think there is a sense in which he was watching himself perform' (DeCurtis, 1994, 51). He is portrayed as some-one who takes on different selves according to the situation he finds himself in, and these selves are drawn from various narratives which have influenced him throughout his life: John Wayne movies, Marxist theory, unspecified B-movies. DeLillo suggests this by depicting Oswald's inner voice as switching between clichés drawn from popular culture: 'My Russian period was over . . .', he thinks at one point, and elsewhere he writes in his diary '*somewhere, a violin plays, as I watch my life whirl away*' (DeLillo, 2006b, 152). Oswald is a man without singular identity – quite unlike the typical autonomous hero of the realist novel. Yet, as Lentricchia suggests, the novel also presents the social backdrop for the presentation of character as utterly different from the world of stable 'social forces' which 'shape as they differentiate the individ-ual', which was central to realism. These have been replaced by a new climate of the image, whose principal effect is to 'realign radically all social agents (from top to bottom) as first-person agents of desire seeking self-annihilation and fulfillment in the magical third' (Lentricchia, 1991, 198). Oswald's aim is thus – to draw on the formulation used by DeLillo in speaking about the novel in interview – to escape the self by 'merging with history' (DeCurtis, 1994, 52).

As well as being seduced by the fantasy identities which the media projects DeLillo's Oswald is acutely conscious of constructing his own image in ways that will determine how others see him. When he initially plans to assassinate General Edwin Walker to help Castro he buys a mail-order rifle and poses with the gun in one hand and a radical publication held aloft in the other imagining that the image will appear on the cover of *Time* or *Newsweek* after Walker is killed. In the end the photograph is indeed the one which featured in the print and visual news media following the assassination of JFK. As media creation, Oswald undergoes the perfect demise, watching his own murder on a TV monitor: 'He could see himself shot as the camera caught it. Through the pain he watched TV. . . . Through the pain, through the losing of sensation except where it hurt, Lee watched himself react to the auguring heat of the bullet' (DeLillo, 2006a, 439).

Bret Easton Ellis, *American Psycho*

The US writer Bret Easton Ellis was associated with the so-called 'Generation X' or 'brat pack' of writers in the 1980s, along with Dennis Cooper, Douglas Coupland, Jay McInerney, and Tama Janowitz, the children of the 'baby-boomer' generation in the decades following the Second World War, writers who present an accurate portrayal of the morally bankrupt, consumerist, celebrity-obsessed culture of late twentieth-century North America. In a different way from J. G. Ballard, the writings of this generation of writers deals head on with the 'death of affect' in contemporary society.

Their writing has been termed 'blank fiction' by James Annesley, to denote a style of novel where plot and character, the traditional staples of realist fiction, are less important than the impression of a detailed '*surface*' created by a surfeit of references to pop-cultural ephemera and consumer products. The subject matter of blank fiction deals with the empty lives of disaffected young people in North American cities in a way which eschews the dense plotting and politically weighty stories of earlier American literary novelists such as Morrison, Pynchon, and Mailer in favour of an episodic, 'glassy' series of impressions or perspectives of the lives of its characters. Rather than a literary movement or genre, 'blank fiction' is a kind of 'scene' or shared context reflecting a 'modern mood' which ultimately is generated by the effects of late-capitalist commodification.

Ellis's first two novels demonstrated his ability to chronicle the society that surrounded him. Both *Less Than Zero* (1985) and *The Rules of Attraction* (1987) depict the lives of disaffected students against the backdrop of the consumerist 1980s. They demonstrate the feeling of alienation suffered by wealthy white Americans who indulge in a never-ending superficial lifestyle of drugs, parties and sex. But his most famous – and notorious – novel is 1991's *American Psycho*, the novel which has been linked most frequently and persuasively to postmodernism.

Ellis's fiction had depicted scenes of sexual violence before (*Less Than Zero* features a snuff movie and the gang rape of a twelve-year-old tied to a bed), but nothing prepares the reader for this novel. To use the author's own words, *American Psycho* is 'a novel about a young, wealthy, alienated Wall Street yuppie named Patrick Bateman who also happened to be a serial killer filled with vast apathy during the height of the Reagan eighties' (Ellis, 2005, 12). The novel alternates between two kinds of narrative sequence. The first, which takes up most of its pages, details at great length the mundane, inconsequential sequence of lunches, parties, meetings, obscure business deals and discussions about investment banking which constitute Bateman's professional and social life, and is punctuated by long ironic, 'anti-narrative' sequences such as going to the drycleaner, the video rental store, the gym, as well as flatly written 'mini-essays' on Bateman's favourite bands like Genesis and Huey Lewis and the News. The chapter titles reflect this mundane succession of routine events: 'Business Meeting', 'Yale Club', 'Lunch With Bethany', etc. Throughout these sections the reader is confronted by a mass of references to designer labels and product names, making reading the novel at times like reading catalogues or stocklists.

The second kind of narrative in *American Psycho* constitutes the only real 'action' in the novel and features scenes (away from the office or the restaurant) in which Bateman tortures and kills a series of harmless victims – women whom he has seduced into returning home with him, business associates, a homeless person, a five-year-old boy. His crimes seem generally to be motiveless, his victims apparently selected at random, but he treats them all with extreme sadism and violence, keeping them conscious for as long as possible, and, even though there is no consistency in either type of victim selected or *modus operandi*, engaging in stock serial killer behaviour such as keeping trophies.

These sections are shocking, and explain why the novel is (after *Crash*) another of the most notorious *succès de scandales* in recent decades, frequently charged with being misogynistic (many of Bateman's mutilated victims are women) and pornographic (i.e. dwelling on sexual violence for titilation rather than any literary merit). The novel is still shelved in shrink wrapping in some countries, or prohibited from being sold to those under eighteen. Anticipating scandal, Ellis's original publishers, Simon & Schuster, famously tore up his contract – even forfeiting the advance they had paid him – while the book was reviewed in the *New York Times* with the headline 'Don't Buy This Book', and condemned by the National Organization of Women.

American Psycho is shocking however one interprets it. However, as with all such cases, popular debate has shown a tendency to fall into the naïve trap of assuming the protagonist's tastes and behaviour are the author's own, rather than a satire on a particular kind of person. Of more interest is the fact that the novel presents the reader with two clear challenges (besides stomaching the detailed mutilation and torture).

The first is that it is unclear how real we are intended to see its contents as being. *American Psycho*'s first-person narration gives it a radical undecideability. It is never clear whether the sections in which Bateman tortures and kills have really happened in the world of the story, or whether he is merely fantasizing or perhaps even hallucinating them. No one sees him commit any murders, and there is only one which leads to any suspicion – the one that is closest to having a motive, that of Paul Owen, one of Bateman's colleagues of whom he appears to be envious and whom he butchers with an axe. Owen's disappearance leads a private detective, Donald Kimball, to investigate, interviewing Bateman, but there is never any real suggestion that Bateman will be found out. The novel is without suspense in this regard. One effect of the novel's indeterminacy about the status of events is that the reader comes to experience a similar dissolution of the boundary between 'reality' and fiction to that experienced by Bateman.

The second challenge *American Psycho* poses to readers is how to relate to each other the two apparently quite different kinds of narrative sequence which make up the novel, one banal, trivial and comic, the other horrifying and brutal (though not without moments of the blackest comedy). The answer is surely that the murderous sections are the reactions to, perhaps even the ultimate expressions of the consumerist lifestyle which dictates Bateman's and his associates' existence. In a world where commodification is all, it follows that human beings become interchangeable commodities.

This would explain Bateman's practice of chopping up his victims' bodies and exploring how they work and feel to the touch with a detached fascination. He *consumes* the bodies of those he tortures and murders, 'experiencing' their smells and textures the same way he would with a new product or a meal. Sometimes he eats or burns them. The listing of mutilated body parts in the murder scenes provides an obvious parallel to the relentless description of the clothes he wears or the hi-fi equipment he has bought in the non-murder sections.

In his study of serial killers, referred to earlier, Mark Seltzer sets out to answer the question: what kind of society can produce something as monstrous as the serial killer? His answer is that it is a supremely homogenized one, which lays the emphasis on human types and repetitive forms of production and consumption. The serial killer, Seltzer says, embodies the mass in a single individual (his amassing of victim after victim in similar 'trademark' style functioning as an ironic reflection of the culture of mass production). Just like Patrick Bateman, serial killers are always remarked upon as being shockingly *ordinary*, just like you or I, able to blend into the crowd, with no-one suspecting the depths of depravity which lie beneath their everyday exteriors. Ellis's novel, Seltzer argues, 'advertises, and trades on, the analogies, or causal relations, between . . . two forms of compulsive repetition, consumerism and serialized killing'. That is, '[t]he question of serial killing cannot be separated from the general forms of seriality, collection, and counting conspicuous in consumer society . . . , and the forms of fetishism – the collecting of things and representations, persons and person-things like bodies – that traverse it' (Seltzer, 1998, 64).

Everything Bateman considers of value – the designer labels, the quality restaurants, even the 'hardbodies' he admires – seem to be selected because of how he thinks others would regard them. In this respect he is just as much a creature of the hyperreal mediatized culture as DeLillo's Oswald. Bateman tends to film his victims, and choose products or lifestyles because of the influence of advertising. Bateman might be regarded as 'the postmodern, pop cultural subject carried to its logical conclusion, its apocalyptic apotheosis' (Blazer, 2002, n.p.) He exists in a world where signifiers float freely, detached from any referent, and consequently he is an extreme demonstration that there is no substance inside the self, simply what it draws from the circulation of signifiers *outside*, the products and fantasies offered by culture.

The novel might also be considered as an illustration of the dangers of postmodern relativism, where every story or *petit récit* is as valid as any other, there are no reliable external moral codes and, as Lyotard says, 'Eclecticism is the degree zero of contemporary general culture: one listens to reggae, watches a western, eats McDonald's food for lunch and local cuisine for dinner, wears Paris perfume in Tokyo and "retro" clothes in Hong Kong' (Lyotard, 1984, 76). If there are no values, no norms, then nothing can have any real meaning. An overall logic of equivalence applies in Bateman's shallow world. Genesis *equals* Drakkar Noir aftershave *equals* high-performance stereo equipment. But if this is the case then nothing has any value. It is but a short step to good being indistinguishable from evil. Bateman is entirely unable to distinguish between the different kinds of consumption he engages in. At one point he fades out of a conversation with his girlfriend Evelyn, and finds himself:

> lost in my own private maze, thinking about other things: warrants, stock offerings, ESOPs, LBOs, IPOs, finances, refinances, debentures, converts, proxy statements, 8-Ks, 10-Qs, zero coupons, PiKs, GNPs, the IMF, hot executive gadgets, billionaires, Kenkichi Nakajima, infinity, Infinity, how fast a luxury car should go, bailouts, junk bonds, whether to cancel my subscription to *The Economist*, the Christmas Eve when I was fourteen and had raped one of our maids, Inclusivity, envying someone's life, whether someone could survive a fractured skull, waiting in airports, stifling a scream, credit cards and someone's passport and a book of matches from La Côte Basque spattered with blood, surface surface surface, a Rolls is a Rolls is a Rolls.   (Ellis, 2004, 331)

This logic of equivalence is paralleled at an aesthetic level in *American Psycho* by the way that the different sections (murder and lifestyle) of the novel are simply set side by side, one following the other, without framing. The first murder, horrifically described, where Bateman savages a down-and-out with a knife, is followed immediately by a deadpan mini-essay in which he extolls the merits of the band Genesis (it is surely appropriate that all the bands he likes are suitably bland, 'middle-of-the-road').

One explanation for the extreme controversy generated by Ellis's book is because, unlike genre fiction, the horrific crimes are not positioned within a clearly defined moral framework which classifies them as evil, and the perpetrator goes unpunished. But its most disturbing feature is the morally bankrupt world in which Bateman's murders take place, which might even *produce* them. In a world where affect has died, just as J. G. Ballard had predicted, people seek ever more desperate ways of interacting with another person, of experiencing emotion. Bateman is almost entirely unable to feel. He responds to what others say in the way he feels he ought to, as if he is from another planet. Before one lunch meeting, for example, he realizes he is feeling 'extremely nervous':

> The cause is hard to locate but I've narrowed it down to one of two reasons. It's either that I'm afraid of rejection (though I can't understand why: *she* called *me*, she wants to see *me*, she wants to have lunch with *me*, she wants to fuck *me* again) or, on the other hand, it could have something to do with this new Italian mousse I'm wearing, which, though it makes my hair look fuller and smells good, feels very sticky and uncomfortable, and it's something I could easily blame my nervousness on.   (Ellis, 2004, 221)

It ought to be apparent by now that Ellis – like Ballard and DeLillo, indeed like any number of postmodern novelists who are mistaken for precisely the opposite – is a moralist. *American Psycho* is an urgent, heartfelt critique of our affectless culture. Its credentials as such are absolutely clear, in fact. The novel's third epigraph is a couplet from a song by the band Talking Heads (surely, we suspect, much more to Ellis's own taste): 'And as things fell apart / Nobody paid much attention'. This raises the uncomfortable possibility that the really disturbing element of *American Psycho*'s shocking narrative is not its violence (for, after all, the most extreme violence is graphically displayed constantly in mainstream American popular culture) but the fact that Bateman's activities go unnoticed, never mind undetected by the police.

A repeated source of black comedy in the novel are the episodes in which Bateman apparently comments out loud on his horrific deeds. It may be that these admissions occur only in his head, or they are provocative boasts which prove just what he can get away with. However, the effect is also to remind us that this is a world which does not care, one which is incapable of dealing with shocking eruptions of violent emotion in the midst of all its relentless consumerism. Thus Bateman announces to two of his friends, 'You know, guys, it's not beyond my capacity to drive a lead pipe repeatedly into a girl's vagina' (312), tells his colleague Armstrong, 'And there are many more people I, uh, want to . . . want to, well, I guess *murder*' (137), and coos to a baby 'Yes I'm a total psychopathic murderer, oh yes I am, I like to kill people, oh yes I do, honey, little sweetie pie, yes I do . . . ' (212). The recipients of such admissions either ignore the remark or assume he is joking.

Ellis's novel is reminiscent here of Browning's 1836 poem 'Porphyria's Lover', in which the psychopathic hero strangles his beloved and complains 'And yet God has not said a word', not because he is pleased not to be punished but because the absence of judgement disturbs him. This logic in fact suggests the significance of the first of *American Psycho*'s three epigraphs. It comes from another nineteenth-century text, Fyodor Dostoevsky's novel *Notes from Underground*, published in 1864. Despite the gulf in history and style, there are obvious similarities in that both novels are first-person narratives by disaffected, alienated city-dwellers. The emblematic nature of each protagonist, the Underground Man and the American Psycho, is suggested by the particular passage Ellis uses for the epigraph. It comes not from Dostoevsky's novel itself but from its preface: 'Both the author of these *Notes* and the *Notes* themselves are, of course, fictional. Nevertheless, such persons as the composer of these *Notes* not only exist in our society, but indeed must exist, considering the circumstances under which our society has generally been formed.' The quotation goes on to note that its hero 'represents a generation that is still living out its days amongst us' and that his narrative is able to 'clarify the reasons why he appeared and was bound to appear in our midst.' Ellis's choice of epigraph signals clearly the sociological intention behind the book: to suggest that a character like Patrick Bateman is the ultimate product of a superficial, uncaring age, in which the logic of consumerism runs rampant.

But the more specific parallel between *American Psycho* and Dostoevsky's *Notes from Underground* also points to another way of reading the novel. Like *Notes from Underground* the book is a confession, though it is easy to miss this. But why else would Bateman be narrating? He even confesses directly on two occasions. Towards the end of the novel he tells Evelyn: 'My...my *need* to engage in...homicidal behavior on a massive scale cannot be, um, corrected.... But I...have no other way to express my blocked...needs'. But she 'misses the essence of what I'm saying' (Ellis, 2004, 325). Soon after he erupts into an even more direct and explicit confession of his guilt to his associate Harold Carnes: 'You don't seem to understand. You're not really comprehending any of this. *I* killed him. *I* did it, Carnes. *I* chopped Owen's fucking head off. *I* tortured dozens of girls. That whole message I left on your machine was *true*' (Ellis, 2004, 373). At first Carnes ignores him, then thinks it's an unfunny joke, then does not believe him as he is convinced he was with Owen himself a few days before and Owen is therefore still alive.

This is a novel which parallels the modernist confessional form, typified by *Notes from Underground*, but in this case is actually about the impossibility of confessing. As a result it puts the onus on the reader to heed what he is saying. There is a subtle metafictional dimension to *American Psycho* which confirms that it requires its reader to be active. The first line of the novel is: 'ABANDON ALL HOPE YE WHO ENTER HERE is scrawled in blood red lettering on the side of the Chemical Bank near the corner of Eleventh and First' (Ellis, 2004, 4). At the most obvious level this refers to a piece of graffiti, but the quotation is from Dante's *Inferno* and relates to the inscription on the gates of Hell. With a sense of circularity, the novel ends with Bateman hearing someone ask 'Why?' and explaining out loud (though of course no-one in the world of the novel is listening):

> 'this is, uh, how life presents itself in a bar or in a club in New York, maybe *anywhere*, at the end of the century and how people, you know, *me*, behave, and this is what being *Patrick* means to me, I guess, so, well, yup, uh...' and this is followed by a sigh, then a slight shrug and another sigh, and above one of the doors covered by red velvet drapes in Harry's is a sign and on the sign in letters that match the drapes' color are the words THIS IS NOT AN EXIT. (Ellis, 2004, 384)

While both opening and closing lines are obviously signs written on the wall, at a symbolic level they are clearly suggesting that the writing (on the wall) ought to convey a message to the reader of *American Psycho*: what the book presents us with is a vision of contemporary Hell, one moreover from which it is impossible to escape. As with *Libra*, while the title of the novel most obviously is a label for its central character, an American 'psycho'(path), it could also of course be read adjectivally, in the way one does with 'American Gothic'. 'American psycho' may be an alternative term for postmodernity.

To take heed of what Bateman says in the last passage of the novel, *American Psycho* is indeed a depiction of 'how life presents itself ... at the end of the century'. Both the first and last words of the novel are metafictional directions to the reader. Unlike the metafiction of an earlier generation of American novelist, such as Barth or Coover, they do not imply that fiction can no longer have a referential function, but instead collapse the distinction between world and book. When we close the book we exist in a world which is essentially a more tempered version of the homogenous, commodified, affectless world of *American Psycho*. The ending is not an exit because we cannot get outside of the book: the book *is* the world.

References

Acker, Kathy (1986) *Don Quixote*. New York: Grove Press.

(1997) *Bodies of Work: Essays*. London: Serpent's Tail.

(2002) From *Great Expectations*. In *Essential Acker: The Selected Writings of Kathy Acker*. Ed. Amy Scholder and Dennis Cooper. New York: Grove Press.

Aldridge, John (1983) *The American Novel and the Way We Live Now*. Oxford University Press.

Annesley, James (1998) *Blank Fictions: Consumerism, Culture and the Contemporary American Novel*. London: Pluto.

Ashcroft, Bill, Gareth Griffiths and Helen Tiffin, eds. (1988) *The Empire Writes Back*. London: Routledge.

eds. (1995) *The Post-Colonial Studies Reader*. London and New York: Routledge.

Atwood, Margaret (1996a) *The Handmaid's Tale*. London: Vintage.

(1996b) *Alias Grace*. Toronto: McLelland & Stewart.

(1997) *In Search of Alias Grace*. Ottowa University Press.

Auster, Paul (1987) *City of Glass*. In *The New York Trilogy*. London: Faber.

Ballard, J. G. (1968) 'Interview with J. G. Ballard'. *Munich Round Up* 100, 104–6. Trans. Dan O'Hara [available on www.ballardian.com].

(1995a) Introduction to *Crash*. London: Vintage.

(1995b) *Crash*. London: Vintage.

Barnes, Julian (1985) *Flaubert's Parrot*. London: Picador.

(2002) 'Julian Barnes in Conversation', *Cercles* 4, 255–69.

Barth, John (1981) 'Lost in the Funhouse'. *Lost in the Funhouse*. New York: Bantam Books.

(2002) 'The Literature of Exhaustion'. In Bran Nicol, ed. *Postmodernism and the Contemporary Novel: A Reader*. Edinburgh University Press. 138–47.

Barthes, Roland (1975) *The Pleasure of the Text*. New York: Hill and Wang.

(1977a) 'Introduction to the Structural Analysis of Narratives'. *Image – Music – Text*. Trans. Stephen Heath. London: Fontana. 79–124.

(1977b) 'The Death of the Author'. *Image – Music – Text*. Trans. Stephen Heath. London: Fontana. 142–8.

(1977c) 'From Work to Text'. *Image – Music – Text*. Trans. Stephen Heath. London: Fontana. 155–64.

(1981) 'The Discourse of History'. Trans. Stephen Bann. *Comparative Criticism*, 3, 7–20.

(1990) *S/Z*. Trans. Richard Miller. London: Jonathan Cape.

Baudrillard, Jean (1994a) 'Aesthetic Illusion and Virtual Reality'. In Nicholas Zurbrugg, ed. *Jean Baudrillard: Art and Artefact*. Sage. 19–27.

(1994b) *Simulacra and Simulation*. Trans. Sheila Faria Glases. Ann Arbon, MI: University of Michigan Press.

Bayard, Pierre (2000) *Who Killed Roger Ackroyd?* London: Fourth Estate.

Beckett, Samuel (1973) *Murphy*. London: Picador.

(1994a) *Three Novels: Molloy, Malone Dies, The Unnamable*. New York: Grove Press.

(1994b) *Watt*. New York: Grove Press/Atlantic Monthly.

Bell, Daniel (1973) *The Coming of Post-Industrial Society*. New York: Basic Books.

Belsey, Catherine (1980) *Critical Practice*. London: Methuen.

Berger, Peter L. and Thomas Luckmann (1991) *The Social Construction of Reality: A Treatise in the Sociology of Knowledge*. Harmondsworth: Penguin.

Blanchot, Maurice (1989) *The Space of Literature*. Trans. Ann Smock. Lincoln, NE: University of Nebraska Press.

Blazer, Alex (2002) 'Chasms of Reality, Aberrations of Identity: Defining the Postmodern through Bret Easton Ellis's *American Psycho*'. *Americana: The Journal of American Popular Culture (1900-Present)*. 1:2 [available at www.americanpopularculture.com/journal/articles/fall`2002/blazer.htm.]

Bloom, Harold (1973) *The Anxiety of Influence: A Theory of Poetry*. Oxford University Press.

Borges, Jorge Luis (1982) *Seven Conversations with Jorge Luis Borges*. Ed. Fernando Sorrentino. Trans. Clark M. Zlotchew. Albany, NY: Whitston Publishing.

(1985) 'The Detective Story'. Trans. Alberto Manguel. *Descant* 16.4, 15–24.

(1989) 'Death and the Compass'. *Labyrinths*. Harmondsworth: Penguin. 106–17.

(1998a) 'Pierre Menard, Author of the *Quixote*'. *Collected Fictions*. Trans. Andrew Hurley. London & New York: Allen Lane/Penguin. 88–95.

(1998b) 'The Garden of Forking Paths'. *Collected Fictions*. Trans. Andrew Hurley. London & New York: Allen Lane/Penguin. 119–28.

(1998c) 'Tlön, Uqbar, Orbis Tertius'. *Collected Fictions*. Trans. Andrew Hurley. London & New York: Allen Lane/Penguin. 68–81.

Bould, Mark (2005) 'Cyberpunk'. In David Seed, ed. *A Companion to Science Fiction*. Oxford: Blackwell. 217–31.

Bradbury, Malcolm (1992) *The Modern American Novel*. 2nd edition. Oxford University Press.

Bradley, A. C. (1926) *Oxford Lectures on Poetry*. London: Macmillan.

Brennan, Teresa (2004) *The Age of Paranoia*. New York: W. W. Norton & Sons.

Brooks, Peter (1993) *Body Work: Objects of Desire in Modern Narrative*. Cambridge, MA: Harvard University Press.

Bukatman, Scott (1993) *Terminal Identity: The Virtual Subject in Postmodern Science Fiction.* Durham, NC: Duke University Press.

Burgin, Victor (1990) 'Paranoiac Space', *New Formations* 12, 61–75.

Burroughs, William S. (1974) *Exterminator!* London: John Calder.

(1982) *A William Burroughs Reader.* London: Picador.

(1993) 'The Fall of Art'. *The Adding Machine: Selected Essays.* New York: Arcade Publishing. 60–4.

(2008) *Naked Lunch.* London: Harper Perennial.

Butler, Judith (1990a) *Gender Trouble: Feminism and the Subversion of Identity.* London: Routledge.

(1990b) 'Performative Acts and Gender Constitution: An Essay in Phenomenology and Feminist Theory'. In Sue-Ellen Case, ed. *Performing Feminisms: Feminist Critical Theory and Theatre.* Baltimore, MD: Johns Hopkins University Press. 270–82.

Carter, Angela (1992) *The Passion of New Eve.* London: Virago.

(1993) *Expletives Deleted: Selected Writings.* London: Vintage.

(1994) *The Infernal Desire Machines of Doctor Hoffman.* London: Penguin.

(1997) 'Notes from the Front Line'. *Shaking a Leg: Journalism and Writings.* London: Chatto and Windus. 36–43.

Castillo, Debra A. (1991) 'Borges and Pynchon: The Tenuous Symmetries of Art'. *New Essays on The Crying of Lot 49.* Cambridge University Press. 21–46.

Chatman, Seymour (1978) *Story and Discourse: Narrative Structure in Fiction and Film.* Ithaca, NY and London: Cornell University Press.

Cohen, Stanley and Laurie Taylor (1992) *Escape Attempts: The Theory and Practice of Resistance to Everyday Life.* 2nd edition. London and New York: Routledge.

Conradi, Peter J. (1982) *John Fowles.* London: Methuen.

Coover, Robert (1973) *Pricksongs and Descants.* London: Picador.

Cundy, Catherine (1996) *Salman Rushdie.* Contemporary World Writers. Manchester University Press.

Day, Aidan (1998) *Angela Carter: The Rational Glass.* Manchester University Press.

DeCurtis, Anthony (1994) '"An Outsider in This Society": An Interview with Don DeLillo'. In Frank Lentricchia, ed. *Introducing Don DeLillo.* Durham, NC: Duke University Press. 43–66.

Deleuze, Gilles and Felix Guattari (1987) *A Thousand Plateaus: Capitalism and Schizophrenia.* Trans. Brian Massumi. Minneapolis, MN: University of Minnesota Press. 7–13.

DeLillo, Don (1984) *White Noise.* London: Picador.

(2006a) *Libra.* London: Penguin.

(2006b) 'Assassination Aura'. In *Libra.* London: Penguin. v–x.

During, Simon (1995), 'Postmodernism or Postcolonialism Today'. In Bill Ashcroft, Gareth Griffiths and Helen Tiffin, eds. *The Post-Colonial Studies Reader.* London: Routledge. 119–29.

Duvall, John N. (2000) *Identifying Fictions of Toni Morrison: Modernist Authenticity and Postmodern Blackness.* Gordonsville, VA: Palgrave Macmillan.

Dworkin, Andrea (1974) *Woman Hating.* New York: Plume.

Eagleton, Terry (1997) *The Illusions of Postmodernism.* Oxford: Blackwell.

Eco, Umberto (1984) *The Name of the Rose.* London: Picador.

    (1985) *Reflections on The Name of the Rose.* London: Secker and Warburg.

    (2002) 'Postmodernism, Irony and the Enjoyable'. In Bran Nicol, ed. *Postmodernism and the Contemporary Novel: A Reader.* Edinburgh University Press. 110–12.

Ellis, Bret Easton (1991) *American Psycho.* London: Vintage.

    (2005) *Lunar Park.* London: Picador.

Ellison, Ralph (1978) 'The Essential Ellison (Interview)', *Y'Bird* 1:1, 130–59. Oxford University Press.

Featherstone, Mike and Mike Burrows, eds. (1995) *Cyberspace/Cyberbodies/Cyberpunk: Cultures of Technological Embodiment.* London: Sage.

Fiedler, Leslie (2002) 'Cross the Border – Close that Gap'. In Bran Nicol, ed. *Postmodernism and the Contemporary Novel: A Reader.* Edinburgh University Press. 162–8.

Fishman, Barry (1989) Graham Swift Hypertext Resource: www.usp.nus.edu.sg/post/uk/gswift/gsov.html.

Foucault, Michel (1995) *Discipline and Punish.* London: Vintage.

Fowles, John (1990) 'Notes on an Unfinished Novel'. In Malcolm Bradbury, ed. *The Novel Today: Contemporary Writers on Modern Fiction.* Revised edition. London: Fontana. 147–62.

    (1996) *The French Lieutenant's Woman.* London: Vintage.

Frank, A. W. (1992) 'Cyberpunk Bodies and Postmodern Times'. *Studies in Social Interaction.* 13, 39–50.

Freud, Sigmund (1991) 'Remembering, Repeating and Working-Through' [1914]. *Art and Literature.* Penguin Freud Library, Vol. 14. Harmondsworth: Penguin.

Friedman, Ellen G. (1989) 'A Conversation with Kathy Acker'. *The Review of Contemporary Fiction,* Special Issue: Kathy Acker/Christine Brooke-Rose/Marguerite Young. *Centre for Book Culture.* 9:3, 12–22. Available at: www.centreforbookculture.org/interviews/interview_acker.html).

Gasiorek, Andrzej (1995) *Post-War British Fiction: Realism and After.* London: Arnold.

    (2007) *J. G. Ballard.* Manchester University Press.

Gates, Henry Louis, Jr. (1989) *Figures in Black : Words, Signs, and the Racial Self.* Oxford University Press.

Genette, Gérard (1980) *Narrative Discourse: An Essay on Method.* Trans. Jane E. Lewin. Oxford: Blackwell.

Gergen, Kenneth J. (1992) *The Saturated Self: Dilemmas of Identity in Contemporary Life.* New York: Basic Books.

Gibson, William (1995) *Neuromancer*. London: Voyager.

Gottschalk, Simon (2000) 'Escape from Insanity: "Mental Disorder" in the Postmodern Moment'. In Dwight Fee, ed. *Pathology and the Postmodern: Mental Illness as Discourse and Experience*. London: Sage. 18–48.

Haffenden, John (1985) 'Angela Carter'. *Novelists in Interview*. London & New York: Methuen. 76–96.

Haraway, Donna J. (1985) 'The Cyborg Manifesto: Science, Technology and Socialist Feminism in the 1980s'. *Socialist Review* 80, 65–107.

Harding, Sandra (1990) 'Feminism, Science and the Anti-Enlightenment Critiques'. In Nancy Fraser and Linda J. Nicholson, eds. *Feminism/Postmodernism*. London: Routledge. 83–106.

Hauck, Richard B. (1971) *A Cheerful Nihilism: Confidence and 'The Absurd' in American Humorous Fiction*. Bloomingdale, IN & London: Indiana University Press.

Hawkins, Susan E. (2004) 'All in the Family: Kathy Acker's *Blood and Guts in High School*'. *Contemporary Literature* 45:4, 637–58.

Holquist, Michael (1990) *Dialogism: Bakhtin and His World*. London: Routledge.

Howells, Coral Ann (2005) *Margaret Atwood*. London: Palgrave Macmillan.

Hutcheon, Linda (1984) *Narcissistic Narrative: The Metafictional Paradox*. London: Methuen.

(1988a) *A Poetics of Postmodernism*. London & New York: Routledge.

(1988b) *The Canadian Postmodern: A Study of Contemporary English-Canadian Fiction*. Oxford University Press.

(1995) 'Circling the Downspout of Empire', in Bill Ashcroft, Gareth Griffiths and Helen Tiffin, eds. in *The Post-Colonial Studies Reader*. London: Routledge. 130–5.

(2002) *The Politics of Postmodernism*. 2nd edn. London: Routledge.

Huyssen, Andreas (2002) 'Mapping the Postmodern'. In Bran Nicol, ed., *Postmodernism and the Contemporary Novel: A Reader*. Edinburgh University Press. 59–71.

Jameson, Fredric (1981) *The Political Unconscious: Narrative as a Socially Symbolic Act*, Ithaca, NY: Cornell University Press.

(1984) 'The Politics of Theory: Ideological Positions in the Postmodernism Debate'. *New German Critique* 33, 53–65.

(1991) *Postmodernism, or the Cultural Logic of Late Capitalism*. London & New York: Verso.

Jencks, Charles (1986) *What is Post-Modernism?* London: Academy.

Johnson, B. S. (1964) *Albert Angelo*. London: Constable.

(1989) 'A Few Selected Sentences'. In Malcolm Bradbury, ed. Modern British Short Stories. Harmondsworth: Penguin. 282–5.

(1990) Introduction to *Aren't You Rather Young to be Writing Your Memoirs?* In Malcolm Bradbury, ed. *The Novel Today*. London: Fontana. 151–68.

King, Noel (1991) 'Reading *White Noise*: Floating Remarks'. *Critical Quarterly* 33:3, 66–83.

Klinkowitz, Jerome (1975) *Literary Disruptions: The Making of a Post-Contemporary Fiction*. Urbana, IL: University of Illinois Press.

Kroker, Arthur and David Cook (1988) *The Postmodern Scene: Excremental Culture and Hyper-Aesthetics*. Basingstoke: Macmillan.

Lauzen, Sarah (1986) 'Notes on Metafiction: Every Essay has a Title', in Larry McCaffery, ed. *Postmodern Fiction: A Bio-Bibliographical Guide*. New York: Greenwood Press. 93–117.

Lee, Alison (1990) *Realism and Power: Postmodern British Fiction*. London & New York: Routledge.

Lentricchia, Frank (1991) '*Libra* as Postmodern Critique'. In Lentricchia, ed. *Introducing Don DeLillo*. Durham, NC: Duke University Press.

Levin, David Michael (1987) *Pathologies of the Modern Self: Postmodern Studies on Narcissism, Schizophrenia and Depression*. New York University Press.

Lovibond, Sabina (1989) 'Feminism and Postmodernism', *New Left Review* 178, Nov/Dec, 5–28.

Luckhurst, Roger (1997) *'The Angle Between Two Walls': The Fiction of J. G. Ballard*, Liverpool University Press.

Lukács, Georg (1983) *The Historical Novel*. Trans. Hannah Mitchell and Stanley Mitchell. Lincoln, NB: University of Nebraska Press.

Lyotard, Jean-François (1984) 'Answering the Question: What is Postmodernism?' Trans. Régis Durand. In *The Postmodern Condition: A Report on Knowledge*. Trans. Geoff Bennington and Brian Massumi. Minneapolis, MN: University of Minnesota Press/Manchester University Press. 71–82.

MacCabe, Colin (1974) 'Realism and the Cinema: Notes on some Brechtian Theses'. In Philip Rice and Patricia Waugh, eds. *Literary Theory: A Reader*. 2nd revised edition. London: Edward Arnold, 1992, 134–42.

Mandel, Ernest (1975) *Late Capitalism*. London: New Left Books.

Martin, Reginald (1984) 'An Interview with Ishmael Reed'. *Review of Contemporary Fiction*. 4:2. Available at: www.centerforbookculture.org/interviews/interview reed.html.

Massumi, Brian (1993) 'Everywhere You Want To Be: Introduction to Fear'. In Massumi, ed. *The Politics of Everyday Fear*. Minneapolis, MN: University of Minnesota Press.

Matus, Jill (1998) *Toni Morrison*. Contemporary World Writers. Manchester University Press.

Mauss, Marcel (2001) *The Gift: The Form and Reason for Exchange in Archaic Societies*. London & New York: Routledge.

McCaffrey, Larry, ed. (1986) Introduction. *Postmodern Fiction: A Bio-Bibliographical Guide*. New York: Greenwood Press.

(1989) 'The Artists of Hell: Kathy Acker and "Punk Aesthetics"'. In Ellen G. Friedman and Mirian Fuchs, eds. *Breaking the Sequence: Women's Experimental Fiction*. Princeton University Press.

(1991a) 'An Interview With William Gibson'. In *Storming the Reality Studio: A Casebook of Cyberpunk and Postmodern Fiction.* Duke University Press. 263–85.

(1991b) Introduction. *Storming the Reality Studio: A Casebook of Cyberpunk and Postmodern Science Fiction.* Durham: Duke University Press.

McCarthy, Mary (2000) 'A Bolt from the Blue: An Introductory Essay'. In Vladimir Nabokov. *Pale Fire.* Harmondsworth: Penguin.

McHale, Brian (1987) *Postmodernist Fiction.* London & New York: Routledge.

(1992) *Constructing Postmodernism.* London & New York: Routledge.

(2002) 'Change of Dominant from Modernist to Postmodernist Writing'. In Bran Nicol, ed. *Postmodernism and the Contemporary Novel: A Reader.* Edinburgh University Press. 278–300.

McHale, Brian and Adriana Neagu (2006) 'Literature and the Postmodern: A Conversation with Brian McHale'. *Kritikos: an international and interdisciplinary journal of postmodern cultural sound, text and image* 3, http://garnet.acns.fsu.edu/~nr03/neagu%20and%20mchale.htm. Accessed: 20/09/07.

Merivale, Patricia and Sweeney, Susan Elizabeth (1999) 'The Game's Afoot: On the Trail of the Metaphysical Detective Story'. In Merivale and Sweeney, eds. *Detecting Texts: The Metaphysical Detective Story from Poe to Postmodernism.* Philadelphia, PA: University of Pennsylvania Press. 1–24.

Morris, Meaghan (2002) 'Feminism, Reading, Postmodernism'. In Bran Nicol, ed. *Postmodernism and the Contemporary Novel: A Reader.* Edinburgh University Press. 390–5.

Morrison, Toni (1987) *Beloved.* London: Picador.

Mukherjee, Ankhi (2005) 'Missed Encounters: Repetition, Rewriting, and Contemporary Returns to Charles Dickens's *Great Expectations*'. *Contemporary Literature* 46:1, 108–33.

Nabokov, Vladimir (2000) *Pale Fire.* Harmondsworth: Penguin.

Nealon, Jeffrey T. (1999) 'Work of the Detective, Work of the Writer: Auster's *City of Glass*'. In Patricia Merivale and Susan Elizabeth Sweeney, eds. *Detecting Texts: The Metaphysical Detective Story from Poe to Postmodernism* Philadelphia, PA: University of Pennsylvania Press. 117–33.

Nesbit, Molly (1995) 'What was an Author'. In Séan Burke, ed. *Authorship: From Plato to the Postmodern: A Reader.* Edinburgh: Edinburgh University Press. 247–62.

Nicholls, Peter (1996) "The Belated Postmodern: History, Phantoms, and Toni Morrison." In Sue Vice, ed. *Psychoanalytic Criticism: A Reader.* Cambridge: Polity Press. 50–74.

Nietzsche, Friedrich (1964) *The Dawn of Day. The Complete Works of Friedrich Nietzsche.* Vol. 9. Trans. J. M. Kennedy. New York: Russell and Russell.

O'Donnell, Patrick (1991) 'Introduction'. *New Essays on The Crying of Lot 49.* Cambridge University Press. 1–20.

Onega, Susan (1995) 'British Historiographic Metafiction'. In Mark Currie, ed. *Metafiction*. London: Longman. 92–103.

Owens, Craig (1983) 'The Discourse of Others: Feminists and Postmodernism'. In Hal Foster, ed. *The Anti-Aesthetic: Essays on Postmodern Culture*. Port Townsend, WA: Bay Press.

Phillips, Rod (1994) 'Purloined Letters: *The Scarlet Letter* in Kathy Acker's *Blood and Guts in High School*'. *Critique* 35:3, 173–80.

Pitchford, Nicola (2002) *Tactical Readings: Feminist Postmodernism in the Novels of Kathy Acker and Angela Carter*. Lewisburgh: PA, Bucknell University Press.

Pynchon, Thomas (1991) *Vineland*. London: Minerva.
    (1995a) *Gravity's Rainbow*. Harmondsworth: Penguin.
    (1995b) 'Introduction'. *Slow Learner*. London: Vintage. 3–23.
    (1998) *The Crying of Lot 49*. London: Vintage.

Reed, Ishmael (1972) *Mumbo Jumbo*. New York: Atheneum.

Reeve, N. H. (1999) 'Oswald Our Contemporary: Don DeLillo's *Libra*'. In Rod Mengham, ed. *An Introduction to Contemporary Fiction*. Oxford: Polity Press. 135–49.

Ricoeur, Paul (1970) *Freud and Philosophy: An Essay on Interpretation*. New Haven, CT: Yale University Press.

Rimmon-Kenan, Shlomith (1983) *Narrative Fiction: Contemporary Poetics*. London: Routledge.

Robbe-Grillet, Alain (1989a) 'From Realism to Reality'. *For a New Novel: Essays on Fiction*. Trans. Richard Howard. Evanston, IL: Northwestern University Press. 157–68.
    (1989b) 'Time and Description in Fiction Today'. *For a New Novel: Essays on Fiction*. Trans. Richard Howard. Evanston, IL: Northwestern University Press. 143–56.

Robinson, Sally (2000) 'The Anti-Hero as Oedipus: Gender and the Postmodern Narrative in *The Infernal Desire Machines of Doctor Hoffman*'. In Alison Easton, ed. *Angela Carter: Contemporary Critical Essays*. Basingstoke: Macmillan, 107–26.

Roth, Philip (1990) 'Writing American Fiction'. In Malcolm Bradbury, ed. *The Novel Today: Contemporary Writers on Modern Fiction*. Revised edition. London: Fontana. 27–43.

Rucker, Rudy (1999) 'What Is Cyberpunk?' *Seek!* New York: Four Walls Eight Windows.

Rushdie, Salman (1981) *Midnight's Children*. London: Picador.
    (1985) '*Midnight's Children* and *Shame*: An Interview'. *Kunapipi* 7:1, 1–19.

Salaam, Kalamu ya (1995) 'It Didn't Jes Grew: The Social and Aesthetic Significance of African American Music'. *African American Review* 29:2, 351–75.

Sarraute, Nathalie (1963) 'The Age of Suspicion'. *The Age of Suspicion: Essays on the Novel*. Trans. Marie Jolas. New York: G. Braziller. 51–74.

Saussure, Ferdinand de (1966) *Course in General Linguistics*. Trans. Wade Baskin. New York: McGraw-Hill.

Schappell, Elissa (1993) Toni Morrison: The Art of Fiction CXXXIV'. *The Paris Review* 128, 83–125.

Scholes, Robert (1979) In *Fabulation and Metafiction*. Urbana, IL: University of Illinois Press.

Schultz, Max F. (1973) *Black Humor Fiction of the Sixties: A Pluralistic Definition of Man and His World*. Athens, OH: Ohio University Press.

Seltzer, Mark (1998) *Serial Killers: Death and Life in America's Wound Culture*. London & New York: Routledge.

Showalter, Elaine (1998) *Hystories: Hysteria, Gender and Culture*. London: Picador.

Siegel, Mark R. (1976) 'Creative Paranoia: Understanding the System of *Gravity's Rainbow*'. *Critique* 18, 39–54.

Simpsons Archive, The. www.snpp.com/episodes/CABF20.

Sloterdijk, Peter (1987) *Critique of Cynical Reason*. London & New York: Verso.

Smith, Zak (2006) *Pictures Showing What Happens on Each Page of Thomas Pynchon's Novel* Gravity's Rainbow. Berkeley, CA: Tinhouse Books.

Sontag, Susan (2001) 'One Culture and The New Sensibility'. *Against Interpretation*. London: Vintage. 293–304.

Spanos, William (2002) 'The Detective and the Boundary: Some Notes on the Postmodern Literary Imagination'. In Bran Nicol, ed. *Postmodernism and the Contemporary Novel: A Reader*. Edinburgh University Press. 169–85.

Suleiman, Susan Rubin (1994) 'The Fate of the Surrealist Imagination in the Society of the Spectacle'. In Lorna Sage, ed. *Flesh and the Mirror: Essays on the Art of Angela Carter*. London: Virago. 98–116.

Swift, Graham (1992) *Waterland*. London: Picador.

Swope, Richard (2002) 'Crossing Western Space, or the HooDoo Detective on the Boundary in Ishmael Reed's *Mumbo Jumbo*'. *African American Review* 36:4, 611–28.

Tanner, Tony (1971) *City of Words: American Fiction 1950–1970*. London: Jonathan Cape.

Tekiner, Christina (1979) 'Time in *Lolita*'. *Modern Fiction Studies* 25, 463–9.

Todorov, Tzvetan (1977) 'The Typology of Detective Fiction'. *The Poetics of Prose*. Trans. Richard Howard. Oxford: Blackwell. 42–52.

Vonnegut, Kurt (2000) *Slaughterhouse-Five*. London: Vintage.

Watt, Ian (1957) *The Rise of the Novel: Studies in Defoe, Richardson, and Fielding*. Berkeley, CA: University of California Press.

Waugh, Patricia (1984) *Metafiction: The Theory and Practice of Self-Conscious Fiction*. London: Methuen.

(1992) 'Modernism, Postmodernism, Feminism: Gender and Autonomy Theory'. In Patricia Waugh, ed. *Postmodernism: A Reader*, Edward Arnold. 189–204.

Weisenburger, Steven (1988) *A Gravity's Rainbow Companion: Sources and Contexts for Pynchon's Novel.* Athens, GA & London: University of Georgia Press.

Wells, H. G. (1917) 'James Joyce', *Nation* 20, 710, 712.

White, Hayden (1984) 'The Question of Narrative in Contemporary Historical Theory'. *History and Theory* 23:1, 1–33

Zimmerman, Bonnie (1986) 'Feminist Fiction and the Postmodern Challenge'. In Larry McCaffery, ed. *Postmodern Fiction: A Bio-Bibliographical Guide.* Westwood, CT: Greenwood Press. 175–88.

Žižek, Slavoj (1991) *Looking Awry.* Cambridge, MA: MIT Press.

(1999) *The Ticklish Subject: Absent Centre of Political Ontology.* London and New York: Verso.

Index

215

Cambridge Introductions to . . .

AUTHORS

Jane Austen Janet Todd

Samuel Beckett Ronan McDonald

Walter Benjamin David Ferris

J. M. Coetzee Dominic Head

Joseph Conrad John Peters

Jacques Derrida Leslie Hill

Emily Dickinson Wendy Martin

George Eliot Nancy Henry

T. S. Eliot John Xiros Cooper

William Faulkner Theresa
M. Towner

F. Scott Fitzgerald Kirk Curnutt

Michel Foucault Lisa Downing

Robert Frost Robert Faggen

Nathaniel Hawthorne Leland S. Person

Zora Neale Hurston Lovalerie King

James Joyce Eric Bulson

Herman Melville Kevin J. Hayes

Sylvia Plath Jo Gill

Edgar Allan Poe Benjamin F. Fisher

Ezra Pound Ira Nadel

Jean Rhys Elaine Savory

Shakespeare Emma Smith

Shakespeare's Comedies Penny Gay

Shakespeare's History Plays Warren
Chernaik

Shakespeare's Tragedies Janette Dillon

Harriet Beecher Stowe Sarah Robbins

Mark Twain Peter Messent

Virginia Woolf Jane Goldman

W. B. Yeats David Holdeman

Edith Wharton Pamela Knights

Walt Whitman M. Jimmie
Killingsworth

TOPICS

The American Short Story Martin
Scofield

Comedy Eric Weitz

Creative Writing David Morley

Early English Theatre Janette Dillon

English Theatre, 1660–1900 Peter
Thomson

Francophone Literature Patrick
Corcoran

Modernism Pericles Lewis

Modern Irish Poetry Justin Quinn

Narrative (second edition) H. Porter
Abbott

*The Nineteenth-Century American
Novel* Gregg Crane

Postcolonial Literatures
C. L. Innes

Postmodern Fiction Bran Nicol

Russian Literature Caryl Emerson

The Short Story in English Adrian
Hunter

Theatre Historiography Thomas
Postlewait

Theatre Studies Christopher
Balme

Tragedy Jennifer Wallace